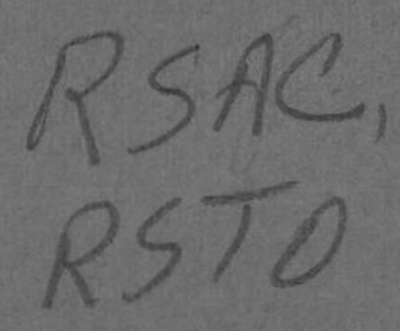

Paul Revere's Engravings

PAUL REVERE'S ENGRAVINGS

CLARENCE S. BRIGHAM

AMERICAN ANTIQUARIAN SOCIETY, WORCESTER, MASS.

ATHENEUM · *NEW YORK*

1969

Library of Congress catalog card number 73–86552
Published simultaneously in Canada by McClelland and Stewart Ltd.
Printed by The Meriden Gravure Company, Meriden, Connecticut
Bound by H. Wolff, New York
Revised Edition

Introductory Note

BY BERNARD BAILYN

FOR those who know this elegant book, with its superb reproductions of all of Paul Revere's engravings, including the famous Massacre and Troop Landing scenes in color, its republication needs no justification. It originally appeared as the collaborative effort of three institutions, equally excellent in their different spheres: The American Antiquarian Society, whose late Director Clarence S. Brigham spent years collecting the material for the book and who wrote the text; the Meriden Gravure Company, whose Director, Harold Hugo, supervised the making of the collotype reproductions; and the Harvard University Printing Office, which designed and printed the book. It was produced for a limited audience of book lovers, print collectors, and connoisseurs, and thought of as a collector's item. And since its distribution was handled more or less informally, mainly for the convenience of the Antiquarian Society's members and for others of like interests, it did not reach far beyond that initial audience, by whom it was, and is, greatly prized.

Its republication now by a general publisher with strong interests in American history has another, wider justification. It reflects not only a broadening popular interest in American antiquities but developments in American historical writing that endow even the crudest of Revere's unsophisticated prints with a fresh significance. Historians are concerned now as never before with the attitudes, beliefs, and ideas that dominate the minds and hence the actions of ordinary people, not simply in order to trace the development of popular taste but to understand how the great movements and events of the past came about. For, however great the political skill and however powerful the intellects of a people's leaders, they can act only within the scope of the people's existing interests and they can only manipulate symbols that are broadly shared. Accurate expressions of these concerns and symbols are therefore important historical documents, and their derivation and character are matters of peculiar interest.

The American Revolution took place in an age of ideology. The attitudes, ideas, feelings, and sensibilities shared by the colonists in the years leading up to the outbreak of hostilities are essential to an understanding of the event itself. They are expressed in many forms: in private correspondence, in newspapers, pamphlets, speeches, and state papers, and they are expressed too in the graphic art of the time. There was not very much of it that has any public reference. There were no artists in pre-Revolutionary America comparable to so prolific and skilled a public commentator as William Hogarth, whose engravings, circulating among a broad middle-class public, expressed popular moral attitudes; depicted, at times in brilliant caricature, aspects of everyday life in Georgian London; and provided for posterity a treasury of popular eighteenth-century iconography. Certainly Paul Revere is in no way to be compared with him.

Revere began his work as a silversmith, and remained a silversmith—a very skilled one indeed—all his life. Copperplate engraving developed naturally from that craft. Much of his engraving consequently—plates for bill forms, paper money, musical scores, and title pages—served strictly commercial purposes, and they have their own interest as the work of an eighteenth-century craftsman. But in his political prints, portraits, and scenic views he went beyond that, to the point of intersection between private, commercial interests and public, social concerns. Deeply committed to the Revolutionary movement, he sought to apply his skill to that cause. He set to work on illustrative prints—propaganda efforts, a later age would call them—and commemorative engravings of popular heroes. His skill as a pictorial engraver was limited: he never developed much beyond the level of a copyist and adapter; but what he did was almost unique, and is of unique historical importance.

Since Revere was a copyist and an adapter, it is one of the special virtues of this book that it presents not only all of Revere's prints but the originals upon which they were based—prints which, because of Revere's adaptations, became sources of American imagery. Such borrowing was not unusual at the time. We know quite well how fully Americans took over the political ideas and attitudes as well as the literary taste of the parent culture, and how directly they applied them to their own affairs despite the incongruities that existed. Revere's work is only a specific example, though a particularly vivid one, of this general phenomenon of eighteenth-century America. He worked from anything that came to hand. A stray cartoon of the 1763 excise controversy in England became the basis of his Stamp Act print, "A View of the Year 1765"; parts of an English cartoon of 1773 satirizing the cabinet's duplicity in relations with France were copied with American adaptations for his plate, "A Certain Cabinet Junto." The adaptations are sometimes extremely superficial: he did not bother to remove certain figures and symbols in the excise print that had no bearing at all on the Stamp Act. But, however closely Revere adhered to his English models, in the end he transformed them all into unmistakable expressions of American Revolutionary thought.

The political prints—modest, simple, almost primitive folk art—are important expressions of popular ideology. Shown here with the sources from which they were derived, they become examples of the cultural transfer from England to America that shaped early American society generally and that provided the ideological basis of the American Revolution. They capture something of the mood of a great event and give it permanent symbolization in visual form.

Preface

THE development of the American Antiquarian Society's collection of Paul Revere's engravings shows how any collection can be enriched by persistent search and acquisition over the years. When the present Director came to the Library in 1908, the Society owned only eight of Revere's seventy-two copper-plate engravings — two of the separately issued engravings, the Landing of the Troops, and the Portrait of William Pitt; three of the engravings published in books, the Plan of the Hemp Mill, and the two cuts in Church's *King Philip's War*; and three of the bookplates. We did not even own an original Boston Massacre, although we knew that Nathaniel Paine's copy would come to us through bequest. We did own most of the woodcut engravings such as the mastheads of newspapers and the several cuts made for almanacs and pamphlets. But the important large engravings were missing, also the numerous trade cards, masonic engravings, and issues of colonial paper money.

None of the English engravings which Revere copied for American publication had been located. That was a task for future research. Nor had the Revere manuscript Day Books been examined, which were to reveal many engravings which could be credited to him, especially bookplates, masonic prints, business cards, and woodcuts for newspapers and almanacs.

Revere had a characteristic style and much of his work can be identified at sight. The close examination of scores of his engravings reveals his peculiar method of lettering, of mantling, and of crudity of original drawing. No other engraver used his abbreviation for the word "Number," following the capital "N" by a superior "o" with two short horizontal lines underneath. When he copied an English print, the faithfulness of his engraving was remarkable.

The fifty or more prints which copied his work, or from which he made copies, all of which are reproduced in this book, were subject to future acquisition. From

1915 to the present day Revere prints have been relentlessly pursued. From dealers, especially Charles E. Goodspeed, Robert H. Dodd, and Robert Fridenburg, several rare engravings, including trade cards and masonic items, were secured. The large engravings, such as the original Massacre, the Obelisk, and the Harvard view, came as gifts from donors who had owned them sometimes for generations. The complete file of the *Royal American Magazine* came from combining the Charles H. Taylor and John W. Farwell sets. The bookplates were added chiefly through the purchase of the Frank E. Marshall collection. The engravings of colonial notes and paper money came primarily through the purchase of the J. N. Spiro collection. The prints in English magazines, from which Revere copied so many of his engravings, were acquired through voluminous correspondence with English booksellers. This latter effort was one of the most rewarding connected with the various fields of research necessary to the building up of the Revere collection.

There are some — a very few — engravings which we have never been able to secure. Josiah Flagg's *Psalm Tunes*, 1764, has never come our way. The portrait of Jonathan Mayhew is still known by only one copy. The earliest edition of the Anatomical Lectures is unique and not in our collection. One paper money bill we never could obtain. Nor have we been able to acquire all three varieties of the Aaron Willard clock label. We have, however, one of the Boston labels, acquired from the J. Cheney Wells collection through the generosity of the Wells Historical Museum. But considering the great size of the Revere collection, with seventy-two copperplate engravings, and about seventy closely related prints and woodcuts, we have been fortunate indeed.

Many people have helped to form this collection. Thousands of letters have been written in the quest to solve minor points. Every effort has been made to insure accuracy of statement, and especially to be conservative in solving problems of debatable ascriptions. Yet errors undoubtedly have crept in, and the compiler would welcome all corrections. To list the names of all those who have helped me in this process of compilation, which has taken nearly forty years, would form a long directory of scholars, collectors, and booksellers. There are several, however, who have constantly answered my numerous queries and have gone beyond the ordinary duties of cooperation in aiding me. Charles E. Goodspeed always maintained an active interest in my work and steered in our direction many otherwise unobtainable prints. His friendliness has been continued by his son, George T. Goodspeed. Robert W. G. Vail, who was conversant with much of the search during his nine years' service here as Librarian, has continued to aid me in later years. Mrs. Muriel D. Taylor, Librarian of the Grand Lodge Library in Boston, has solved many of my problems in Masonic history. Edward H. R. Revere, great-grandson of Paul Revere, presented to the Society his copy of the 1770 *New-England Psalm-Singer*, and has helped me in many ways. Valentine Hollingsworth, Jr., loaned for reproduction his invaluable copy of the engraving of the Landing of the Troops. Frederic C. C. Boyd, of Ringoes, New Jersey, has loaned to me for examination many of the Massachusetts bills in his collection of colonial currency. Dard Hunter, the well known authority on paper-making, has helped me often in the identification of water-marks. Sinclair Hamilton has made valuable suggestions, particularly in the chapter on metal cuts. Stephen T. Riley has constantly opened up his knowledge and the collections of which he is in charge. It is to the Massachusetts Historical Society, moreover, that I owe the favor of the long loan of the photostat copy of the two Revere Day Books, probably the greatest single source of help in producing this volume. Clifford K. Shipton has read the copy for arrangement and style, and has given much help in the solving of technical problems. Rae M. Spencer has frequently given aid in the settling of disputed points upon printing and illustration. Ruth R. Merrill has ably typed all of the manuscript of this volume. But to more than anyone I am indebted to Dorothea E. Spear, Assistant Librarian of the Society, who has given much time to the reading of copy and proof, has contributed innumerable suggestions for the improvement of the narrative, and has made the invaluable Index.

The late William B. Goodwin, of Hartford, Connecticut, worked for several years, twenty years ago, in collecting Revere Massacre prints and planning to write for the Walpole Society a monograph on the subject. He acquired nearly all of the contemporary prints, both American and English, and also most of the nineteenth-century versions and restrikes. He finished a short outline entitled "Remarks on the Four Salient Prints of the Boston Massacre," after he was informed by the Walpole Society that it could not afford to publish an extended volume on the subject. Mr. George F. Dow, of Topsfield, in 1934 had the first part of this outline set up in type covering eight pages, planning to print it in the Society's *Note Book*, but it was never published. Mr. Goodwin died in 1950, confining his later years to the study of American archeology and Norse voyages to New England. The American Antiquarian Society owns his truly vast correspondence with George F. Dow relating to his study on the Boston Massacre prints.

C. S. B.

Contents

LIST OF PLATES, WITH SIZE AND OWNERSHIP

Paul Revere's Engravings

Introduction

THE FAME of Paul Revere rests largely upon a poem written by Henry W. Longfellow, first published in book form in 1863. No dictionary of American biography, before that date, even included his name. Neither Hardie's *New Universal Biographical Dictionary*, with three editions from 1802 to 1808, nor John Eliot's *Biographical Dictionary*, 1809, nor William Allen's *American Biographical and Historical Dictionary*, 1809, with a third edition in 1857 containing seven thousand sketches, mentioned the name of Paul Revere. Then in 1860 Henry W. Longfellow composed his famous poem.

> Listen, my children, and you shall hear
> Of the midnight ride of Paul Revere,
> On the eighteenth of April, in Seventy-five;
> Hardly a man is now alive
> Who remembers that famous day and year.

This was published in his *Tales of a Wayside Inn*, which was brought out in 1863 in an edition of fifteen thousand copies. Immediately it was quoted and republished all over the country. Its lilt and its patriotism made it a favorite with school-boy orators, and few poems in American literature have been declaimed more frequently. As a result, American biographical annalists became conscious of Revere's existence, and Francis S. Drake, in his *Dictionary of American Biography*, 1872, gave him a sizable sketch, the first time that his name had ever appeared in a biographical reference book. Since then his fame has been secure. As instanced by Barbara Frietchie and The Old Stone Mill, the poet popularized, and even created, the subject.

Revere's ride was made to alarm the patriots and to prepare them for the British troops who were secretly attempting to leave Boston and march to Concord to destroy the cannon and supplies which were stored there. William Dawes, who left Boston by a different route, but was equally a participant in the alarm, because of the vagaries of fate is scarcely known in Revolutionary annals. Helen F. More, a little-known poetess, wrote a poem entitled "What's in a Name."

> 'Tis all very well for the children to hear
> Of the midnight ride of Paul Revere;
> But why should my name be quite forgot,
> Who rode as boldly and well, God wot?
> Why should I ask? The reason is clear —
> My name was Dawes and his Revere.

Yet Revere's ride, as commemorated by Longfellow, was but one of the many incidents of a noteworthy and varied life. The silver which he engraved for many churches and private homes was widely sold, his caricatures and engravings were treasured in many families, his masonic connections gave him fame in fraternal circles, the bells which he manufactured hung in many New England steeples, and the copper foundry which he established prospered and still exists today, known by his name.

Paul Revere was born in Boston in 1735, the son of Apollos Rivoire, a French Huguenot who emigrated from the Isle of Guernsey at the age of thirteen and began life in Boston as an apprentice to the silversmith, John Coney. After Coney's death in 1722 he established himself as a gold- and silversmith, changing his name, for convenience of pronunciation, to Paul Revere. The son Paul, under the tutelage of his father, became proficient in his calling. The graceful designs of his silver objects and the artistic embellishments which he engraved on their surfaces made his work much in demand in the colonial period, and even more so to-day. By 1764 he became interested in copper engraving, and thereafter for several years he issued many examples of portraits, cartoons, and advertising cards, gradually finding his most notable outlet, because of his pronounced patriotism, in producing political caricatures attacking British control over the colonies. He married in 1756 Sarah Orne of Boston who bore him eight children, of whom one, Paul, left a numerous progeny.

When the Revolution broke out, Revere was among the leading patriots. As a member of the Sons of Liberty, he took an important part in their secret caucuses and in the plans of the Boston Tea Party in December, 1773. At this time Revere entered upon his career as a messenger to carry dispatches from Boston to the other colonies. He rode to New York to take the news of the destruction of the Tea, then in May, 1774, journeyed to New York and Philadelphia to carry the news of the Boston Port Bill. As the friend and trusted messenger of Samuel Adams, Joseph Warren, and John Hancock, he made various trips by horseback in 1774 and 1775 to nearby colonies, giving personal information as well as bearing the official dispatches. Then in April, 1775, came his famous ride to Lexington, previously referred to, the details of which are related carefully in his own narrative transmitted several years later to the Massachusetts Historical Society and printed in their *Collections* for 1798.

At the beginning of the Revolution, Revere was chosen Lieutenant-Colonel in the Massachusetts State's Train, and was put in charge of Castle Island. He also participated in ventures for the manufacture of gunpowder and the casting of cannon. His most important services, however, were employed in engraving and printing the Massachusetts paper currency and Treasurer's notes in 1775–1776, a task for which he was particularly fitted, and which took much of his time in the early period of the War. The necessary duties kept him out of the Continental service, despite his voiced wish to enlist.

In July, 1779, Revere accompanied the unfortunate Penobscot expedition, intended to dislodge the English forces at Castine, Maine. He held an important office in the expedition, having complete charge of the artillery. After initial setbacks had occurred, he advocated abandoning the expedition, but not in time to prevent a complete rout of the Massachusetts forces. When the troops returned to Boston, officers whom Revere considered personal enemies brought charges of insubordination against him, and he was brought to trial, without definite result. Bound to vindicate his honor, he persisted in obtaining a court-martial to settle the matter, and finally, in February, 1782, he was acquitted of all charges, "with equal Honor as the other officers in the Expedition."

After the Revolution Revere continued as a silversmith, and in 1783 also opened a hardware store in Boston, although his chief income came from his work in silver. In 1788 he established a small iron foundry, and soon began the casting of cannon, to which he added the making of church bells. His first bell was cast in 1792 for the New Brick Church in Boston, and still exists to-day in Saint James's Church, North Cambridge. By 1803 he had cast sixty church bells of different sizes, the forerunners of many more to follow, and their manufacture became an important part of his business. Many of them are still in use throughout New England. In the 1790's he cast cannon for the State and Federal Governments, and in 1794 received the contract for all the brass and copper work on the Frigate *Constitution.* This was but the beginning of an extensive industry. He built in 1800 a mill for rolling sheet copper, furnished the copper, over six thousand feet, for the dome of the State House in Boston in 1802, re-coppered "Old Ironsides" in 1803, and furnished Robert Fulton copper boilers for Hudson river boats in 1809. The Revere Copper Company continued in the hands of his family as an important American industry, providing the United States Government with hundreds of cannon during the Civil War. It exists today as one of the country's leading concerns in its field, and although out of the control of the family, still has a Revere on the board of directors.

Revere's first wife had died in 1773. Before the end of the year, with a numerous progeny to care for, he was married for the second time, to Miss Rachel Walker. Like his first wife, she bore him eight children, two of whom, Joseph Warren and John, lived to carry on the family name. Revere himself died May 10, 1818, at the age of eighty-three. His tomb is still to be seen in the Granary Burying Ground on Tremont Street, Boston. Three portraits of him were painted during his lifetime. The first, by Copley, shows him at about the age of forty, seated at his work-table as a silversmith, in his shirt-sleeves, with a silver tea-pot in his hand, and with engravers' tools scattered on the table. This portrait, owned by the Revere family, was resuscitated from the attic only in comparatively recent years, and was given by the family to the Boston Museum of Fine Arts. Perhaps, because of its artisan appearance, it was not regarded highly, and it is not even reproduced in Goss's exhaustive *Life of Paul Revere*, with its one hundred and thirty engravings, yet it is a striking and unique portrait. A curious copy of this portrait was made about 1872 by Joseph Warren Revere (1812–1880) of Morristown, New Jersey, grandson of Paul Revere. General Revere was an amateur artist and painted landscapes and an occasional portrait. The story in the family is that his Aunt Harriet did not like the Copley portrait of her father portrayed in shirt-sleeves, so General Revere copied the face, but inserted a red uniform and a gorget of crossed cannon. After the General's death the portrait went to the Washington Headquarters at Morristown, where it now hangs. The American Antiquarian Society has a photograph.

The second life portrait of Paul Revere is a crayon made in 1800 by the celebrated Saint-Mémin, formerly belonging to Priscilla Riddle Knight of Jamaica Plain, a direct descendant of Paul Revere, but now hanging in the Revere Room of the Boston Museum of Fine Arts. The third portrait, painted in Revere's advanced years by Gilbert Stuart, the original of which now belongs to the Boston Museum of Fine Arts, is the one which has been copied most frequently in reproductions. In 1891 Elbridge H. Goss published his elaborate *Life of Paul Revere* in two large volumes. Goss's correspondence, including most of the letters of information which he received regarding Revere, is in the American Antiquarian Society. In 1942 appeared *Paul Revere and the World he Lived In*, the most outstanding of all his biographies — authoritative, imaginative, and comprehensive. This book was written by Esther Forbes, aided by her mother, Mrs. William T. Forbes, largely in the Library of the American Antiquarian Society, so much so that we call the alcove where mother and daughter worked, "The Forbes Alcove."

This has been but a brief summary of the career of a man who lived a notable life through the most stirring scenes in American history. Although his name, as it happens, has come down to us chiefly in connection with his famous Midnight Ride, it means much more to us, both as historians and collectors. He was an important figure in his day, the friend of Revolutionary leaders and himself an active participant in the Revolution. His marked ability as a craftsman, both as a silversmith and as an engraver, has made his name familiar in these fields more than any other American of the eighteenth century.

Paul Revere's silver would be collected eagerly to-day even if he had never taken his Midnight Ride. The gracefulness of his designs, the artistry of his engraving, and the variety of his pieces, make his work among eighteenth-century silversmiths especially sought by collectors. But it is true that the glamor of his name gives added value, commercial if not historical, to everything that came from his hand.

It is difficult to realize the great number of silversmiths who practised their art during the colonial period. Mr. R. T. H. Halsey collected the names of about four hundred who flourished in Boston, New York, and Philadelphia prior to 1800, and this number might be doubled if all the other towns in the colonies were included. But of all early American silversmiths probably none produced so many pieces as Revere. He devoted many years of his long life to the art, and his Day Books, which contain only his charge accounts, are filled almost exclusively with charges for the making or engraving of silver. The variety of his pieces was astonishing. Porringers, cups, ewers, tea-pots and coffee-pots, tankards, flagons, urns, sugar bowls, trays, platters, salt-cellars, candlesticks, are only some of the numerous pieces which he fashioned. His most famous piece, and probably the most historic example of colonial silverware in this country, is the large silver punch bowl which he made to commemorate the action of those members of the Massachusetts House of Representatives who voted not to rescind a certain vote of 1768 which was objectionable to the British Crown. This bowl finally came into the possession of the late Marsden J. Perry of Providence and in 1949 was acquired from his widow by the Museum of Fine Arts in Boston.

No American silversmith has been so much counterfeited as Revere. The ease with which a facsimile die could be made and be pressed into another less valuable piece of silver has made all collectors wary of any but pieces with the most authentic lineage. I knew an antiques dealer in Worcester some thirty years ago who prided himself on his ability to buff out a silversmith's mark and substitute for it the mark of "P. Revere." Under a floorboard in his office he had accumulated a collection of over twenty different silversmiths' dies, which he would press into any piece of silver which was brought to him, at an average cost of $25 each. He seldom sold pieces himself, but worked chiefly on consignment. But the arrest in Boston of an unprincipled antiques dealer frightened him, and he abandoned his nefarious practices and destroyed his dies. It is safe to say that much of the Revere silver scattered through the country to-day is fraudulent, although the improper design often immediately shows its falsity.

After Revere's death in 1818, the Boston newspapers all carried obituary notices emphasizing his integrity and commenting upon his honorable and useful life. There was no mention of his outstanding work as a silversmith and an engraver. In 1832 Joseph T. Buckingham, who edited the *New England Magazine*, in his issue for October, Volume 3, pages 307–314, wrote an eight-page sketch of Revere outlining the important phases of his career and providing a frontispiece portrait after Stuart. Buckingham was a publisher of newspapers and magazines in Boston in the first half of the nineteenth century, and must have seen Revere frequently during his last years. In 1853 Buckingham compiled the *Annals* of the Massachusetts Charitable Mechanics Association, a thick volume filled with sketches of early members. On pages 17–21, he contributed a sketch of Revere, abridging his article written in 1832. In 1856 Samuel G. Drake issued his *History and Antiquities of Boston*, in which he included several references to Revere and reproduced some of his engravings. The above three volumes were about the only books of local history which referred to the career of Revere, the patriot. But Longfellow's poem had not been written, and did not appear until 1863. Then came fame and hero-worship, and Revere came into his own.

Esther Forbes, in the closing paragraph of her biography of Paul Revere, after quoting a sentence from one of his obituaries, reading "Seldom has the tomb closed upon a life so honourable and useful," concludes: "That the tomb had also closed on one of America's most legendary heroes they could have had no idea, for the legend had not as yet risen up to swallow the actual man. They, who had so recently seen the stocky, benevolent old gentleman, walking the streets of Boston, could hardly have guessed that he was destined forever to ride a foaming charger, his face enveloped in the blackness of a famous night of almost half a century before, to become in time hardly a man at all — only a hurry of hooves in a village street, a voice in the dark, a knock on a door, a disembodied spirit crying the alarm."

Revere's Day Books

PAUL REVERE'S two Ledgers, or Day Books, as they are generally called, in the Massachusetts Historical Society, constitute the best existing source for information regarding his engraved prints. Long owned in the family, the books were deposited with the Society by William B. Revere in 1920. At that time two sets of photostats of the two volumes were made for Mrs. Pauline Revere Thayer. One set she gave to the Boston Museum of Fine Arts, and in July, 1935, soon after her death, the second set was given to the Historical Society by her estate. Through the courtesy of the Society I have been privileged to use its photostat set during the recent years of my researches.

The earliest book contains 91 pages. Its first entry is on January 3, 1761, and thereafter it runs regularly to April 1, 1775. The charge accounts are chiefly for the making and repairing of silver, with occasionally the record of work in gold, and frequently the engraving on copper of prints, such as advertising cards, book-plates, plates for magazines or music books, and specially designed plates or maps. There are many instances of woodcuts, or rather cuts made in lead for newspapers and almanacs. When accounts were paid they were scratched off by crossed lines. In April, 1775, Revere was engaged by the Province in the laborsome project of engraving paper money, and so continued until his services in the Revolutionary struggle caused him to abandon his trade as a silversmith and engraver. None of this engraving was entered as a charge account as he was paid officially by vote of the Assembly or of a committee. The Day Book begins again with December 19, 1778, mostly with charges for hardware, dry-goods, and supplies, since Revere was then partially supporting himself by engaging in a mercantile business. This continued until early in 1781, but from March 13, 1781, to October 10, 1783, the old familiar charges for silver and prints cropped up with some regularity. The pages towards the end of this first volume contain memoranda as to rents, long-standing charges, and family accounts, mostly for years previous to 1784. Page 51 of the first Day Book, in 1774, is reproduced on Plate no. 1.

51

1774

Boston New-England

June

	£	s	d
Mr John Piemont Dr			
To two Hundred print	0	8	0
Mr John Homer Dr			
To a Pr Flucks & Tongues	0	1	4
To mending Buckle		0	6
Mr Ezra Collings Dr			
To 100 Hall Bills	0	2	8
July 6			
~~Mr Isaiah Thomas Dr~~			
~~To Engraving heding plate for News~~	0	12	0
9			
~~Capt Bernard Romans Dr~~			
~~To Engraving a Copper Plate for part of a map of Florida~~	7		
~~To Smoothing Plate~~	1		
~~To Cash paid for two letters~~		2	3
~~To Cash paid for bring plate from Providence~~			
~~To Ditto for carrying it to Salem~~		1	4
~~Mr Joseph Eustice Dr~~			
~~To Mending a Shoe Buckle~~	0	0	6
17			
Capt Nehemiah Ingersol Drs			
To a pr of Sugar tongs	0	16	0
Capt Frances Free Dr			
To Mending ...			

Plate 1. Page from Revere's Day Book, 1774.

The second volume of the Day Book begins in January, 1784, when Revere took his son Paul in with him, with a careful record of every amount which each took from the business. This volume takes one hundred and sixty-seven pages and continues to September 25, 1797. There are many charges for work in gold and silver, engraved prints, dies for medals and coins, and frequently Masonic jewels. But this period of his work was not so lively nor apparently so lucrative as in earlier years. Many of his wealthy customers had died or departed from the country. In fact the social structure of Boston was completely altered.

The two volumes of Day Books cover nearly all of Revere's work in engraving for a period of thirty-six years. Many of his engravings of prints, and also for making of silver, are not included. Work done on his own initiative, or for immediate cash, or with the charge awaiting the decision of some organized body, whether the Legislature or some Society or group, was evidently excluded. The Day Books constitute a charge account, a record of work and payments, and not a list of his engravings. Altogether, it is a remarkable tabulation of his handiwork, and should be reprinted, with an index of names and objects.

In the Massachusetts Grand Lodge Library is a small account book in Revere's hand, containing a large number of miscellaneous accounts and charges from 1784 to 1793. It includes his accounts with Saint Andrew's Lodge in 1784, with one record of engraving a copper-plate for a summons, and with Rising States Lodge, as Saint Andrew's Lodge renamed itself, in 1785. The rest of the book is taken up with charges for the Iron Furnace, business accounts with individuals, and miscellaneous memoranda. There are photostat copies of this volume in the American Antiquarian Society and the Massachusetts Historical Society.

North Battery, about 1762

UNTIL recent years the only known representation of Revere's engraving of the North Battery was the original copper-plate owned for eighty years or more by the Massachusetts Historical Society. About twenty years ago an original impression of the plate, filled in with the names of the officers concerned, was found in the possession of Mrs. William H. Eddy, of Providence, Rhode Island, and in 1949 was acquired by the American Antiquarian Society.

The copper-plate owned by the Historical Society was first brought to light in 1877, when in the *Proceedings* of the Society for that year, Volume 15, page 364, it was reproduced in an impression from the copper. J. H. Daniels, copper-plate printer of Boston, pulled the impressions. In 1882 it again appeared, as a restrike, in J. H. Stark's *Antique Views of Boston*, page 193. In 1903, in Samuel A. Green's *Ten Fac-simile Reproductions relating to Various Subjects*, it was once more struck from the original copper. John L. Watson, in his *Paul Revere's Signal*, 1880, reproduced as a frontispiece to his pamphlet only the pictorial part of the engraving, omitting the certificate, as also in *Boston in the Revolution*, 1888, page 16. It appeared in reduced form in E. H. Goss's *Life of Paul Revere*, 1891, Volume 1, page 76, and entirely and inaccurately redrawn as a line cut in Justin Winsor's *Memorial History of Boston*, 1881, Volume 2, page 130.

Restrikes were frequently issued separately, some on early crown water-marked paper. One restrike in the Massachusetts Historical Society has only the engraved view, with descriptive title below, "The North Battery, Boston," and is endorsed "Gift of J. H. Daniels, Apr. 30, 1885." Another restrike has the endorsement "Gift Thos. G. Frothingham, Jan. 28, 1896."

The original impression, size 5⅞ inches high by 7⅝ wide, the only known copy owned by the American Antiquarian Society, is shown on Plate no. 2. It has the water-mark "G R," with parallel chain-marks from top to bottom of

P Revere Sculp

This may Certify all whom it may Concern; *that the Bearer hereof*
Ralph Morgan *is an Inlisted* MONTROSS *at his*
MAJESTY'S *NORTH-BATTERY,* *in* Boston *under my Command.*
Given under my Hand this 18 *April* *In the* *Tenth*
Year of his Majesty's reign *John Ruddock Captain*

PLATE 2. NORTH BATTERY, ABOUT 1762.

plate exactly one inch apart. Several gouges and defects on the copper-plate, as shown in the restrikes, do not show in the original impression. The view shows the buildings and fortification of the North Battery, with a background of the North end, with Christ Church prominently displayed, and that part of Charlestown beyond Charles River. It was engraved by Paul Revere in the early 1760's and must have been one of his first engravings. North Battery was built at Merry's Point in the mid-seventeenth century, and was continuously repaired to the time of the Revolution. It was destroyed late in the eighteenth century and no remains, at the present site of Battery Wharf, are to be seen today.

The certificate is filled in with the name of Ralph Morgan as montross, or artilleryman, April 18, "in the Tenth Year of his Majesty's reign," hence 1770, and is signed by John Ruddock, Captain. Ralph Morgan came from Dorchester, but was married to Elizabeth Parker in Boston, August 11, 1768. John Ruddock was prominent in Boston official life, was a selectman and Justice of the Peace and of the Quorum for Suffolk County. He commanded the North Battery for thirteen years. The *Boston Evening Post* of September 7, 1772, prints a long obituary, stating that Justice Ruddock died September 2, in the sixtieth year of his age. In a letter of John Andrews, printed in the *Proceedings* of the Massachusetts Historical Society in 1865, Volume 8, page 322, he records under date of September 3, 1772: "Yesterday died old Justice Ruddock, the most corpulent man among us, weighing, they say, between 5 and 600 weight." John Ruddock was the direct ancestor of Mrs. William H. Eddy, from whom the American Antiquarian Society acquired the print. The line of ancestry went as follows — Ruth Story Devereux Eddy, Robert Devereux, Robert W. Devereux, Tabitha Story who married Nathaniel K. Devereux, Ruth Ruddock who married Elisha Story, John Ruddock.

Flagg's Collection of Psalm Tunes, 1764

A *Collection of the Best Psalm Tunes*, by Josiah Flagg, Boston, 1764, has an interesting title-page engraved by Paul Revere. Since the title is reproduced, the exact wording is not here repeated.

The title-page is highly ornamental, with its Chippendale border, but it is not an original design. It is almost an exact copy of the Henry Dawkins title-page of James Lyon's *Urania*, Philadelphia, 1761. The only changes made by Revere are the omission of the shell designs at the upper right and left corners and of a series of inner border lines, and the substitution of a basket of fruit and flowers in place of a seated female figure. Both title-pages are here reproduced, Plate no. 3.

The collation of the book is as follows: Title-page on first leaf, with verso blank; Preface on second leaf, with recto blank; Index on third leaf, with verso blank; Introduction on fourth leaf, numbered page 4, with recto blank; Analysis of music, numbered page 5 and signature B, with verso blank; Different Moods of music, no page numbering, but evidently page 6, with recto blank. All of these preliminary pages are engraved except the leaf of Preface, which is set in type. Then follows pages 7 to 66 of engraved music, with the backs of each page, facing each other, all blank. The signatures are apparently A in four, B in two, C to I in eight, and K in four. The size of the book is 5¼ inches high, by 8⅝ inches wide.

In the Preface is the following statement: "It is hoped, it will not diminish the Value of this Book, in the Estimation of any, but may in some Degree recommend it even to those who have no peculiar Relish for the Musick, That however we are oblig'd to the other Side the Atlantick chiefly, for our Tunes, the Paper on which they are printed is the Manufacture of our own Country." The Index lists the titles of the tunes through page 66. The water-mark is a fleur-de-lis, with the letters "IV" underneath. Mr. Dard Hunter informs me that although the paper-maker cannot be identified, "the paper is American made and the moulds upon which it was formed were made in this country."

A Collection of
The best Psalm Tunes, in two, three, and four Parts,
From the most approv'd Authors, fitted to all Measures, and approv'd
of by the best Masters, in Boston New England; to which are added
some Hymns and Anthems the Greater part of them never before Printed
in America By Josiah Flagg
Engrav'd by Paul Revere; Printed & sold by him
and Josiah Flagg — BOSTON,
1764

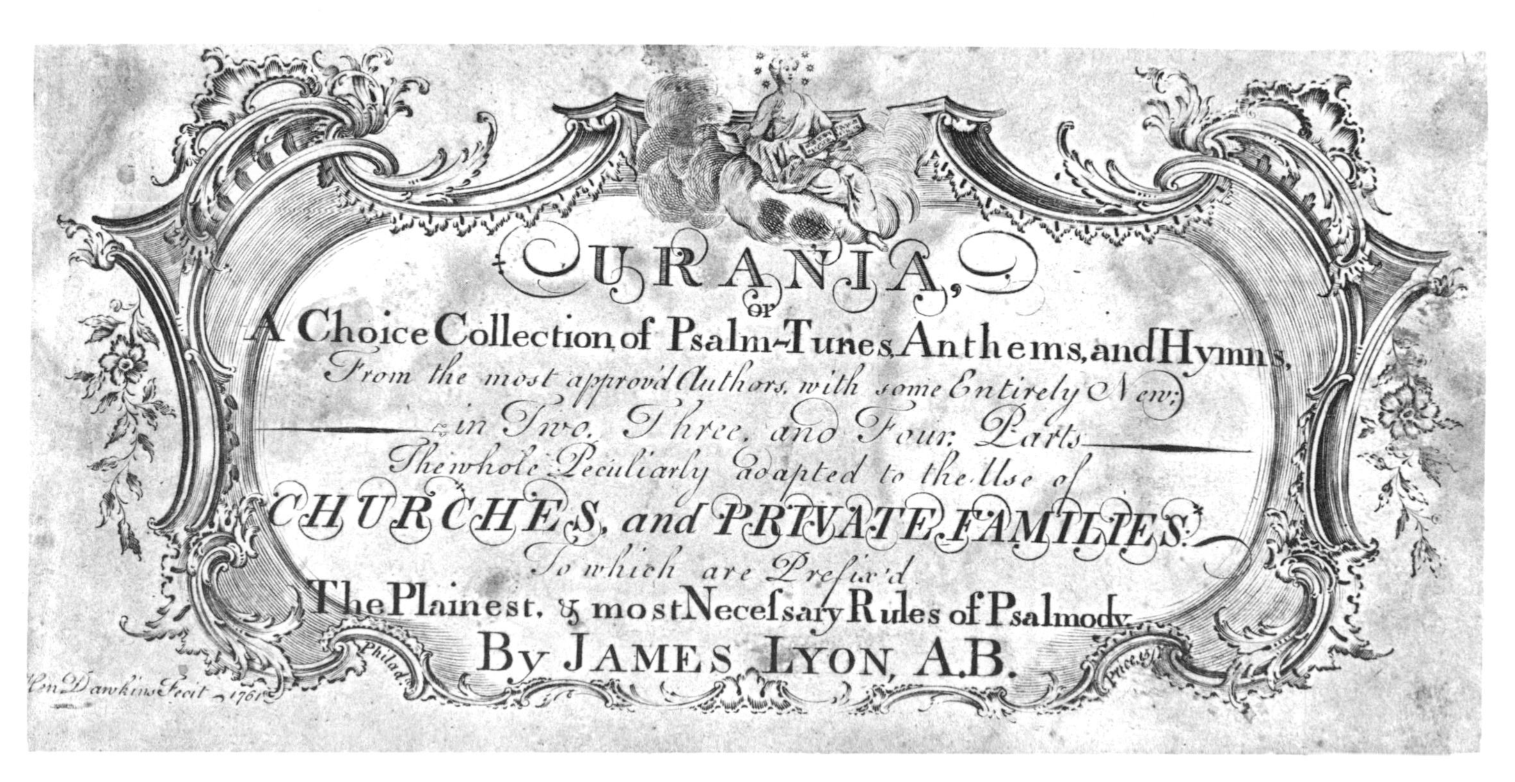
URANIA,
or
A Choice Collection of Psalm-Tunes, Anthems, and Hymns,
From the most approv'd Authors, with some Entirely New;
in Two, Three, and Four Parts
The whole Peculiarly adapted to the Use of
CHURCHES, and PRIVATE FAMILIES.
To which are Prefix'd
The Plainest, & most Necessary Rules of Psalmody.
By JAMES LYON, A.B.
Hn. Dawkins Fecit 1761
Philad.

PLATE 3. FLAGG'S PSALM TUNES, 1764, AND LYON'S URANIA, 1761.

The announcement of the publication of the book is in the *Boston Gazette* of November 5, 1764, as "Just Published." The same advertisement appears in the *Boston News-Letter* of November 8, and is continued in the newspapers as late as February 4, 1765.

According to E. H. Goss's *Life of Paul Revere*, 1891, Volume 1, page 54, a charge is entered in Revere's Day Book against Josiah Flagg: "To one half of Engraving Copper Plates for Singing Book — £150–0–0." The account is accompanied by other charges and has every appearance of being correctly copied. Yet it cannot be found in either of Revere's Day Books, and may have been copied from a separate document or from some other Day Book now unlocated.

Josiah Flagg, described in early life as a jeweller, was well known in Boston as a publisher of psalm-books, a musician, and a concert master. He was born in 1737, the son of Gershom Flagg, and married Elizabeth Hawkes, April 7, 1760. He took a prominent part in the Revolution serving as Lieutenant-Colonel in the Rhode Island line. He died in December, 1794 (see *Massachusetts Magazine*, December, 1794, Volume 6, page 764, *Flagg Family Records*, 1907, page 156, and J. T. Howard's sketch in *Our American Music*, third edition, 1946, page 64.

At least six copies of this book have been located, as follows:

American Antiquarian Society. Title-page and part of page 19 reproduced. Acquired from the Rev. Charles L. Atkins, Boxford, Massachusetts, 1955.

Newberry Library. Page 34 missing, and title-page torn and mended. Presented by Jessie F. Root of Evanston in 1935.

Library of Congress. Index leaf, and pages 8, 41, 44, and 54 missing. Purchased at Libbie Sale of October 10, 1906, number 1534, for $38.

Boston Public Library. Pages 25–28, 41–44, 57–60, and 62 missing; and several pages mutilated. Purchased at Libbie Sale, January 27, 1903, number 1322, for $52.50.

Massachusetts Historical Society. Pages 7–8, 40–41, 45–47, and 49–53 missing, and pages 39 and 65 mutilated.

New York Public Library. Title-page badly mutilated, and pages 34 and 36 missing. It was accessioned in 1900, source not known.

Plan of a Hemp Mill, 1765

REVERE'S Plan of a Hemp Mill was engraved in 1765 to accompany Edmund Quincy's *Treatise of Hemp-Husbandry*, printed at Boston by Green & Russell, in a pamphlet of thirty-five pages, in 1765, by order of the House of Representatives. The author acknowledges that he has done little more than collect "the best experiments and observations he could meet with, from Europe, and in America, relative to the growth and management of Hemp." Marcandier's treatise on hemp had been translated from the French and published in London in 1764, and the subject was engrossing space in the newspapers.

Revere's plate, which appears following page 32 of the pamphlet, is headed "Plan of a Hemp Mill to go by Water," and measures 4⅞ high by 5 inches wide. It is signed below by "G. Flagg Inv." and "P. Revere sculp." (See Plate no. 4.) The Massachusetts Historical Society, in its Quincy Papers, has the original manuscript of Edmund Quincy's *Treatise*. This includes the original plan of the Hemp Mill, entitled "Plan of a Hemp Mill Model, P M [Per Mr.] Gershom Flag." Gershom Flagg was a Boston housewright and glazier, born April 20, 1705, married Lydia Callender in 1731 and second, Elizabeth Pitson in 1736, had seven children, lived on Hanover street in Boston, removed to Harvard about 1769, and died at Boston, March 23, 1771. The Thwing card index in the Massachusetts Historical Society has many references to his purchases of land and the settlement of his estate, and J. W. North's *History of Augusta, Maine*, 1870, page 859, has an excellent sketch of the family.

Quincy's pamphlet was advertised as "This day is Published" in the *Boston Post-Boy & Advertiser* of April 8, 1765, and in the *Massachusetts Gazette and Boston News-Letter* of April 4, 1765.

The Massachusetts House *Journal*, under date of March 1, 1765, page 283, mentions the treatise and says: "The Committee appointed to consider of the Util-

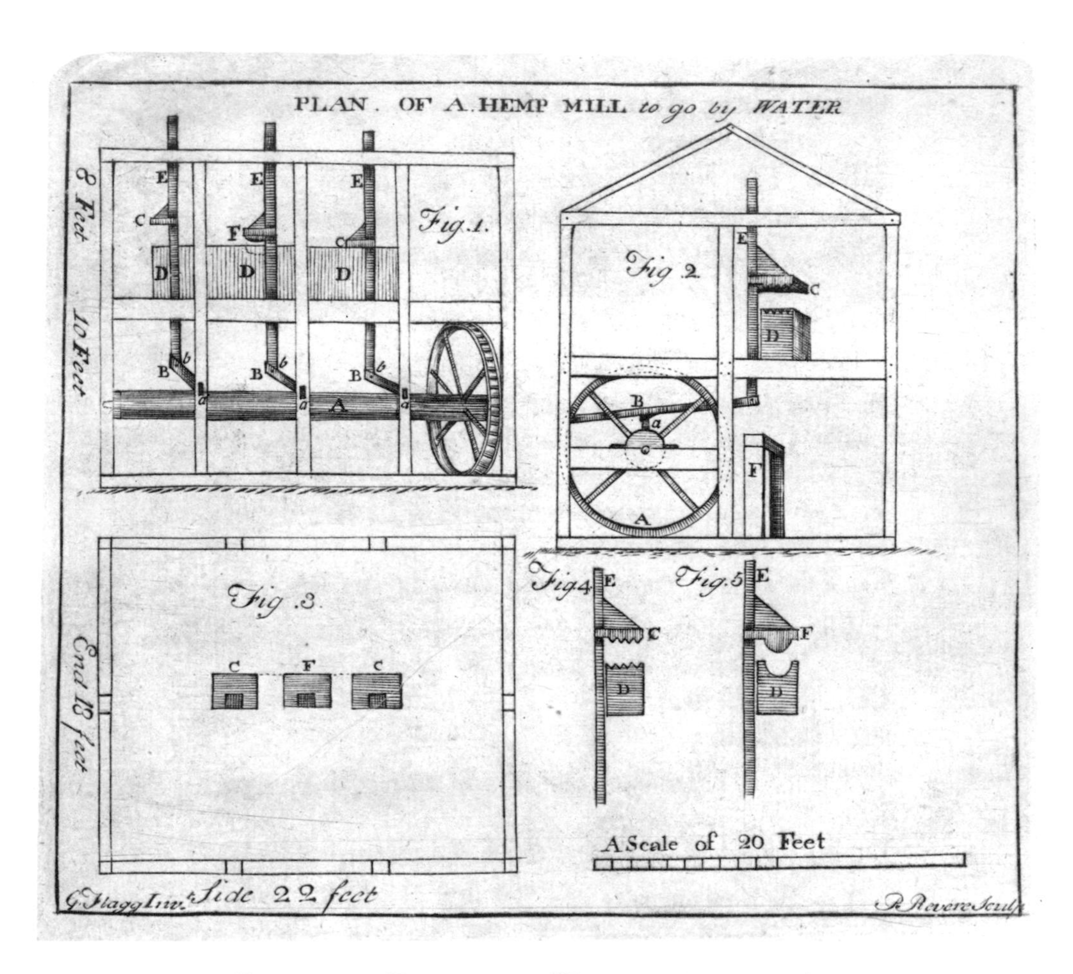

PLATE 4. PLAN OF A HEMP MILL, 1765.

ity of the Treatise of Hemp Husbandry reported . . . that it is adviseable for this Court to order the printing of four hundred Copies of the said Treatise."

Revere does not enter the charge in his Day Book. But W. G. A. Turner of Malden sent me about twenty years ago the wording of an original document which he had seen, as follows:

MAR. 6TH, 1765

MR. PAUL RIVERRE

You are desired by the Committee of the House of Representatives, who were to agree for an Impression of 400 copies of a treatise of hemp husbandry, to cut the view of a hemp mill Model, & to impress 400 Copies thereof — to be delivered to Mess. Green and Russell, — for which (including the paper) you are to be paid, Forty four shillings —

THO. CLAPP
JNO. WINSLOW
JOS. WILLIAMS

The only charges in Revere's Day Book against Edmund Quincy, whom he calls "Edmund Quincy Tertius," are two accounts for the making and engraving of silver, both in January, 1768. In the charge of January 5, 1768, Revere also includes an expense of £2 for "Printing 100 Prints." I do not know what these prints were. Edmund Quincy did not have a bookplate or an advertising card, so far as is known. It is remotely possible that Quincy had more copies printed of his Treatise on Hemp, and needed more copies of the plate.

Copies of Quincy's *Treatise* are to be found in the American Antiquarian Society and in most of the larger libraries which have collections of Americana.

View of the Year 1765

REVERE'S engraving, "A View of the Year 1765," is known apparently by four copies, one owned by the American Antiquarian Society (acquired in 1913 from Goodspeed's and formerly the William E. Spalding copy), one owned by the Worcester Art Museum, one owned by the Bostonian Society (presented by Robert C. Mackay in 1883), and a fourth formerly owned by James Lovell Little and now by Dr. Clarence C. Little of Bar Harbor, Maine.

The size of the plate is 6 1/16 by 7 5/8 inches. At the lower right corner it is signed "Engrav'd Printed & Sold by P. Revere Boston." The three columns of verse underneath are not quoted here since they are shown in Plate no. 5. The allegorical scene shows a dragon, representing the Stamp Act, carrying a scroll labeled "Magna Charta" facing a group of ten figures, four of whom are lettered "U," meaning United Provinces. Then follows "V" for Virginia, "H" for Hampden, the seventeenth-century Englishman who was regarded as the symbol of resistance against taxes, "N Y" for New York, an unnamed figure in clerical costume, "R I" for Rhode Island, and "B" for Boston. On the ground, under the dragon's claws, are two bodies, one holding a scroll lettered Pym, who represented the imposition of the excise tax of 1643, and the other with a scroll lettered "Anti-Sejanus" recognizing Dr. William Scott's "Anti-Sejanus" letters in the London *Public Advertiser*. At the right is the Liberty Tree, with the date of August 14, 1765, commemorating the outbreak on that day, when a crowd opposed to the Stamp Act hanged an effigy of Andrew Oliver, the stamp-master, on the tree and demolished several houses. On the tree is shown the figure of John Huske, who was hanged in effigy on November 1, 1765, in retaliation for his reported efforts to have the Stamp Act passed. Huske was a native of New Hampshire who removed to England and was elected a member of the House of Commons, and whether the allegation was well founded or not, his name was synonymous with

PLATE 5. VIEW OF YEAR 1765, AND ENGLISH PRINT.

opposition to the colonies. Above is the flying figure of Minerva opposing two flying harpies. The verse underneath is in three columns, and could have been written by some patriot poet or by Revere himself.

The copy of the engraving owned by J. Lovell Little in 1891 was accompanied by a card, in Revere's handwriting, describing the print. Goss, in his *Life of Revere*, 1891, Volume 1, page 35, quotes the card as follows: "The odious Stamp Act represented by the Dragon confronted by Boston with drawn sword. The colonies New York and Rhode Island support Hampden. New Hampshire and Virginia with the other United Colonies are also represented. While from the Liberty Tree hangs the officer of the Crown." I have been unable to locate this card.

Revere copied this plate largely from an English caricature entitled "View of the present Crisis," which was published in April, 1763, both as a large print 13⅝ by 8⅜ inches, and as a smaller engraving reproduced in the *Scots Scourge*, Volume 2, plate 24. Revere evidently used the smaller print. The English caricature was issued to signalize opposition to the Excise Bill of 1763. Excise is depicted as a huge dragon-like monster wearing on his head a Scotch bonnet and grasping a large scroll, or Magna Charta. He is opposed by Wilkes, with drawn sword, backed by Charles Churchill, with pointed gun. The Duke of Newcastle and Earl Temple are standing behind Churchill. The Duke of Cumberland, sword in hand, the Duke of York, who is urging the British lion to the rescue, Britannia, and William Pitt are hastening against the monster. In the air are two flying demons, one Lord Mansfield with Scotch bonnet and armed with a syringe with which he sprinkles the group, and the other the Duke of Bedford with one leg encased in a jack-boot, alluding to his supposed subservience to Lord Bute, and the other leg made of wood furnished with a spike. He has a bull's head and two fans serve him for wings. On the other side of the sky Minerva is flying to the rescue. Overthrown on the ground are Arthur Murphy, promoter of the *Auditor*, and Tobias Smollett, promoter of the *Briton*. At the right is a group composed of Lord Bute, Lord Holland portrayed as a fox, and two figures representing France and England (summarized from description of plate in *Catalogue of Prints in British Museum . . . Satires*, 1883, Volume 4, number 4037, page 262).

In adapting his plate for American consumption, Revere omitted Lord Bute's group at the right and substituted the Liberty Tree with the hanging of Huske. He copied the group opposing the dragon to include the figure of Britannia and then added four more figures to depict the United Provinces. The flying figures above are copied faithfully, as are also the two prostrate figures below, although the latter carry signs to denote their identity. Both the English and the American prints are reproduced, the former from the *Scots Scourge* owned by the Harvard College Library, and the latter from the copy owned by the American Antiquarian Society.

The *Boston Evening Post* of November 4, 1765, prints a long account of the popular outbreak of November 1, with the hanging of the effigy of John Huske. In the same issue is an advertisement of the publication of "A Caricatura, being a Representation of the Tree of Liberty, and the Distresses of the present Day. Sold by N. Hurd, near the Exchange." The *Boston Gazette* of January 27, 1766, advertises as "Just Published, (Price Half a Pisterene) And to be Sold by Paul Revere, near Dr. John Clark's, at the North End, by Adam Collson, under Liberty Tree, and by the Printer hereof: A Hieroglyphical View of the Year 1765, neatly engraved."

Revere's print of "A View of the Year 1765" is reproduced in the *Magazine of American History*, 1886, Volume 15, page 14, in E. H. Goss's *Life of Paul Revere*, 1891, Volume 1, page 33, and in William Murrell's *History of American Graphic Humor*, 1933, Volume 1, page 26, all much reduced, and almost full size in Harriet O'Brien's *Paul Revere's Own Story*, 1929, page 37.

The Obelisk, 1766

QUITE the scarcest of Revere's large engravings is his "View of the Obelisk," as it is known by only one copy. When Samuel G. Drake published his *History and Antiquities of Boston* in 1856, the only copy of the print which he could find was owned by John F. Eliot (page 722). It descended to his nieces, Misses Emily B. and Mary L. Eliot of Roxbury, and later of Cambridge. Upon Mary Eliot's death in 1927, the print was bequeathed to the American Antiquarian Society. No other copy of the original print can be traced today.

The story of the erection of the Obelisk and the celebration for the repeal of the Stamp Act is told in full in the newspapers of the day. The Act was repealed March 18, 1766, but not until May 16 did the news reach Boston. The *Boston Gazette* of May 19, 1766, announced that the news of the repeal had been officially received and that the evening of that day would be given to public rejoicing. It also stated that there would "be exhibited on the Common, an Obelisk — A Description of which is engraved by Mr. Paul Revere; and is now selling by Edes & Gill."

The *Massachusetts Gazette. And Boston News-Letter*, in an "Extraordinary" issue of May 22, 1766, graphically records the program of entertainment, quite different in its fullness from the average account of a local event in an eighteenth-century newspaper. Bells were rung, cannon discharged, colors displayed on ships and many of the houses, and bonfires built. The newspaper states: "In the Evening the whole Town was beautifully illuminated: — On the Common the Sons of Liberty erected a magnificent Pyramid, illuminated with 280 Lamps: The four upper Stories of which were ornamented with the Figures of their Majesties, and fourteen of the worthy Patriots who have distinguished themselves by their Love of Liberty. The following Lines were on the four Sides of the next Apartment, which referred to the Emblematical Figures on the lower Story, the whole supported by a large Base of the Doric Order." The lines are completely quoted, and then the account continues: "On the Top of the Pyramid was fix'd a round Box of Fireworks horizontally. . . . At Dusk the Scene opened by the Discharge of twelve Rockets from each Stage; after which the Figures on the Pyramid were uncovered, making a beautiful Appearance. . . . At Eleven o'clock the Signal being given by a Discharge of 21 Rockets, the horizontal Wheel on the Top of the Pyramid or Obelisk was play'd off, ending in the Discharge of sixteen Dozen of Serpents in the Air, which concluded the Shew. . . . The Pyramid, which was designed to be placed under the Tree of Liberty, as a standing Monument of this glorious Aera, by accident took Fire about One o'clock, and was consumed." The newspaper further records that a copper-plate print of the Obelisk had been published.

The print is entitled "A View of the Obelisk erected under Liberty-Tree in Boston on the Rejoicings for the Repeal of the — Stamp-Act 1766." Underneath is a long dedication to "every Lover of Liberty," and the plate is signed "Paul Revere Sculp." It shows all the portraits, poetry, and allegorical views on each of the four sides of the Obelisk. Since these elaborate details are shown in the reproduction, they are not repeated here. (See Plate no. 6.)

The names of the sixteen English "worthy patriots" who befriended the colonies are indicated only by initials at the top of the print, as will be noted in the reproduction. On the original print someone has penned, or pencilled, in contemporary or early hand, the full names, omitting only one — "Lord D — l." Later writers, such as Lucius M. Sargent in his *Dealings with the Dead*, 1856, page 145; S. G. Drake in his *History of Boston*, 1856, page 725; and E. H. Goss in his *Life of Paul Revere*, 1891, Volume 1, page 40, give fourteen of the names, as follows: Duke of York, Marquis of Rockingham, Queen Charlotte, King George III, General Conway, Colonel Barré, William Pitt, Lord Dartmouth, Alderman Beckford, Charles Townshend, Lord George Sackville, Mr. Dennis De Berdt, John Wilkes, and Lord Camden. The name which is at the top of the second pyramid is "L — d T — l" in the original print (changed with a pen to "T — n"), but in the copper-plate it is "L — d D — ll." This might refer to William Dowdeswell, a member of the House of Commons and an influential friend of the colonies, except for the fact that he was not a Lord. There was no

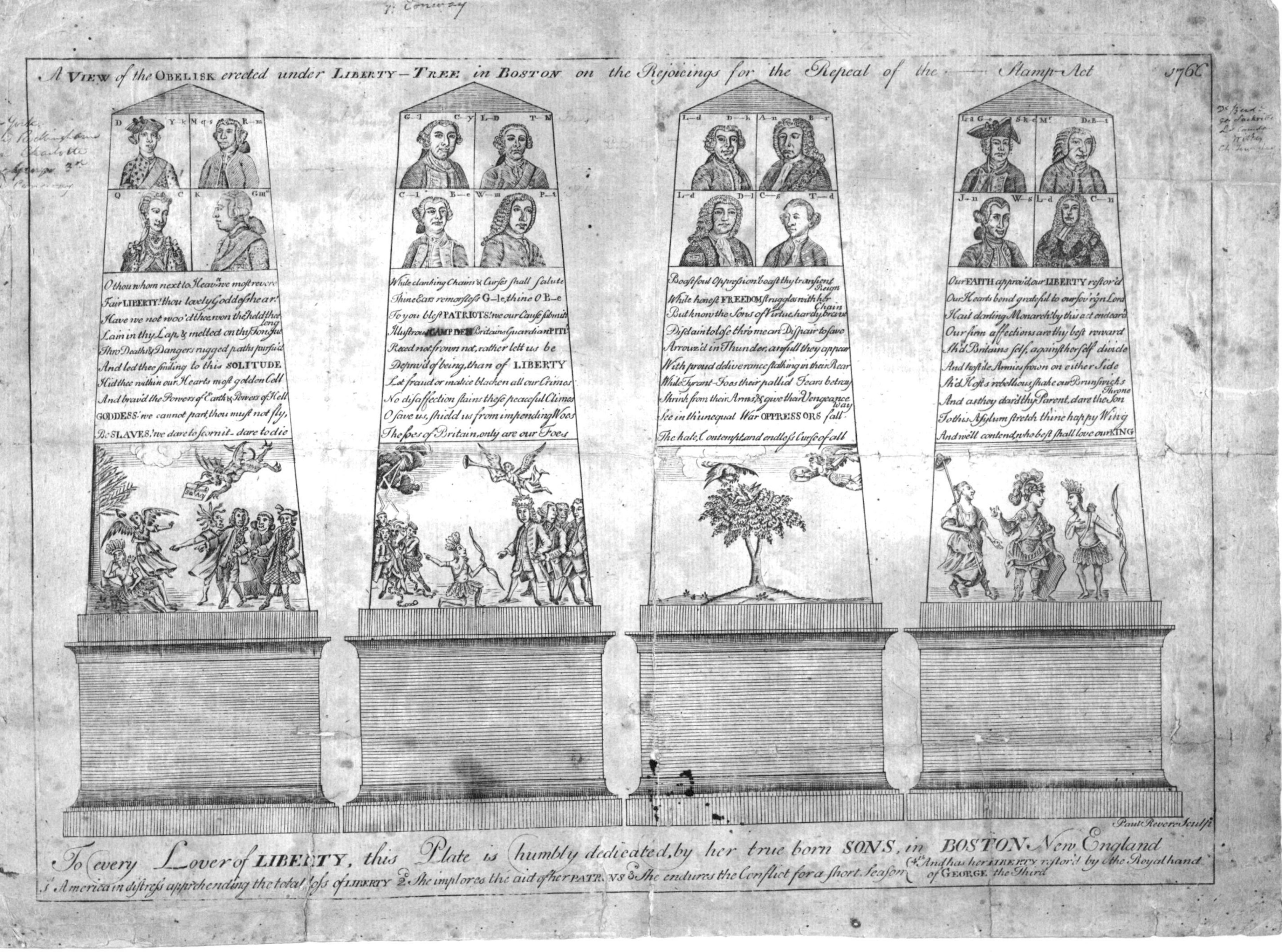

PLATE 6. THE OBELISK, 1766.

Lord bearing a name such as either of the two unidentified. Except possibly for the King and Queen none of the portraits bear the slightest similarity to the original persons.

Although the print stated that the Obelisk was erected under the Liberty Tree, it actually was first erected on the common, with the intention of removing it later to the Liberty Tree. Evidently the print was engraved before the final arrangements for the celebration were made.

The size of the print, to the border lines, is 9⅜ inches high, by 13¼ inches wide. The original copper-plate of the Obelisk print is still in existence today. When Revere, a few years later, was commissioned to engrave a Masonic certificate, he found that the obelisk copper was the right size and used the reverse for his Masonic print. I believe that this design was made about 1773 and altered in 1796. The original bill for the latter design is in the Gay collection in the Harvard College Library. The bill reads:

Elias Perkins Boston Jany 4, 1796.
Bo't of Paul Revere
One Engravd Copper-plate £6.00
for Mason Certificates
Receivd pay
PAUL REVERE

Ernest Gay showed me this manuscript about thirty years ago, telling me, as I remember it, that it had been acquired from a dealer in Connecticut. Upon his death it went to the Harvard College Library. The copper was bought and paid for by Elias Perkins of New London, Connecticut, who was Senior Warden of Union Lodge of New London (see E. G. Storer's *Records of Freemasonry in Connecticut*, 1859, pages 73, 76). He evidently wanted the plate to serve as a certificate for members of his own Lodge. The subject is treated in my chapter on Revere's Masonic engravings, where the print is reproduced. It is also shown in Goss's *Life of Paul Revere*, Volume 2, page 477, the impression being taken from the original copper. The size of the print is 13⅞ inches high by 10 inches wide, to the edges of the plate mark.

The next heard of the copper-plate was in 1839, when on January 16, Francis

A. Perkins of Norwich, Connecticut, sent an impression of the Obelisk engraving to the American Antiquarian Society. It has his inscription on the restrike, and his gift is recorded in the Society's Donation Book on January 24, 1839. Francis Perkins was a prominent citizen of Norwich and its Mayor in 1834. Although he lived in a nearby town, he was not related to Elias Perkins who ordered the plate from Revere. The water-mark is "Pro Patria" and apparently of Dutch manufacture. Mr. Dard Hunter informs me that the paper long antedates the year 1839, and probably was made about the year 1800, or even a few years earlier.

The 1839 impression of the Obelisk side of the plate has the same defects shown in recent restrikes — the letters "P R" and "D," reversed, at the left side, the letter "D" in the margin above the left pyramid, a gouge under the tree in the third pyramid, and occasional scratches on the copper.

Francis A. Perkins died in 1863. About 1890 the Revere copper-plate was acquired by Thomas S. Collier of New London. Collier, who was a poet of some distinction, a collector of books, relics and autographs, and Secretary of the New London County Historical Society, died September 21, 1893. The plate went to his widow, Annie C. Collier, and after her death in 1919, it was bought by R. B. Jacobs, an antiques dealer of Hartford. Mr. Jacobs showed me the plate, and although I was intensely interested, it was a purchase which we could not afford. It was sold to Dr. Rosenbach, who advertised it in one of his Catalogues in 1926 at a price of $5,500. It was purchased by Lessing J. Rosenwald of Jenkintown, Pennsylvania, who in 1943 included it in the collection of prints which he gave to the National Gallery in Washington. Mr. Rosenwald in 1943 engaged Richard E. Bishop of Germantown, Pennsylvania, to pull nineteen proofs from the plate, both sides, which were presented to various interested collectors and institutions. The proofs show all the defects on the plate.

In 1881 two Boston antiquarians, R. D. Child and A. O. Crane, discovered the plate in Connecticut, and issued a facsimile reproduction. This was published, as they state in their circular, in three forms: "one on Bristol board, wide margin, suitable for framing, price 75 cents; one on plate paper, 50 cents; one on strong, thin paper, designed for inserting in Drake's Boston and New England History, 25 cents." Child was Richard D. Child who liked antiquarian matters, and Crane was Albert O. Crane who conducted an art and bric-a-brac store on Washington Street, was especially interested in Revere, and often helped Mr. Goss in preparing the Revere biography. The publishers, in issuing their facsimile, omitted the defects, although they retained the reversed letters on the left margin. The American Antiquarian Society has examples of all the restrikes.

Portrait of Jonathan Mayhew, 1766

PAUL REVERE'S engraving of the Reverend Jonathan Mayhew is one of the scarcest of his prints, and is known only by the copy in the New York Public Library. It carries the inscription "The Revd Jonathan Mayhew. D.D. Pastor of the West Church. Boston. N.E. OBt July 9th 1766. AEt 46," and is signed "P Revere sculp." It was not found by Goss, Sidney L. Smith, Stauffer, or William Loring Andrews. The last writer, in his *Paul Revere and his Engraving*, 1901, page 13, says: "I have grown sceptical in regard to its existence and a little weary in the chase for this elusive will-o'-the-wisp of an effigy of the eminent New England divine."

Samuel G. Drake, in his *History of Boston*, 1856, page 666, says: "Paul Revere engraved a portrait of Doctor Mayhew, which accompanied a volume of the Doctor's sermons. It is the most perfectly awful-looking thing of the kind I have ever seen." Thomas C. Amory, writing on Paul Revere in *Student and Schoolmate* for May, 1869, page 218, says: "One of his earliest works was an engraving of his friend, Dr. Mayhew." Augustus T. Perkins, in his *Sketch of J. S. Copley*, 1873, page 17, says that Revere "made an engraving on copper from a portrait of the Reverend Dr. Mayhew." Daniel T. V. Huntoon, in his *History of Canton*, 1893, page 534, stated that Augustus Gill of Canton owned Revere's engraving of Jonathan Mayhew. The print owned by Augustus Gill descended to Joseph P. Draper, his grandson, and in 1950, after considerable correspondence, I learned that the engraving in question was the 1767 portrait of Mayhew by Cipriani. Therefore this ghost was laid at rest.

The Cipriani portrait of Mayhew was sponsored and paid for by Thomas Hollis of England, one of Mayhew's best friends and admirers. In the *Memoirs of Thomas Hollis*, London, 1780, Volume 1, pages 371, 373, 380, there are references to this portrait which was believed to have been taken from a head either engraved in Boston or drawn there in crayon. Judging from the drawing in the

PLATE 7. JONATHAN MAYHEW, 1766.

Cipriani print (reproduced in the *Memoirs*, Volume 1, page 371), it was based on the 1766 mezzotint by Richard Jennys. In a letter recently discovered and now in the Boston University Library, from Hollis to Mrs. Mayhew, dated August 18, 1767, the writer says: "Inclosed in this Box are three hundred impressions from an Etching of the late excellent Dr. Mayhew, your Husband."

Drake's statement that Revere's portrait of the Reverend Jonathan Mayhew accompanied a volume of his sermons is presumably erroneous, although it might have been inserted in some copy. Mayhew died July 9, 1766, and since the engraving notes the date of his death, it could not have accompanied any of the numerous sermons which Mayhew published during his life. Nor were any of his sermons published posthumously, except a second edition of his Thanksgiving Discourse on the Stamp Act, entitled *The Snare Broken*, which was published August 14, 1766. But none of the eight copies of this pamphlet examined show a portrait or any evidence that there was a portrait.

Three funeral discourses were printed in 1766, by John Browne, Charles Chauncy, and Ebenezer Gay, and I have examined half a dozen copies of each of these sermons. None bears evidence of ever having had such a portrait. An *Eclogue sacred to the Memory of Rev. Jonathan Mayhew*, generally credited to Joseph Green but sometimes to Mather Byles, was printed in 1766 and was advertised as "This Day Published" in the *Massachusetts Gazette and Boston News-Letter* of July 17, 1766. Also Benjamin Church's *Elegy on the Death of Rev. Jonathan Mayhew*, advertised as "just published" in the *Boston Gazette* of September 8, 1766, was printed in that year. But neither pamphlet shows any evidence of a portrait.

About forty years ago the long-sought engraving was found in the print collection of the New York Public Library. It was reproduced in Frank Weitenkampf's *American Graphic Art*, 1912, page 62; again in the 1924 edition of the same work, page 45; and again in the *New York Public Library Bulletin* for March, 1928. Its exact size is 5 11/16 by 4 inches, to the edges of the engraved surface. In his 1924 edition Mr. Weitenkampf states that Mr. Brigham has discovered a second copy, but this unfortunately is not true, and he can rest assured that his is the only copy known to me. (See Plate no. 7.)

Revere copied his engraving of Mayhew, in much reduced form, from the large Richard Jennys mezzotint of the Reverend Jonathan Mayhew, which was painted and cut by Richard Jennys, Jun., and published by Nathaniel Hurd. In the *Massachusetts Gazette and Boston News-Letter* of July 17, 1766, is an advertisement of this mezzotint, showing that it was issued only a few days after Mayhew's death. Very little is known about the life of Richard Jennys, Jun., the portrait painter. Even the excellent monograph on Jennys by Frederic F. Sherman, published in 1941, gives almost no biographical details. He was the son of Richard Jennys who was a notary public in Boston in 1756 (*New England Historical and Genealogical Register*, Volume 30, page 19), and administration was granted on his property in 1768 (Suffolk County Probate Records, number 14358). Nicholas Coxe of Newington Green, England, in 1765 made bequests to his nephew Richard Jennys of Boston in New England, to Richard Jennys, Jun., to his niece Elizabeth Jennys, and to her sister, Rebecca Armstrong, wife of Martin Armstrong of Jamaica (Waters's *Genealogical Gleanings*, Volume 2, page 1094). Richard Jennys, Jun., and his wife Sarah had a son Richard, born in Boston, December 28, 1771.

Revere probably copied his small engraving from the mezzotint because of his long friendship with Jonathan Mayhew, whose views and personality he greatly admired. It was Jonathan Mayhew who so attracted him that when a boy of fifteen he entered the West Street Church to hear Mayhew preach. Although family tradition says that Paul was whipped for going to this church, it was evident that the punishment did not deter him from later absorbing some of Mayhew's views, for it was Mayhew who preached resistance to England's tyranny. If Mayhew had not suffered an early death, he would have become one of the most prominent advocates of the Revolution.

Sixteen Anthems, 1766

JOSIAH FLAGG in 1766 published at Boston a music book entitled *Sixteen Anthems*. The exact title is as follows:

> Sixteen/ Anthems,/ collected/ From Tan'sur, Williams, Knapp, Ashworth & Stephenson./ To which is added,/ a few Psalm Tunes./ Proper to Entertain and Improve those who have made some Proficiency in the Art of/ Singing./ Engraved and Printed by Josiah Flagg, and Sold by him at his House near the Old-North Meeting-House, and at/ his Shop in Fish-Street, also by the Booksellers in Boston, New-England. (Price 6 Shillings.)

The American Antiquarian Society copy contains title-page [p. 1], with reverse blank [p. 2], blank page recto [p. 3], page with "To the Reader," "Explanation of foreign Words," and "An Alphabetical Table," [p. 4]. These preliminary pages were in type, followed by pages 5 to 60, all engraved on one side of the leaf with reverse blank. The Table indexes the first lines of the tunes, comprising eighteen Anthems, six Psalm Tunes, and one Song. There is no tune indexed beyond page 60, and page 60 seems, according to the appearance of the book and the binding, which is original, to be the final page. The size of the book is 5¼ inches high by 8¾ wide.

The Library of Congress copy is identical, except that it has ten unnumbered pages beyond page 60, or pages 61 to 70, apparently engraved by the same hand and in the same style as the earlier part of the book. The ten pages contain an Anthem, Psalm 29, by William Knapp, beginning "Bring unto the Lord, O ye mighty"; and including A Hymn for Ester, by W. S., beginning "Jesus Christ is ris'n today"; and an Anthem out of the second chapter of Luke, beginning "Behold I bring you glad Tidings." Assumedly these ten pages were engraved and added in a later issue and binding. None of them are called for in the Table.

SIXTEEN

ANTHEMS,

COLLECTED

From TANS'UR, WILLIAMS, KNAPP, ASHWORTH & STEPHENSON.

To which is added,

A FEW PSALM TUNES.

Proper to ENTERTAIN and IMPROVE thoſe who have made ſome Proficiency in the ART of SINGING.

Engraved and Printed by JOSIAH FLAGG, and Sold by him at his Houſe near the Old-North MEETING-HOUSE, and his Shop in FISH-STREET, alſo by the BOOKSELLERS in BOSTON, NEW-ENGLAND. (Price 6 Shillings.)

[1766]

PLATE 8. SIXTEEN ANTHEMS, 1766.

The book is advertised in *The Massachusetts Gazette and Boston News-Letter* of October 2, 1766, as follows:

> A Collection
>
> Of all Tansu'r's, and a Number of other Anthems, from Williams, Knapp, Ashworth, and Stephenson. To which are added, some Tunes from Lion, Smith, Ravencraft, &c — Just Published and to be sold by Josiah Flagg (who teaches Psalmody, on Monday and Thursday Evenings) at his House near the Old North Meeting House; also to be sold at his Shop in Fifth Street, by Mess'rs Thomas Leveret, and Samuel Webb in Cornhill, and the rest of the Booksellers in Boston, by Benjamin Loring, at the Head of the Long Wharff, and by Mr. Salmon, at his House near the Sign of the Lamb.
>
> N.B. A sufficient Number of Persons appearing that want any particular Anthem, or Tune, may have it struck off immediately.

In this advertisement it is noticeable that Flagg states that he published and sold the book, but he does not state that he engraved it, as is the inference in the imprint. A careful reading of the imprint would lead to the conclusion merely that the book was engraved, but that it was printed and published by Flagg. The statement in the advertisement that buyers could have individual tunes or pages struck off immediately is interesting. No such individual printings are known.

Revere undoubtedly engraved the music for this volume. It is exactly like his work in the 1764 volume, and even more like the later *New England Psalm Singer* of 1770. The lettering, notes of music, and clef signs were all characteristically his, and unlike any of the other engravers of music of his period — Benjamin Pierpont, J. W. Gilman, S. Wightman, or J. Norman. Flagg himself, in spite of the imprint, was not an engraver. He was a close friend of Revere and presumably would have engaged no other engraver to do his work.

The book is rare, with the only known copies in the American Antiquarian Society and the Library of Congress.

View of the Colleges in Cambridge, 1767

ONE of the rarest and most desirable of Revere's engravings is the Harvard view of 1767. It is entitled "A Westerly View of The Colledges in Cambridge New England." It is signed "Josh. Chadwick, del" and "P Revere sculp." At the bottom are the words "A Harvard Hall B Stoughton C Massachusetts D Hollis E Holden Chapel," the letters referring to the college buildings. The size of the print, to the border lines, is 9¼ by 15⁵⁄₁₆ inches.

The view is of the greatest historical interest. Since no description of the scene could be more authoritative or detailed than that given by Hamilton V. Bail in his *Views of Harvard*, 1949, pages 43–44, it is here quoted entire:

"This view is taken from approximately the present site of the Unitarian Church, facing somewhat to the north and not squarely in front of the first Stoughton as in Burgis's drawing. The second Harvard has disappeared — burned down on the night of 24 January 1764 — and the third and present one is found on its site; Stoughton and Massachusetts appear as previously; and there are two new buildings appearing for the first time — Holden Chapel built in 1744 and Hollis Hall built in 1763. The tree in the old quadrangle is still standing and a smaller one (later to be called the Class Day Tree) is seen in the yard between Harvard, Hollis, and Holden. The fence appears to be lower than in the Burgis View, and bears vertical subdivisions, but these differences may be merely adventitious. There have been general indications that the fence appearing in the Burgis View was built of stone, but the evidence of the District Reports suggests that it was of wood and continued so until the fence first appearing in the *Massachusetts Magazine* View — stone below surmounted by a picket top — was built. The Revere View shows an entrance for pedestrians in front of Hollis and one for carriages to the south of Massachusetts, as well as the entrance in front of Stoughton which appeared in the Burgis View. There is no indication here that the fence surrounds the buildings entirely, although it is known that such was the case. A four-horse carriage is again seen in the road — probably the Governor's, from the out-riders who accompany it. There are also numerous other figures both within and without the Yard, with their costumes shown in considerable detail."

The date of the engraving is well chronicled in Revere's Day Book. Under date of July 4, 1767, is the following entry: "Capt Josep Chadwick Dr/ To one half of the Engraving a Plate/ for a Perspective View of the Colleges/ To Printing/ 4–0–0." No Boston newspaper between August and December, 1767, mentions the publication of the engraving.

It is evident from the charge, that Revere and Chadwick were partners in publishing the print. Joseph Chadwick was well known during the period as a surveyor and engineer. Mr. Bail recounts several instances of his career as a surveyor and artillery officer, to which account I can add little except the date of his death in 1783, based upon his Will signed July 26, 1783, and probated August 14, 1783, in the Suffolk County Probate Records, number 18004.

I can locate only four copies of this print. The Essex Institute has an excellent copy which it has owned for many years. Matthew A. Stickney owned a copy which was sold at the sale of his library at Libbie's, November 25, 1907. A group of seven Harvard alumni purchased the print for $700 and presented it to the Harvard Library. It was described in the catalogue, number 1617, as a fine perfect copy and was reproduced opposite page 152. Zachary T. Hollingsworth owned a copy and upon his death in 1925 bequeathed it to his son Valentine, who upon his death in 1942, bequeathed it to his son Mark Hollingsworth. The fourth located copy was owned by Daniel Denison Slade of Chestnut Hill, Massachusetts. Dr. Slade obtained the print in 1891 from Miss A. P. Rogers, who in turn had acquired it from Mrs. M. B. Blanchard of Harvard, Massachusetts. Dr. Slade upon his death in 1896, bequeathed the print to his daughter, Margaret B. Slade, who upon her death in 1939 left it to her sister, Mrs. Henry E. Warner of South Lincoln, Massachusetts. Mrs. Warner allowed Goodspeed to price it for sale in 1939, but soon asked for its return and in 1950 presented it to the American Antiquarian Society. This copy has two slight mutilations in the sky and the foreground, not affecting the printing, and the print has lately been restored. It is the only copy which has

AMBRIDGE, 1767.

open out

Open Out

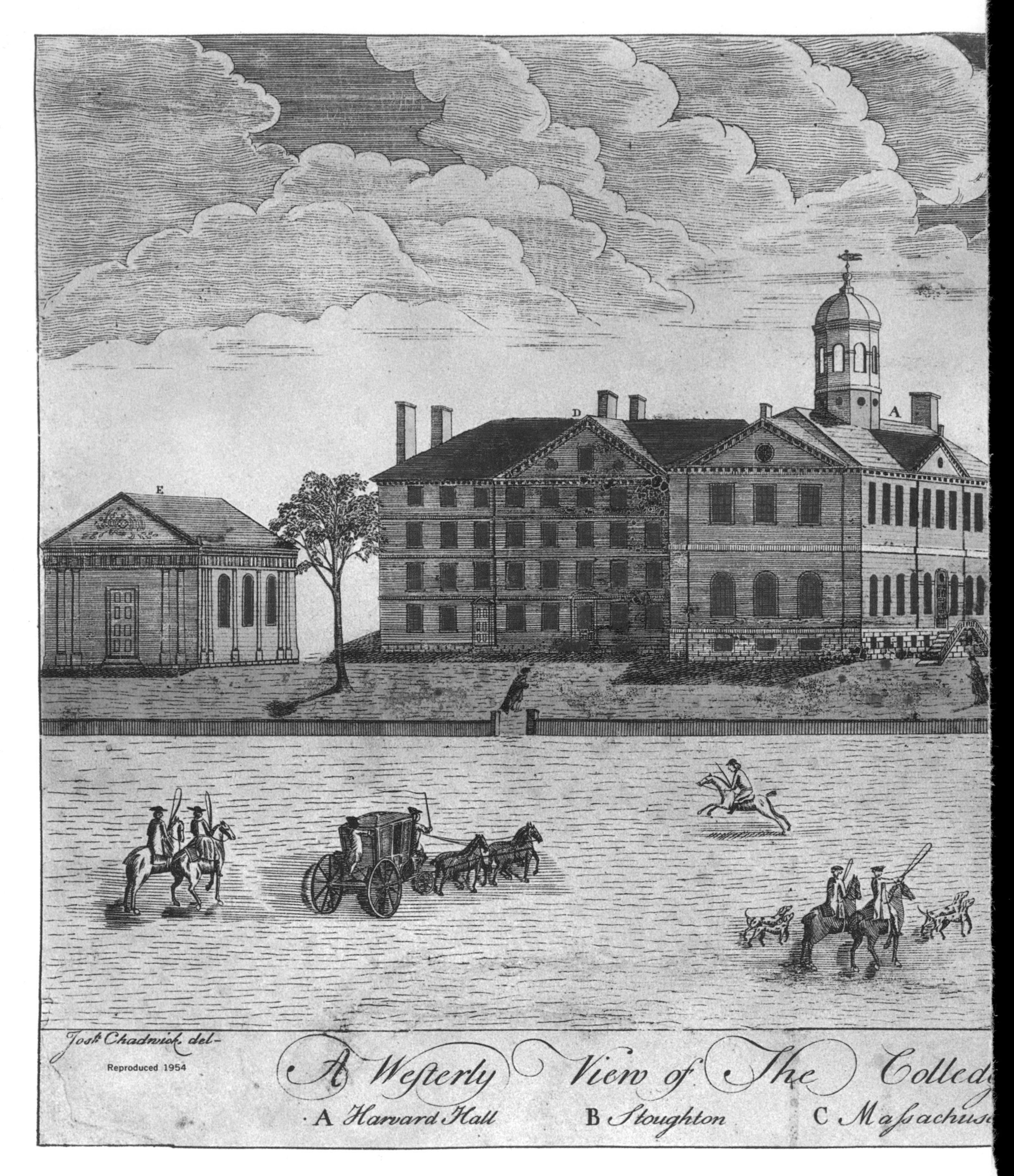

PLATE 9. COLLEGES IN C

been contemporaneously colored, and is the copy which is herewith reproduced. Mr. Bail mentions two other copies, but that owned by Frederick L. Gay was a restrike, and the Margaret Slade copy was the same as that owned by Mrs. Warner.

The Harvard view has been reproduced many times. Mr. Bail lists over a dozen references, to which should be added the reproductions in the Libbie Catalogue of November 25, 1907, and Goodspeed's *Month* for March, 1939. The most noteworthy reproduction, as Mr. Bail states, is the re-engraving executed in exact facsimile (9 11/16 x 15½ inches) by Sidney L. Smith in 1916 with the following additional inscription in the lower left-hand corner: "Engraved by Sidney L. Smith for the/ Club of Odd Volumes/ from the original print in the possession of the/ Essex Institute, Salem, Mass./ 110 Copies printed October, 1916. Copyrighted." The print was published November 28, 1916, and entered for copyright December 1, 1916. Smith's re-engraving is described under Item B–68 in Stokes's *American Historical Prints* (New York, 1932) and also in the *Catalogue of the Collection of Engravings in the University Club* (New York, 1926), as well as in several of the contemporary Goodspeed sales catalogues.

In May, 1775, the Massachusetts Provincial Congress ordered that the sum of £26,000 should be issued in paper bills, to provide advance pay for the soldiers. Paul Revere was commissioned to engrave them, and they were engraved on three plates. They were dated May 25, 1775. One plate was for the bills of 20, 14, and 6 shillings, the second for 18, 12, and 10 shillings, and the third for 16, 15, and 9 shillings. Revere obtained the copper for his three plates by cutting down the plates of the Harvard View, the Boston Massacre, and another copper of a portrait of the Reverend Samuel Willard. The subject is fully discussed in my chapter on Paper Money.

In July, 1775, the Provincial Congress, desiring to raise more money, found that the coppers were still useable and requested Revere to alter the date on the bills from May 25, 1775, to July 8, 1775. That is the date on the bills last impressed from the copper-plates. All three original coppers are in the office of the Massachusetts Archives. The plate of the Harvard View was cut almost in half, leaving the right half for the engraving of the bills. The size of the copper-plate is 10¼ inches high by 7⅜ wide, to the outside of the plate marks. Restrikes have been made many times from this copper-plate. Some restrikes were made in the late 'sixties. A copy owned by Conrad Slade, of Hollywood, California, has written on the back: "Bought in Harvard Square, Cambridge, about 1869 by father [Dr. D. D. Slade]. There were a number of impressions for sale at the time." Another restrike made by Conrad Blackden of the American Bank Note Company in 1913 was owned by Francis R. Hart of Boston and was given to the American Antiquarian Society in 1928. Hamilton Bail says that a reproduction of the half print was used in a newspaper advertisement of the Bank of New York and Trust Company in 1933. Anyone could obtain a restrike from the original copper if he could get permission from the proper State authority.

A Warm Place — Hell, 1768

THE Rescinders print, entitled "A Warm Place — Hell," is one of the rarest of Revere's engravings and is known by only two copies. One, now reproduced, was owned for many years by the Misses Emily B. and Mary L. Eliot of Roxbury, and later of Cambridge, who were the daughters of Nathaniel G. Eliot, the son of Ephraim Eliot who married Elizabeth Fleet, the daughter of John Fleet, the son of Thomas Fleet, Senior. The print was acquired by Ephraim Eliot (*Publications*, Colonial Society of Massachusetts, Volume 25, pages 47–50). It was bequeathed to the American Antiquarian Society by Miss Mary L. Eliot upon her death on January 15, 1927. Another copy was acquired several years ago by a Providence book-dealer, James A. Tyson. The John Carter Brown Library obtained this copy in October 1960.

The story told in the print is well known. On February 11, 1768, the Massachusetts House of Representatives voted to approve a "Circulatory Letter" opposing the various Acts of Parliament levying taxes on the colonies, and ordered that copies should be sent to the legislatures of all the colonies (letter printed in Massachusetts House *Journal* for 1767–1768, appendix, pages 20–23). The letter greatly disturbed Parliament, and Governor Bernard was ordered to demand that the vote of the House should be rescinded, under penalty of his dissolving the General Court. On June 30, 1768, the House put the motion to vote whether the resolution of the House authorizing the circular letter should be rescinded. Upon a yea and nay vote, 92 members voted not to rescind, and 17 voted to rescind. The names are carefully recorded in the House *Journal* for June, 1768, pages 89–90.

The vote aroused great excitement in Massachusetts, especially as the General Court was promptly dissolved by Governor Bernard on July 1. Everywhere toasts were drunk to "the glorious ninety-two," and the seventeen rescinders were held up to public obloquy.

It set the scene for one of Paul Revere's best known caricatures. He issued a print entitled "A Warm Place — Hell," showing the devil with a pitchfork pushing seventeen men into the yawning, fiery jaws of a monster representing the mouth of Hell. Above is a flying devil, crying "push on Tim," referring to Timothy Ruggles, an active Loyalist and one of the seventeen. Another member of the group is shown bearing a calf's head, an evident reference to Dr. John Calef. Ephraim Eliot preserves an interesting reminiscence of the print. He showed it to Paul Revere, then eighty years of age, who observed that he had not seen a copy for forty years. He said that "he was a young man, zealous in the cause of liberty when he sketched it & had forgotten the circumstances — but this he did remember, that while he was doing it, the famous Doct Church (then considered a leading whig, though he afterwards proved defective) came into his shop & seeing what he was about, took a pen & wrote the following lines as an accompaniment. The Colonel then delivered them with much pathos exactly as they are on the print. He was asked to call over their names, but could recall only the above named Timothy Ruggles, & Doctor Robert [error for John] Calef of Ipswich, whom he had particularized in the print with a Calfs head." (*Publications* of the Colonial Society of Massachusetts, Volume 25, page 49, quoting from Ephraim Eliot's commonplace book, which manuscript is now owned by Samuel Eliot Morison of Cambridge, Massachusetts. The same incident is told in the sketch of Paul Revere written for the *New England Magazine* for October, 1832, page 309.)

It was Revere, too, who had a hand in honoring the ninety-two patriots who refused to rescind. Fifteen patriots, or "Sons of Liberty," commissioned Revere to make a large silver punch bowl, which bore this inscription, "To the memory of the glorious Ninety-two Members of the Honbl House of Representatives of the Massachusetts-Bay, who, undaunted by the insolvent Menaces of Villains in Power, from a strict Regard to Conscience, and the Liberties of their Constituents, on the 30th of June 1768, Voted, NOT TO RESCIND." The names of the fifteen patriots were engraved around the top of the bowl, and Revere's name is stamped underneath. The bowl descended to Robert C. Mackay of Boston and was displayed to the Massachusetts Historical Society in 1873 (see *Proceedings*, 1873–1875, page 199). It later was acquired by Marsden J. Perry of Providence, and

PLATE 10. WARM PLACE – HELL, 1768. ENGLISH AND AMERICAN PRINTS.

*W*HILE *gasping Freedom waits her future Fate,*
And Commerce sickens with the sick'ning State;
What Tennes, Mentor, Judas, more than Fiend,
Their Country's last Resort wou'd vote RESCIND?
Cou'd Hope, cou'd Fear, cou'd weighty Cudgels maul,
A very Camel to relinquish all?
And shall the Hero, Sage, and Prophet say,
To save our RIGHTS, *we shou'd them all betray.*
Resign, RESCIND, *submit to sov'reign Will,*
Aw'd by meer brutal Force, be passive still,
Then by kind Suff'rance you may sleep on Snow;
And feast on Winds, or browse as Goats shou'd do—
Much have you dar'd, fierce Anger to provoke,
Your patient Masters but delay the Stroke:
The Tempest rages shou'd you disobey,
Confess the Power, and fall an easy Prey.
Is this the Language of the brave, the just,
The Guardian-Gods in whom the People trust?
Detested TRAYTORS, *fly the Sight of Men,*
And never dare to mention RIGHT *again.*

The Seventeen Proselytes to his E——y's Doctrinal Faith of Submission!

William Brown,	*Salem,*	His E——y's Interpreters of hard Sayings.
Peter Frye,		His E——y's Viceroy, and Comptroller of the Fish Flakes.
Jacob Fowle,	*Marblehead,*	Apothecary to his E——y.
John Calef,	*Ipswich,*	Groom of the Stool to his E——y with the Reward of a Coach-man's Livery.
Richard Saltonstall,	*Haverhill,*	His E——y's great Chamberlain.
Israel Williams,	*Hatfield,*	Under Graduates in his E——y's political Academy for teaching passive Obedience and Non-Resistance.
Jonathan Bliss,	*Wilbraham,*	
Jonathan Ashley, junr.	*Deerfield,*	His E——y's Branch of human Weakness.
Joseph Root,	*Sunderland,*	Keeper of the Key of his E——y's privy Custom-House and covert Ways, with a Pension of a £.100 per Ann.
Timothy Ruggles,	*Hardwick,*	His E——y's Ahithophel.
Chillingsworth Foster,	*Harwich,*	His E——y's chief Soothsayer, and grand Oracle of Infallibility.
Jonathan Sayward,	*York,*	His E——y's necessary Man in Times of Distress.
William Jernigan,	*Edgartown,*	His E——y's Instructor in the Indian Tongue, and Corrector of his false Grammar.
Matthew Mayhew,	*Chilmark,*	His E——y's Inspector of the Fiery Furnace.
Josiah Edson,	*Bridgewater,*	Register of his E——y's "merely ministerial" circular Letters.
John Ashley,	*Sheffield,*	Surveyor and Searcher of his E——y's Provincial Grant.
John Chadwick,	*Tyringham,*	

Q.——*Whether Those, who consent to be Slaves to usurping Tyrants of the Earth, are fit to enjoy the glorious Liberty of the Sons of God in Heaven?*

O Fools! Who fear to speak a Truth well known,
That what a Man possesses is his OWN.

PLATE 11. RESCINDERS BROADSIDE, 1768.

in 1949 was obtained from Mr. Perry's widow, through a public subscription chiefly raised by Mr. Mark Bortman of Boston, and presented to the Museum of Fine Arts in Boston, there to be permanently preserved.

The Rescinders engraving has been often reproduced. E. H. Goss, in his *Life of Paul Revere*, 1891, Volume 1, page 60, first showed it in reduced form. The Colonial Society of Massachusetts reproduced it in exact size in the program for its annual dinner on November 21, 1922, and again in its *Publications*, Volume 25, page 49, printed in 1924, where Samuel Eliot Morison exhibited the print and made comment upon it. William Murrell, in his *History of American Graphic Humor*, 1933, prints a reduced reproduction in Volume 1, page 26. Esther Forbes, in her *Paul Revere*, 1942, page 146, shows the print, and also its English original, both somewhat reduced.

A recent discovery has been made in Sheffield, England, of a different and interesting impression of the "Rescinders" print. In the Sheffield City Library, in the Wentworth Woodhouse Collection, there was found in 1949 a broadside poem, with the engraving of "A Warm Place — Hell" placed at the top. It was found in a bundle of Boston papers of July, 1768. The broadside is 13¾ inches high by 8 inches wide, to the edges of the printing. A twenty-line poem is followed by a list of the seventeen rescinders, each described in uncomplimentary terms (see Plate no. 11, slightly reduced). Evidently Edes & Gill printed this patriotic broadside and ornamented it with the original engraved cut of "A Warm Place — Hell." The Massachusetts Historical Society has a copy of the broadside, but with its most important element, the engraved cut, carefully torn off.

As was usual, Revere obtained the model for his print from an English original. A small volume of political caricatures, entitled *The Scots Scourge, being a Compleat Supplement to the British Antidote to Caledonian Poison*, was published in 1765. There was no date on the title-page, but in the American Antiquarian Society copy the date of "1765" has been inserted in the handwriting of Isaiah Thomas. The work was in two volumes and went through six editions. Plate 22 in the first volume is entitled "A Warm Place — Hell" and shows the devil with a pitchfork pushing six miscreants into the fiery jaws of a monster representing Hell. A verse in the text thus describes the print:

> Hell open its jaws! lo! the train is arriv'd!
> They may bless their good fortune so long they surviv'd!
> *Reynard* backs the *gude* L — as he us'd to do here,
> While the Devil pricks *Law*, and the rest in the rear.

Revere's print is almost an identical copy of the English caricature, except for increasing the number of figures to seventeen, inserting a flying devil above, and placing over the dragon's eye a representation of the cupola of the Province House, with Shem Drowne's familiar Indian with bow and arrow. The size of the English print is 3 7/16 high by 3 15/16 inches wide, to the edge of the border lines. Revere's print measures 3 3/8 by 4 15/16 inches to the border lines of the cut, and 4 1/2 by 4 15/16 inches to the edge of the printing. The same English print also appeared in *The North Briton. Extraordinary. No 1763. Or, A Peep into Futurity.* This was the caption title of an undated pamphlet, evidently issued in 1765. It had nothing to do with the long series known as *The North Briton* conducted by John Wilkes in 1763. Both of the English originals are in the American Antiquarian Society's Library. The cut in the *Scots Scourge*, as well as Revere's print, is reproduced, Plate no. 10.

In his print Revere inserted at the lower right corner "Pubd Accord'g to Act by M Darly." Matthew Darly was the most famous publisher of satirical prints in London in the 1750's and 1760's, and frequently his imprint carried the approval of the Act of Parliament. A vast amount of information regarding this period of English caricature is contained in Frederic G. Stephens's lengthy Introduction to Volume 4 of the *Catalogue of Prints and Drawings in the British Museum — Political and Personal Satires*, 1883.

Lord God Omnipotent, 1768

THE allegorical frontispiece in *Edes & Gill's North-American Almanack* for 1769, Boston, printed by Edes and Gill in Queen-Street, is headed in a motto at the top: "The Lord God Omnipotent reigneth. let all the Earth rejoice!" A detailed description of the plate is given on the title-page of the almanac, as follows: "Two Female Figures. The principal, richly decorated, is seated on a Throne with an Imperial Diadem on her Head, and a Spear in her left Hand. The other Figure exhibits a Virgin with a Civic Crown, in the utmost Agonies of Distress and Horror. The Cap of Liberty falling from the Spear of one, and tottering to fall from the other. The Label of one, is Collidimur; of the other, Frangimur. Two Ships are represented to View in a Tempest in the Instant of dashing to Pieces against one another, and sinking between the Rocks of Sylla and Caribdis. In the Interim are seen two Arch Angels, flying as 'on the Wings of the Wind.' The Label of the one is, 'Shall not the Lord of all the Earth do Right.' The other is, 'The Fool' only 'hath said in his Heart there is no God.' Above all, in a Glory, is inscribed these Words, 'The Lord GOD Omnipotent reigneth, let the Earth rejoice!' "

The almanac was reissued in a Second Edition, with the same plate and with the text in the same type set-up.

The plate is signed "P Revere sculp." No charge against Edes & Gill is entered in Revere's Day Book. Apparently Revere himself designed the plate, as well as engraving it. The size of the plate is 5⅛ high by 3¼ inches wide. (See Plate no. 12.)

The copy of the almanac in the Massachusetts Historical Society has written in contemporaneous hand on the lower border of the frontispiece: "This plate was struck in ye Fall 1768 when a large Naval Force, and 4 Regimts arrived." Above the engraving is the following manuscript note: "This represents ye sad State of

Britain and America, by the Taxes laid on ye Latter &c The Figure (1) Britannia wth Cap of Liberty totterg. (2) America with Cap off. 3. She Breaks on ye Rocks." The British fleet arrived at Boston on September 28, 1768, and landed their troops on October 1. The *Boston Gazette*, published by Edes & Gill, in the issue of October 31, 1768, states that "Edes & Gill's North-American Almanack for 1769, will be published on Thursday next [November 3]." In the issue of November 7, the almanac is announced as "This Day published." The announcement carries a long advertisement of the almanac, with a full description of the plate, the same as it appears on the title-page.

Both editions of the almanac are in the American Antiquarian Society and one or other of the editions are in several libraries.

PLATE 12. LORD GOD OMNIPOTENT, 1768.

Boston Massacre, 1770

PAUL REVERE'S "Boston Massacre" is the most famous and most desirable of all his engravings. It is the corner-stone of any American collection. This is not because of its rarity. More than twenty-five copies of the original Revere could be located, and the late Charles E. Goodspeed handled at least a dozen. But it commemorated one of the great events of American history, it was engraved by a famous artist and patriot, and its crude coloring and design made it exceedingly decorative. The mystery of its origin and the claims for priority on the part of at least three engravers constitute problems that are somewhat perplexing and are still far from being solved.

There were three prints of the Massacre issued in Massachusetts in 1770, as far as the evidence goes — those by Pelham, Revere, and Mulliken. The sequence of the advertisements in the newspapers is important. The *Boston Evening Post* of March 26, 1770, carried the following advertisement, "To be Sold by Edes and Gill (Price One Shilling Lawful) A Print, containing a Representation of the late horrid Massacre in King-street." In the *Boston Gazette*, also of March 26, 1770, appears the same advertisement, only the price is changed to "Eight Pence Lawful Money." On March 28, 1770, Revere in his Day Book charges Edes & Gill £5 for "Printing 200 Impressions of Massacre."

On March 29, 1770, Henry Pelham, the Boston painter and engraver, wrote the following letter to Paul Revere:

"THURSDAY MORNG. BOSTON, MARCH 29, 1770.

SIR,

When I heard that you was cutting a plate of the late Murder, I thought it impossible as I knew you was not capable of doing it unless you coppied it from mine and as I thought I had entrusted it in the hands of a person who had more regard to the dictates of Honour and Justice than to take the undue advantage you have done of the confidence and Trust I reposed in you. But I find I was mistaken and after being at the great Trouble and Expence of making a design paying for paper, printing &c. find myself in the most ungenerous Manner deprived not only of any proposed Advantage but even of the expence I have been at, as truly as if you had plundered me on the highway. If you are insensible of the Dishonour you have brought on yourself by this Act, the World will not be so. However, I leave you to reflect upon and consider of one of the most dishonorable Actions you could well be guilty of.

H. Pelham.

P S. I send by the Bearer the prints I borrowed of you. My Mother desired you would send the hinges and part of the press, that you had from her." (Massachusetts Historical Society *Collections*, 1914, Volume 71, page 83, and also photostat of original which is in Entry Book of letters dispatched, in the British Public Record Office, Colonial Office Record, C.O. 5/39, Part I, f. 1.) Following the letter is also a bill from Daniel Rea, Jr., March, 1770, for "Printing 575 of your Prints @ 12/Pr.Hund. 3:9:" (Idem, page 84).

In the *Boston Evening Post* of April 2, 1770, appeared this advertisement, "To be sold by T. & J. Fleet, and Edes & Gill, [Price Eight Pence] The Fruits of Arbitrary Power: An Original Print, representing the late horrid Massacre in Kingstreet, taken on the Spot." The same advertisement, except for a transposition of the names of the printers, was in the *Boston Gazette* of the same date.

In the American Antiquarian Society collection is an engraving of the Massacre with the following inscription at the top: "The Fruits of Arbitrary Power, or the Bloody Massacre, perpetrated in King Street Boston, on March 5th 1770, in which Messrs. Saml. Gray: Saml. Maverick. James Caldwell. Crispus Attucks. Patrick Carr were killed. Six Others Wounded Two of them Mortally." Underneath is a quotation from the Ninety-fourth Psalm, with a skull and cross-bones in the lower left-hand corner and a sword broken by lightning in the right-hand corner. The size of the print is 9⅜6 by 8¾ inches, within the rectangular lines. The print is unsigned, and this copy, one of two known and the only perfect copy, is partially colored. There is a water-mark of a crown, with the letters "LVG," which Dard Hunter assures me is probably the water-mark of Lubertus van Gerrevink, a highly regarded paper-maker of Holland.

There is not the slightest question in my mind but that the print entitled "The

PLATE 13. PELHAM'S BOSTON MASSACRE, 1770.

Fruits of Arbitrary Power" in the American Antiquarian Society collection is the engraving by Henry Pelham. Revere's print, which was described in the Boston newspapers as a "Representation of the late horrid Massacre in King-street" was first advertised on March 26, 1770, and put on sale. Revere entered his charge against Edes & Gill on March 28 for printing 200 impressions of the Massacre. Pelham, on March 29, wrote his letter upbraiding Revere for surreptitiously copying his print. Then, in the Boston newspapers of April 2, 1770, a week later, he advertised his print, "The Fruits of Arbitrary Power," and described it as "An Original Print . . . taken on the Spot." Note the word "Original." By the time Pelham's prints reached the street, Revere's print had already flooded the market. In a letter of May 1, 1770, to Charles Pelham, Henry Pelham records that he is sending to his brother at Newton "two of my prints of the late Massacre."

That Henry Pelham could engrave prints is well known to the antiquarian, although I have not been able to locate some of those which he made in Great Britain after his departure to that country. William H. Whitmore, in his article on "Painters and Engravers in New England" in the Massachusetts Historical Society *Proceedings*, May, 1866, Volume 9, page 204, says that Henry Pelham "certainly painted and engraved a picture on The Finding of Moses." The London *Notes and Queries*, Series 1, Volume 4, page 306, contains an article by A. B. Rowan, noting a mezzotint by Henry Pelham of Katharine Fitzgerald, Countess of Desmond, published by him June 4, 1806. He says that Pelham executed "a great part of a large county and baronial map," and gives considerable information regarding Pelham's later life in Ireland, where he died in 1806. Martha B. Amory's *Life of John S. Copley*, 1882, pages 3–5, quotes a letter by John Singleton, written in 1859, which notes several of Henry Pelham's engravings, including the 1777 Map of Boston, and the map of County Clare in Ireland, and calls him both an engraver and a painter. The Map of Boston, published in London in 1777 is well engraved and a highly valuable map. There are copies in the American Antiquarian Society and in most of the Boston libraries, and it is reproduced in full size in the *Celebration of the Centennial Anniversary of the Evacuation of Boston*, 1876. The best sketch of Henry Pelham, by Denison R. Slade, is in the

Publications of the Colonial Society of Massachusetts, 1898, Volume 5, pages 193–211.

Pelham's letter to Revere did not come to light until 1893, when Paul Leicester Ford contributed an article on the Copley-Pelham letters to the *Atlantic Monthly* for April of that year, in which he printed the Pelham-Revere letter. In May, 1893, William H. Whitmore read the letter at a meeting of the Massachusetts Historical Society and it was printed in the Society's *Proceedings*, Series 2, Volume 8, page 227. In 1902 Paul Leicester Ford printed the letter in the March issue of the *Bibliographer*, page 117. Then in 1914 Worthington C. Ford had all of the Pelham letters copied from the manuscripts in the Public Record Office and printed by the Massachusetts Historical Society in Volume 71 of its *Collections*. All of Pelham's letters were in the form of rough drafts, which has caused some sceptics to query whether Pelham's letter was written only in draft form, and never delivered. No comment upon the matter by Revere has ever been found. It was customary in the eighteenth century for engravers to copy anything which came their way, without credit or acknowledgment. Perhaps Revere did not know that Pelham intended to publish the print, or possibly he even shared with Pelham some portion of the profit. It is all a matter of surmise. Certain it is that Revere was an outstanding patriot and saw the opportunity of furthering the patriot cause by circulating so significant a print. Certain also it is that he never could have designed it. He was an engraver, not an artist, and could only copy the designs of others.

The Revere engraving is too well known to need a detailed description. The size of the print is 7⅞ inches high by 8 11/16 wide for the size of the cut, or 9¾ inches high by 8¾ wide to the edges of the text. The water-mark in the Revere print, at least in some copies which I have seen, is a capital letter "W." In other copies the water-mark is a crown, and underneath are the letters L V G, supposedly standing for Lobertus van Gerrevink of Holland, the same water-mark which was used in the Pelham "Fruits of Arbitrary Power." As can be seen in the reproductions, the differences between the Pelham and Revere engravings are many, although at first glance they seem identical. The Revere print has the moon facing to the left, has seven columns instead of eight in the cupola of the First Church

Unhappy BOSTON! see thy Sons deplore,
Thy hallow'd Walks besmear'd with guiltless Gore:
While faithless P—n and his savage Bands,
With murd'rous Rancour stretch their bloody Hands;
Like fierce Barbarians grinning o'er their Prey,
Approve the Carnage, and enjoy the Day.

If scalding drops from Rage from Anguish Wrung
If speechless Sorrows lab'ring for a Tongue,
Or if a weeping World can ought appease
The plaintive Ghosts of Victims such as these;
The Patriot's copious Tears for each are shed,
A glorious Tribute which embalms the Dead.

But know, FATE summons to that awful Goal,
Where JUSTICE strips the Murd'rer of his Soul:
Should venal C—ts the scandal of the Land,
Snatch the relentless Villain from her Hand,
Keen Execrations on this Plate inscrib'd,
Shall reach a JUDGE who never can be brib'd.

The unhappy Sufferers were Messrs SAML GRAY, SAML MAVERICK, JAMS CALDWELL, CRISPUS ATTUCKS & PATK CARR

Killed. Six wounded; two of them (CHRISTR MONK & JOHN CLARK) *Mortally*

PLATE 14. REVERE'S BOSTON MASSACRE, 1770.

to the left of the Town House, omits a smoking chimney behind the figure of the unicorn, omits a slender steeple to the right of this chimney, has no clear design of the sun-dial on the Town House, and inserts the words "Butcher's Hall" on the second story of the "Custom House." The chief difference between the two engravings is the inscription above and below, as will be seen in the reproductions. The Pelham engraving is drawn with a much freer hand, has more depth and artistic expression, and gives a more lifelike feeling to the figures of the soldiers — all of which would be expected from an artist of Pelham's ability.

The third engraving of the Massacre, apparently contemporaneous, is that inscribed "Jona. Mulliken Newbury Port sculp." This follows the Revere print almost exactly, except that there are a sufficient number of differences, such as having only six columns in the cupola of the First Church, the use of "ye 29th Regt" instead of "the 29th Regt," and many variations in the drawings of lines and letters, to show that it was an independent print, and not a restrike. The size of the Mulliken print is 9⅞ inches high by 8⅝ wide, to the edges of the text. Jonathan Mulliken was a clock-maker of Newburyport who was born in 1746 and died in 1782. Although he is not credited with any other printed engravings, he is known to have executed some etching on the brass faces of clocks. The Newburyport *Essex Journal* of May 25, 1774, has his advertisement as a clock- and watch-maker. From the appearance of his print of the Massacre it would seem to be a fairly faithful copy of Revere's work and was probably issued contemporaneously for sale in Newburyport. There was no Newburyport newspaper in 1770 to advertise such a print, and no other paper in Salem or Boston mentioned it. There are copies of this print owned by the American Antiquarian Society, Harvard College, Henry L. Shattuck of Boston, Miss Caroline C. Hollingsworth of York, Maine, Charles F. Rowley of Boston, the Winterthur Museum, and the William B. Goodwin Estate of Hartford. Most of these copies are colored.

In connection with Revere's print, it should be noted that there was a variant, with the hands of the clock on the First Church pointed to 8 o'clock, instead of 10.20 o'clock. This was first noticed, so far as I can find, in the 1902 Catalogue Number 8 of Burnham's Antique Book Store, number 41, priced at $700 and reproduced in the catalogue. This copy was previously owned by Francis LeBaron

Goodwin, a surgeon's mate in the Revolution. It is advertised in the Anderson Auction Catalogue, April 11, 1905, no. 685, $700; in George D. Smith's Catalogue in 1908, no. 334, $1200; in the Rosenbach Catalogue of March, 1913, no. 497, $1000. Apparently these sales were of the same copy, now owned by J. Wm. Middendorf, II, of Greenwich, Connecticut. The Rosenbach copy was sold to Dr. A. H. Rich of New York, and, after his death in 1956, to Mr. Middendorf. This so-called "eight o'clock" print has the hands at 8:10. The "ten o'clock" print has the hands at 10:20. Revere could not copy the time on the clock from the indistinct Pelham print. Presumably the hands, in any case, could not be easily seen by moonlight; according to the *Short Narrative of the Massacre*, the height of the disturbance in King Street occurred just before 10 P.M.

Edes & Gill not only published Revere's print of the Boston Massacre, but they used it in issuing late in March, 1770, a large broadside, 19 inches high by 15⅜ wide, printing the account of the Massacre taken from the *Boston Gazette* of March 12 and 19, 1770, and also using the copper-plate of the engraving, 8⅝ x 9¹⁄16 inches, exactly as originally issued. The broadside took five columns of printed matter, with the cut taking three columns at the top. It was headed "An Account of a late Military Massacre at Boston, or the Consequences of Quartering Troops in a populous well-regulated Town, taken from the Boston-Gazette, of March 12, 1770." (See Plate no. 16, slightly reduced.) The only known complete copy is owned by the New-York Historical Society, and is reproduced in the Society's *Annual Report* for 1930. A defaced copy, showing the print only, with part of the title at the top, is owned by Frank H. Schramm, of Burlington, Iowa.

The original copper-plate of Revere's Massacre is now in the State House in Boston, in the Archives Office. It was used by Revere when he was engaged to engrave the Massachusetts paper money issue of May 25, 1775, altered for date only in the issue of July 8, 1775. To reduce the plate to proper size he cut it off at the top, removing the title, and at the bottom, removing all of the verses. As reduced it measured 8⅛ by 9¼ inches. On the reverse he engraved the 10, 12, and 18 shilling notes. The Massacre side of the plate shows several smooches and scratches. Restrikes have been made from this defaced copper many times. The American Antiquarian Society has a dozen varieties. Two of them are old, perhaps early in

PLATE 15. MULLIKEN'S BOSTON MASSACRE, 1770.

the nineteenth century, one showing all of the smooches on the copper, and another with such defects carefully removed.

An interesting side-light on Revere's connection with the Boston Massacre is his pen-and-ink plan of the scene of the massacre which was used in the trial of the British soldiers. This plan was formerly owned by Mellen Chamberlain, and was first reproduced in his chapter on "The Revolution Impending" in Justin Winsor's *Narrative and Critical History*, 1888, Volume 6, page 48. Chamberlain says that it was drawn by Revere, and the lettering and figures are undoubtedly in Revere's hand. It was again reproduced in E. H. Goss's *Life of Paul Revere*, 1891, Volume 1, page 73. Neither Chamberlain nor Goss reproduced the original designations for the streets and house owners shown in the original, but substituted a key to describe all such locations. William Loring Andrews, in his *Paul Revere and his Engraving*, 1901, page 99, reproduces the plan, engraved by Sidney L. Smith, reduced from the original size of 12½ by 8 inches. In Esther Forbes's *Paul Revere*, 1942, following page 146, the original is photographically reproduced, with identification of the victims killed. The plan is now in the Chamberlain collection in the Boston Public Library.

It has been frequently supposed that the *Short Narrative of the Horrid Massacre*, Boston, 1770, carried the view of the massacre as a frontispiece. John Doggett's edition of the Narrative, 1849, showed a frontispiece view, but stated that it was a facsimile of the original engraving by Paul Revere, yet it was far from an exact facsimile as all of the lettering and much of the design were omitted. Sabin's *Dictionary of Books relating to America*, 1869, number 6739, in listing the *Short Narrative*, calls for a plate, although later in his work, in 1891, number 80,668, he omits mention of a plate. Frederic Kidder, in the *History of the Boston Massacre*, 1870, used the same small frontispiece plate as Doggett, except that the Kidder plate has a line below the print, "Am. Photo-Litho. Co. N. Y. (Osborne's Process)." Kidder does not mention the plate or its source. Justin Winsor, in the *Memorial History of Boston*, 1881, Volume 3, page 39, implies that the Boston, 1770, *Short Narrative* was accompanied by a folding plate of the Massacre, and in his *Narrative and Critical History*, 1888, Volume 6, page 47, says definitely: "Revere engraved a large folding picture of the massacre, which appeared in the official *Short Narrative.*" E. H. Goss, in his *Life of Paul Revere*, 1891, Volume 1, page 66, says that Revere's view of the Massacre "was a large, folded plate, issued in the 'Short Narrative' by the Town, and printed by Edes & Gill." W. L. Andrews, in his *Paul Revere and his Engraving*, 1901, page 104, says that the "first copy" of Revere's engraving of the Massacre is the one which forms the frontispiece of the official *Short Narrative* of 1770, that it measures only 6⅝ by 4¼ inches and has no inscription at the top, and has an inscription below reading: "The Massacre perpetrated in King Street Boston on March 5th 1770, in which Messrs. Saml. Gray, Saml. Maverick, James Caldwell, Crispus Attucks Patrick Carr were Killed, six other Wounded two of them Mortally." He continues: "It is not improbable that this engraving is the handiwork of Paul Revere, but it cannot be identified as such." Andrews reproduces the engraving on page 109, and the inscription above is taken from the reproduction. But it turns out that this plate is the exact frontispiece of the Dilly edition printed at London in 1770. I have seen it inserted in at least one copy of the Boston, 1770, *Short Narrative*, the Brinley copy sold to the American Antiquarian Society in 1878, I suppose because it was of small size, unlike the large plates engraved by Revere and others. There is no evidence that a plate was issued with the Boston, 1770, edition of the *Short Narrative*, and much evidence to show that it was not.

Christian Remick, mariner and artist, has for a century or more been credited with coloring Revere's print of the Boston Massacre. It is the crude, but effective, coloring — red for the British uniforms and the blood, blue, green, brown and black — that gives charm to the print and makes it more desirable for the collector. Yet there is no documentary proof to show that Remick was the colorist, except that the copy in the Boston Museum of Fine Arts has in the lower right corner the inscription, in contemporary hand, "Cold by Christn Remick," apparently written by Remick himself. There is reason to support the assumption, as only a few weeks earlier, in the *Boston Gazette* of October 16, 1769, Christian Remick had advertised that "he performs all sorts of Drawing in Water Colours, such as Sea Pieces, Perspective Views, Geographical Plans of Harbours, Sea-Coasts, &c. Also, Colours Pictures to the Life, and Draws Coats of Arms, at the most reasonable Rates." Revere used him to color his View of Boston and the Landing of the

An Account of a late Military Massacre at Boston, or the Consequences of Quartering Troops in a populous well-regulated Town, taken from the Boston-Gazette, of March 12, 1770.

BOSTON, March 12, 1770.

THE Town of Boston affords a recent and melancholy Demonstration of the destructive Consequences of quartering Troops among Citizens in a Time of Peace, under a Pretence of supporting the Laws and aiding Civil Authority; every considerate and unprejudic'd Person among us was deeply imprest with the Apprehension of these Consequences when it was known that a Number of Regiments were ordered to this Town under such a Pretext, but in Reality to inforce oppressive Measures; to awe and controul the legislative as well as executive Power of the Province, and to quell a Spirit of Liberty, which however it may have been basely oppos'd and even ridicul'd by some, would do Honor to any Age or Country. A few Persons amongst us had determin'd to use all their Influence to procure so destructive a Measure with a View to their securely enjoying the Profits of an American Revenue, and unhappily both for Britain and this Country they found Means to effect it.

It is to Governor Bernard, the Commissioners, their Confidents and Coadjutors, that we are indebted as the procuring Cause of a military Power in this Capital.—The Boston Journal of Occurrences, as printed in Mr. Holt's York Gazette, from Time to Time, afforded many striking Instances of the Distresses brought upon the Inhabitants by this Measure; and since those Journals have been discontinued, our Troubles from that Quarter have been growing upon us: We have known a Party of Soldiers in the face of Day fire off a loaden Musket upon the Inhabitants, others have been prick'd with their Bayonets, and even our Magistrates assaulted and put in Danger of their Lives, when Offenders brought before them have been rescued; and why those and other bold and base Criminals have as yet escaped the Punishment due to their Crimes, may be soon Matter of Enquiry by the Representative Body of this People.—It is natural to suppose that when the Inhabitants of this Town saw those Laws which had been enacted for their Security, and which they were ambitious of holding up to the Soldiery, eluded, they should more commonly resent for themselves—and accordingly it has so happened; many have been the Squabbles between them and the Soldiery; but it seems their being often worsted by our Youth in those Rencounters, has only serv'd to irritate the former.—What passed at Mr. Gray's Rope-walk, has already been given the Public, and may be said to have led the Way to the late Catastrophe.—That the Rope-walk Lads when attacked by superior Numbers should defend themselves with so much Spirit and Success in the Club-way, was too mortifying, and perhaps it may hereafter appear, that even some of their Officers were *unhappily* affected with this Circumstance: Divers Stories were propagated among the Soldiery, that serv'd to agitate their Spirits; particularly on the Sabbath, that one Chambers, a Serjeant, represented as a sober Man, had been missing the preceeding Day, and must therefore have been murdered by the Townsmen; an Officer of Distinction so far credited this Report, that he enter'd Mr. Gray's Rope-walk that Sabbath; and when required of by that Gentleman as soon as he could meet him, the Occasion of his so doing, the Officer reply'd, that it was to look if the Serjeant said to be murdered had not been hid there; this sober Serjeant was found on the Monday unhurt, in a House of Pleasure.—The Evidences already collected shew, that many Threatnings had been thrown out by the Soldiery, but we do not pretend to say that there was any preconcerted Plan, when the Evidences are published, the World will judge.—We may however venture to declare, that it appears too probable from their Conduct, that some of the Soldiery aimed to draw and provoke the Townsmen into Squabbles, and that they then intended to make Use of other Weapons than Canes, Clubs or Bludgeons.

Our Readers will doubtless expect a circumstantial Account of the tragical Affair on Monday Night last; but we hope they will excuse our being so particular as we should have been, had we not seen that the Town was intending an Enquiry and full Representation thereof.

On the Evening of Monday, being the 5th Current, several Soldiers of the 29th Regiment were seen parading the Streets with their drawn Cutlasses and Bayonets, abusing and wounding Numbers of the Inhabitants.

A few minutes after nine o'clock, four youths, named Edward Archbald, William Merchant, Francis Archbald, and John Leech, jun. came down Cornhill together, and seperating at Doctor Loring's corner, the two former were passing the narrow alley leading to Murray's barrack, in which was a soldier brandishing a broad sword of an uncommon size against the walls, out of which he struck fire plentifully. A person of a mean countenance armed with a large cudgel bore him company. Edward Archbald admonished Mr. Merchant to take care of the sword, on which the soldier turned round and struck Archbald on the arm, then pushed at Merchant and pierced thro' his cloaths inside the arm close to the arm-pit and grazed the skin. Merchant then struck the soldier with a short stick he had, and the other Person ran to the barrack and bro't with him two soldiers, one armed with a pair of tongs the other with a shovel: he with the tongs pursued Archbald back thro' the alley, collar'd and laid him over the head with the tongs. The noise bro't people together, and John Hicks, a young lad, coming up, knock'd the soldier down, but let him get up again; and more lads gathering, drove them back to the barrack, where the boys stood some time as it were to keep them in. In less than a minute 10 or 12 of them came out with drawn cutlasses, clubs & bayonets, and set upon the unarmed boys and young folks, who stood them a little while, but finding the inequality of their equipment dispersed.—On hearing the noise, one Samuel Atwood, came up to see what was the matter, and entering the alley from dock-square, heard the latter part of the combat, and when the boys had dispersed he met the 10 or 12 soldiers aforesaid rushing down the alley towards the square, and asked them if they intended to murder people? They answered Yes, by G—d, root and branch! With that one of them struck Mr. Atwood with a club, which was repeated by another, and being unarmed he turned to go off, and received a wound on the left shoulder which reached the bone and gave him much pain. Retreating a few steps, Mr. Atwood met two officers and said, Gentlemen, what is the matter? They answered, you'll see by and by. Immediately after, those heroes appeared in the square, asking where were the boogers? where were the cowards? But notwithstanding their fierceness to naked men, one of them advanced towards a youth who had a split of a raw stave in his hand, and said damn them here is one of them; but the young man seeing a person near him with a drawn sword and good cane ready to support him, held up his stave in defiance, and they quietly passed by him up the little alley by Mr. Silsby's to Kingstreet, where they attacked single and unarmed persons till they raised much clamor, and then turned down Cornhill street, insulting all they met in like manner, and pursuing some to their very doors. Thirty or forty persons mostly lads, being by this means gathered in Kingstreet, Capt. Preston, with a party of men with charged bayonets, came from the main guard to the commissioners house, the soldiers pushing their bayonets, crying, Make way! They took place by the custom-house, and continuing to push to drive the people off, pricked some in several places; on which they were clamorous, and, it is said, threw snow-balls. On this, the Captain commanded them to fire, and more snow-balls coming, he again said, Damn you, Fire, be the consequence what it will! One soldier then fired, and a townsman with a cudgel struck him over the hands with such force that he dropt his firelock; and rushing forward aimed a blow at the Captain's head, which graz'd his hat and fell pretty heavy upon his arm: However, the soldiers continued the fire, successively, till 7 or 8, or as some say 11 guns were discharged.

By this fatal manœuvre, three men were laid dead on the spot, and two more struggling for life; but what shewed a degree of cruelty unknown to British troops, at least since the house of Hanover has directed their operations, was an attempt to fire upon or push with their bayonets the persons who undertook to remove the slain and wounded!

Mr. Benjamin Leigh, now undertaker in the Delph Manufactory, came up, and after some conversation with Capt. Preston, relative to his conduct in this affair, advised him to draw off his men, with which he complied.

The dead are Mr. Samuel Gray, killed on the spot, the ball entering his head and beating off a large portion of his skull.

A mulatto man, named Crispus Attucks, who was born in Framingham, but lately belonged to New-Providence and was here in order to go for North-Carolina, also killed instantly; two balls entering his breast, one of them in special goring the right lobe of the lungs, and a great part of the liver most horribly.

Mr. James Caldwell, mate of Capt. Morton's vessel, in like manner killed by two balls entering his back.

Mr. Samuel Maverick, a promising youth of 17 years of age, son of the Widow Maverick, and an apprentice to Mr. Greenwood, Ivory-Turner, mortally wounded, a ball went through his belly, and was cut out at his back: He died the next morning.

A lad named Christopher Monk, about 17 years of age, an apprentice to Mr. Walker, Shipwright; wounded a ball entered his back about 4 inches above the left kidney, near the spine, and was cut out of the breast on the same side; apprehended he will die.

A lad named John Clark, about 17 years of age, whose parents live at Medford, and an apprentice to Capt. Samuel Howard of this town; wounded, a ball entered just above his groin and came out at his hip, on the opposite side, apprehended he will die.

Mr. Edward Payne, of this town, Merchant, standing at his entry-door, received a ball in his arm, shattered some of the bones.

Mr. John Green, Taylor, coming up Leverett's Lane, received a ball just under his hip, and lodged in the under part of his thigh, which was extracted.

Mr. Robert Patterson, a seafaring man, who was the person that had his trowsers shot through in Richardson's affair, wounded; a ball went thro' his right arm, and he suffered great loss of blood.

Mr. Patrick Carr, about 30 years of age, who work'd with Mr. Field, Leather-Breeches-maker in Queen-street, wounded, a ball enter'd near his hip and went out at his side.

A lad named David Parker, an apprentice to Mr. Eddy the Wheelwright, wounded, a ball entered in his thigh.

The People were immediately alarmed with the Report of this horrid Massacre, the Bells were set a Ringing, and great Numbers soon assembled at the Place where this tragical Scene had been acted; their Feelings may be better conceived than express'd; and while some were taking Care of the Dead and Wounded, the Rest were in Consultation what to do in those dreadful Circumstances.—But so little intimidated where they, notwithstanding their being within a few Yards of the Main-Guard, and seeing the 29th Regiment under Arms, and drawn up in King-Street; that they kept their Station and appear'd as an Officer of Rank express'd it ready to run upon the very Muzzles of their Muskets.—The Lieut. Governor soon came into the Town-House, and there met some of his Majesty's Council, and a Number of Civil Magistrates; a considerable Body of the People immediately entered the Council Chamber, and expressed themselves to his Honor with a Freedom and Warmth becoming the occasion. He used his utmost Endeavours to pacify them, requesting that they would let the Matter subside for the Night, and promising to do all in his Power that Justice should be done, and the Law have its Course; Men of Influence and Weight with the People were not wanting on their part to procure their Compliance with his Honor's Request by representing the horrible Consequences of a promiscuous and rash Engagement in the Night, and assuring them that such Measures should be entered upon in the Morning as would be agreeable to their Dignity, and a more likely way of obtaining the best Satisfaction for the Blood of their Fellow-Townsmen.—The Inhabitants attended to these Suggestions, and the Regiment under Arms being ordered to their Barracks, which was insisted upon by the People, they then separated and returned to their Dwellings by One o'Clock, at 3 o'Clock Capt. Preston was committed, as were the Soldiers who fir'd, a few Hours after him.

Tuesday Morning presented a most shocking Scene, the Blood of our Fellow Citizens running like Water thro' King-Street, and the Merchants Exchange the principal Spot of the Military Parade for about 18 Months past. Our Blood might also be track'd up to the Head of Long-Lane, and through divers other Streets and Passages.

At eleven o'clock the inhabitants met at Faneuil-Hall, and after some animated speeches becoming the occasion, they chose a Committee of 15 respectable Gentlemen to wait upon the Lieut. Governor in Council, to request of him to issue his Orders for the immediate removal of the troops.

The Message was in these Words:

THAT it is the unanimous opinion of this meeting that the inhabitants and soldiery can no longer live together in safety; that nothing can rationally be expected to restore the peace of the town and prevent further blood and carnage, but the immediate removal of the Troops; and that we therefore most fervently pray his Honor that his power and influence may be exerted for their instant removal.

His Honor's Reply, which was laid before the Town then Adjourn'd to the Old South Meeting-House, was as follows,

Gentlemen,

I AM extremely sorry for the unhappy differences between the inhabitants and troops, and especially for the action of the last evening, and I have exerted myself upon that occasion that a due enquiry may be made, and that the law may have its course. I have in council consulted with the commanding officers of the two regiments who are in the town. They have their orders from the General at New-York. It is not in my power to countermand those orders. The Council have desired that the two regiments may be removed to the Castle. From the particular concern which the 29th regiment has had in your differences, Col. Dalrymple who is the commanding officer of the troops has signified that that regiment shall without delay be placed in the barracks at the Castle until he can send to the General and receive his further orders concerning both the regiments, and that the main guard shall be removed, and the 14th regiment so disposed and laid under such restraint that all occasion of future disturbances may be prevented.

The foregoing Reply having been read and fully considered—the question was put, Whether the Report be satisfactory? Passed in the Negative, (only 1 dissentient) out of upwards of [illegible] Voters.

It was then moved & voted that John Hancock, Esq; Mr. Samuel Adams, Mr. William Molineux, William Phillips, Esq; Dr. Joseph Warren, Joshua Henshaw, Esq; and Samuel Pemberton, Esq; be a Committee to wait on his Honour the Lieut. Governor, and inform him, that it is the unanimous Opinion of this Meeting, that the Reply made to a Vote of the Inhabitants presented his Honor in the Morning, is by no means satisfactory; and that nothing less will satisfy, than a total and immediate removal of all the Troops.

The Committee having waited upon the Lieut. Governor agreeable to the foregoing Vote; laid before the Inhabitants the following Vote of Council received from his Honor.

His Honor the Lieut. Governor laid before the Board a Vote of the Town of Boston, passed this Afternoon, and then addressed the Board as follows.

Gentlemen of the Council,

"I lay before you a Vote of the Town of Boston, which I have just now received from them, and I now ask your Advice what you judge necessary to be done upon it."

The Council thereupon expressed themselves to be *unanimously* of opinion, "that it was absolutely necessary for his Majesty's service, the good order of the Town, and the Peace of the Province, that the Troops should be immediately removed out of the Town of Boston, and thereupon advised his Honor to communicate this Advice of the Council to Col. Dalrymple, and to pray that he would order the Troops down to Castle-William." The Committee also informed the Town, that Col. Dalrymple, after having seen the Vote of Council, said to the Committee, "That he now gave his word of Honor that he would begin his Preparations in the Morning, and that there should be no unnecessary delay until the whole of the two Regiments were removed to the Castle."

Upon the above Report being read, the Inhabitants could not avoid expressing the high Satisfaction it afforded them.

After Measures were taken for the Security of the Town in the Night by a strong Military Watch, the Meeting was Dissolved.

The 29th Regiment have already left us, and the 14th Regiment are following them, so that we expect the Town will soon be clear of all the Troops. The Wisdom and true Policy of his Majesty's Council and Col. Dalrymple the Commander appear in this Measure. Two Regiments in the midst of this populous City; and the Inhabitants justly incensed: Those of the neighbouring Towns actually under Arms upon the first Report of the Massacre, and the Signal only wanting to bring in a few Hours to the Gates of this City many Thousands of our brave Brethren in the Country, deeply affected with our Distresses, and to whom we are greatly obliged on this Occasion—No one knows where this would have ended, and what important Consequences even to the whole British Empire might have followed, which our Moderation and Loyalty upon so trying an Occasion, and our Faith in the Commander's Assurances have happily prevented.

Last Thursday, agreeable to a general Request of the Inhabitants, and by the Consent of Parents and Friends, were carried to their Grave in Succession, the Bodies of *Samuel Gray, Samuel Maverick, James Caldwell,* and *Crispus Attucks,* the unhappy Victims who fell in the bloody Massacre of the Monday Evening preceeding!

On this Occasion most of the Shops in Town were shut, all the Bells were ordered to toll a solemn Peal, as were also those in the neighboring Towns of Charlestown, Roxbury, &c. The Procession began to move between the Hours of 4 and 5 in the Afternoon; two of the unfortunate Sufferers, viz. Messi. *James Caldwell* and *Crispus Attucks,* who were Strangers, borne from Faneuil Hall, attended by a numerous Train of Persons of all Ranks; and the other two, viz. Mr. *Samuel Gray,* from the House of Benjamin Gray, (his Brother) on the North-side the Exchange, and Mr. *Maverick,* from the House of his distressed Mother Mrs. *Mary Maverick,* in Union-Street, each followed by their respective Relations and Friends: The several Hearses forming a Junction in King-Street, the Theatre of that inhuman Tragedy! proceeded from thence thro' the Main-Street, lengthened by an immense Concourse of People, so numerous as to be obliged to follow in Ranks of six, and brought up by a long Train of Carriages belonging to the principal Gentry of the Town. The Bodies were deposited in one Vault in the middle Burying-ground: The aggravated Circumstances of their Death, the Distress and Sorrow visible in every Countenance, together with the peculiar Solemnity with which the whole Funeral was conducted, surpass Description.

BOSTON, March 19.

Last Wednesday Night died, *Patrick Carr,* an Inhabitant of this Town, of the Wound he received in King-Street on the bloody and execrable Night of the 5th Instant.—He had just before left his Home, and upon his coming into the Street, received the fatal Ball in his Hip which passed out at the opposite Side; this is the fifth Life that has been sacrificed by the Rage of the Soldiery, but it is feared it will not be the last, as several others are dangerously languishing of their Wounds. His Remains were attended on Saturday last from Faneuil-Hall by a numerous and respectable Train of Mourners, to the *same* Grave, in which those who fell by the *same* Hands of Violence were interred the last Week.

The Bloody Massacre perpetrated in King Street BOSTON on March 5th 1770 by a party of the 29th REGt

Engrav'd Printed & Sold by PAUL REVERE BOSTON

Unhappy Boston! see thy Sons deplore,
Thy hallow'd Walks besmear'd with guiltless Gore:
While faithless P—n and his savage Bands,
With murd'rous Rancour stretch their bloody Hands;
Like fierce Barbarians grinning o'er their Prey,
Approve the Carnage, and enjoy the Day.

If scalding drops from Rage from Anguish Wrung
If speechless Sorrows lab'ring for a Tongue,
Or if a weeping World can ought appease
The plaintive Ghosts of Victims such as these;
The Patriot's copious Tears for each are shed,
A glorious Tribute which embalms the Dead.

But know, Fate summons to that awful Goal,
Where Justice strips the Murd'rer of his Soul:
Should venal C—ts the scandal of the Land,
Snatch the relentless Villain from her Hand,
Keen Execrations on this Plate inscrib'd,
Shall reach a Judge who never can be brib'd.

The unhappy Sufferers were Messrs. SAMl. GRAY, SAMl. MAVERICK, JAMs. CALDWELL, CRISPUS ATTUCKS & PATk. CARR *Killed. Six wounded; two of them* (CHRISTr. MONK & JOHN CLARK) *Mortally*

PLATE 16. BROADSIDE ACCOUNT OF MASSACRE, 1770.

Troops, issued in April, 1770, and a copy of this latter print, owned by the late Valentine Hollingsworth, bears the signature "Cold. by Chn. Remich," apparently in Remick's own hand.

Remick also drew and painted a "Perspective View of Boston Harbour," showing the landing of the British troops in October, 1768. There are at least six different copies of this view, generally dedicated to the purchaser or owner. They vary in size and coloring, but most of them are about five feet wide by one foot high. Five of the views are described in Henry W. Cunningham's *Christian Remick*, published by the Club of Odd Volumes in 1904. A sixth copy, recently revealed, owned by Henry L. Shattuck and formerly belonging to William G. Shillaber, was reproduced in 1950 by the Iconographic Society of Boston in a collotype facsimile of 110 copies. Christian Remick also made a water-color view of Boston Common, showing the Hancock house and other houses on Beacon Street, drawn and painted October 1, 1768. This view was reproduced by Charles E. Goodspeed in 1902 in an edition of seventy-five copies, engraved by Sidney L. Smith, from the original in the Concord Antiquarian Society. One copy is reproduced in James H. Stark's *Antique Views of Boston*, 1888, page 205; another in the William H. Whitmore Auction Sale Catalogue of November 11, 1902, much reduced and reissued in an edition of fifty-one copies for the Club of Odd Volumes. The Whitmore copy, purchased by the Club of Odd Volumes, was reproduced in facsimile in 1904, in an edition of one hundred copies, by Sidney L. Smith.

Christian Remick was a little known figure of the eighteenth century, but researches of recent years have pieced together many details of his life. He was born at Eastham, Massachusetts, in 1726, married at Harwich in 1752 Sarah Freeman, and followed the sea as a mariner and pilot. His advertisement as an artist and colorist, and the several examples of his work which have survived, reveal that interesting side of his career. During the Revolution he served on various vessels, the details of which service are given in the official record published by the State. He is mentioned in the Will of his father, Christian Remick, in 1783; but nothing is known of his later life or of the date of his death. Perhaps he was lost at sea. The best summaries of his career are in Mr. Cunningham's volume published in 1904, and Winifred L. Holman's *Remick Genealogy*, 1933, pages 91–94.

A woodcut of the Boston Massacre, size 4¾ inches high by 3⅞ wide to the border lines, was published in two forms in 1771–1772. Isaiah Thomas published *The Massachusetts Calendar, or an Almanac for 1772*, containing a woodcut of the Massacre, drawn closely after the Revere print, on the reverse of the first leaf, and below the cut an eight-line patriotic verse. It was unquestionably engraved by Thomas's friend, Paul Revere, as it was characteristically his work, and of the Boston engravers he was the only one who excelled in engraving on wood. In the *Massachusetts Spy* of October 3, 1771, Thomas advertised that the almanac would be published on "Monday next," which was October 7. There are copies of the almanac in the American Antiquarian Society and several other libraries, and it was sold at a Libbie Sale of April 13, 1904, number 1422, for $44, and at the E. B. Holden Sale of April 18, 1910, number 3694, for $1.50. W. L. Andrews, in *Paul Revere and his Engraving*, 1901, used the woodcut, somewhat enlarged, as lining-papers for the covers of his book.

The second publication of the woodcut was in a broadside entitled *A Monumental Inscription on the Fifth of March. Together with a few Lines On the Enlargement of Ebenezer Richardson, Convicted of Murder.* The size of the broadside, to the border lines, is 17½ inches high by 9¾ wide. The woodcut occupies the upper left corner; below it is a featured summary of the events of the Massacre and the previous murder by Ebenezer Richardson, who was still in jail on March 5, 1772, and to the right is the poetical inscription on the "enlargement" (release) of Ebenezer Richardson. Richardson was released from jail on March 10, 1772, according to the *Boston Gazette* of March 16, 1772. Isaiah Thomas, in his *Massachusetts Spy* of March 5, 1772, printed the summary of the murderous events in the same type as that of the broadside, and evidently, a few days later, printed the broadside, although like most broadsides and leaflets it was not advertised. There are original copies of the broadside in the American Antiquarian Society, Massachusetts Historical Society and New York Public Library. It is reproduced in Ola E. Winslow's *American Broadside Verse*, 1930, page 97. Both the almanac woodcut and the broadside are herewith reproduced, Plates nos. 17 and 18.

There were three English reprints of the Boston, 1770, engravings of the

The BOSTON MASSACRE, perpetrated on
March the 5th, 1770.

WHILE BRITONS view this ſcene with conſcious dread,
And pay the laſt ſad tribute to the dead ;
What though the ſhafts of juſtice faintly gleam,
And ermin'd miſcreants ridicule the ſcene ;
Ne'er let one breaſt the generous ſigh diſclaim,
Or ceaſe to bow at FREEDOM's hallow'd fane ;
Still with the thought let Fame's loud Clarion ſwell,
And Fate to diſtant time the MURDER tell.

PLATE 17. MASSACHUSETTS CALENDAR WOODCUT OF MASSACRE, 1771.

AMERICANS!
BEAR IN REMEMBRANCE
The HORRID MASSACRE!
Perpetrated in King-ſtreet, BOSTON,
New-England,
On the Evening of March the Fifth, 1770.
When FIVE of your fellow countrymen,
GRAY, MAVERICK, CALDWELL, ATTUCKS,
and CARR,
Lay wallowing in their Gore!
Being *baſely*, and moſt *inhumanly*
MURDERED!
And SIX others badly WOUNDED!
By a Party of the XXIXth Regiment,
Under the command of Capt. Tho. Preſton.
REMEMBER!
That Two of the MURDERERS
Were convicted of MANSLAUGHTER!
By a Jury, of whom I ſhall ſay
NOTHING,
Branded in the hand!
And *diſmiſſed*,
The others were ACQUITTED,
And their Captain PENSIONED!
Alſo,
BEAR IN REMEMBRANCE
That on the 22d Day of February, 1770.
The infamous
EBENEZER RICHARDSON, Informer,
And tool to Miniſterial hirelings,
Moſt *barbarouſly*
MURDERED
CHRISTOPHER SEIDER,
An innocent youth!
Of which crime he was found guilty
By his Country
On Friday April 20th, 1770;
But remained *Unſentenced*
On Saturday the 22d Day of February, 1772.
When the GRAND INQUEST
For Suffolk county,
Were informed, at requeſt,
By the Judges of the Superior Court,
That EBENEZER RICHARDSON'S *Caſe*
Then lay before his MAJESTY.
Therefore ſaid *Richardſon*
This day, MARCH FIFTH! 1772,
Remains UNHANGED!!!
Let THESE things be told to Poſterity!
And handed down
From Generation to Generation,
'Till Time ſhall be no more!
Forever may AMERICA be preſerved,
From weak and wicked monarchs,
Tyrannical Miniſters,
Abandoned Governors,
Their Underlings and Hirelings!
And may the
Machinations of artful, *deſigning* wretches,
Who would ENSLAVE THIS People,
Come to an end,
Let their NAMES and MEMORIES
Be buried in eternal oblivion,
And the PRESS,
For a *SCOURGE* to Tyrannical Rulers,
Remain FREE.

A MONUMENTAL INSCRIPTION

ON THE

Fifth of March.

Together with a few LINES

On the Enlargement of

EBENEZER RICHARDSON,

Convicted of MURDER.

AWAKE my drowſy Thoughts! Awake my muſe!
Awake O earth, and tremble at the news!
In grand defiance to the laws of God,
The Guilty, Guilty murd'rer walks abroad.
That city mourns, (the cry comes from the ground,)
Where law and juſtice never can be found:
Oh! ſword of vengeance, fall thou on the race
Of thoſe who hinder juſtice from its place.
O MURD'RER! RICHARDSON! with their lateſt breath
Millions will curſe you when you ſleep in death!
Infernal horrors ſure will ſhake your ſoul
When o'er your head the awful thunders roll.
Earth cannot hide you, always will the cry
Of Murder! Murder! haunt you 'till you die!
To yonder grave! with trembling joints repair,
Remember, SEIDER's corps lies mould'ring there;
There drop a tear, and think what you have done!
Then judge how you can live beneath the Sun.
A PARDON may arrive! You laws defy,
But Heaven's laws will ſtand when KINGS ſhall die.
Oh! Wretched man! the monſter of the times,
You were not hung " by reaſon of *old* Lines,"
Old Lines thrown by, 'twas then we were in hopes,
That you would ſoon be hung with *new made* Ropes
But neither *Ropes nor Lines*, will ſatisfiy
For SEIDER's blood! But GOD is ever nigh,
And guilty ſouls will not unpuniſh'd go
Tho' they're excus'd by judges here below!
You are enlarg'd but curſed is your fate
Tho' *Cuſhing*'s eas'd you from the priſon gate
The *Bridge* of *Tories*, *it* has borne you o'er
Yet you e'er long may meet with HELL's dark ſhore.

+ "Lines" - the name of one of the Judges
* Name of another Judge, newly appointed
† Do. of another of the Judges
‡ Trowbridge another Judge.

PLATE 18. BROADSIDE MONUMENTAL INSCRIPTION, 1772.

Boston Massacre, all of them of much historical interest. The English Whigs were only too willing to capitalize on any happening that would annoy the Conservative Tories. Edes & Gill, in the *Boston Gazette* of March 26, 1770, state that they have been hastening the printing of the *Short Narrative of The Horrid Massacre in Boston*, as follows: "The Betsey Packet, a prime sailing Schooner . . . has been hired by this Town, to carry to England, a full Representation of the tragical Affair on the Evening of the 5th of this Month; and we hear will sail the first Wind . . . our whole Time has been taken up in printing the Narrative and Depositions of the late horrid Massacre in this Town, to go by the above Express to England." On April 2, 1770, the *Gazette* stated: "The Betsey, Capt. Andrew Gardiner, hired by this Town, to carry a particular Account of the late horrid Massacre, sail'd Yesterday for London." The vessel arrived at Bristol, England, on May 1, according to the *Massachusetts Gazette. and Boston News-Letter Extraordinary* of June 21, 1770, which also stated that a faster vessel had arrived in England on April 22, and that the news of the Massacre was immediately forwarded to London. In the *London Chronicle* of May 5, 1770, is the advertisement: "This Day was published, Price 2s. Ornamented with a Frontispiece representing the Soldiers in the very Action, A Short Narrative of the Horrid Massacre . . . Boston, printed by Messrs. Edes and Gill, by Order of the Town of Boston; re-printed for W. Bingley, in Newgate-street, London." The news reached Boston in time for the newspapers of June 18. The *Boston Gazette* of June 18, 1770, announced that the *Short Narrative* has been reprinted by William Bingley and concluded: "With this authenticated Narrative Mr. Bingley received a copper plate print, representing the soldiers firing on the unarmed townsmen of Boston, while they were removing their murdered countrymen. The plate he has had engraved, and has prefixed it to the Narrative by way of frontispiece."

The Bingley edition of the *Short Narrative*, London, 1770, is to be found at the American Antiquarian Society, John Carter Brown Library, American Philosophical Society, Harvard, Massachusetts Historical Society, Yale, British Museum, and other libraries. It went through two editions, differing in pagination and even in set-up of title-pages. The engraved frontispiece was also sold separately, as is shown in the imprint of the engraving, where the price of it alone is given as 6d. Also in the *North Briton*, for May 12, 1770, London, printed for W. Bingley, page 398 (copy in American Antiquarian Society), Bingley advertises his publication of the *Short Narrative*, stating that the frontispiece is sold separately, price 6d. The British Museum copy of the engraving, which was presented by Thomas Hollis, May 14, 1770, has never been folded or creased. The copy of the frontispiece in the American Antiquarian Society collection is a proof before letters, with no text whatever. The title-page of the Bingley edition is reproduced in the E. D. Church Catalogue, Volume 5, page 2145, also in C. F. Heartman's Auction Catalogue, February 22, 1927, number 30, where the copy was sold to L. C. Harper for $325.

When Bingley had the plate engraved, he evidently had both the Pelham and Revere plates before him. As will be seen by the reproductions, Bingley copied both of the plates for his text. For the heading he copied the heading of the Pelham plate, except that he omitted the date "on March 5, 1770," omitted "by a Party of the XXIXth Regt.," and added the names of the two wounded, "Christopher Monk and John Clark." For the inscription below, he preserved Pelham's design of the skull and cross-bones and the broken sword, but split the quotation from Psalms into two sections, at the lower left and right. He used Revere's eighteen-line, three-column poem, splitting it into two columns of eight and ten lines. He inserted the imprint "Printed for and sold by W. Bingley, in Newgate-Street, Price 6d."

As for the design of the Massacre, he followed Pelham's drawing, with the moon facing right, eight columns in the steeple of the Church, and the smoking chimney to the right of the Town House tower. He omitted, as Revere did, the narrow church spire in the far right background. The only items which he took from Revere's design were the words "Butchers Hall" and "Custom House" for the building at the right. Bingley also improved and lightened the print by drawing in the panes of windows and the texture of the brick in the Town House. The detail and carefulness of his design were much superior to either Pelham's or Revere's. The measurements of the Bingley plate are 9 1/16 inches high by 8 5/8 wide to the border lines of the Massacre design, and 13 7/16 by 9 inches to the extreme margins of the text. (See Plate no. 19.)

PLATE 19. BINGLEY REPRINT OF MASSACRE, 1770.

The second English printing of *The Short Narrative* was that published by E. and C. Dilly. The title-page follows closely the Boston edition. The imprint reads: "Printed by Order of the Town of Boston: London, Re-printed for E. and C. Dilly, in the Poultry; and J. Almon, in Piccadilly. M.DCC.LXX." In the *London Chronicle* of May 8, 1770, its publication is recorded as follows: "This Day was published, Price 2s, 6d. Printed on a fine Paper, with a Copper Plate, representing the Scene of Action near the Town Hall of Boston, A Narrative of the Horrid Massacre . . . London reprinted for E. and C. Dilly, in the Poultry; and J. Almon, Piccadilly." Copies are in the American Antiquarian Society and other libraries. The frontispiece plate, omitting the inscription, measures 6 inches high by 4⅛ wide. It follows the Pelham plate carefully. The engraved inscription below the plate follows Pelham's title, omitting only the words "The Fruits of Arbitrary Power, or the Bloody," and beginning "The Massacre." It copies Pelham in detail, even to the slender spire in the upper right background, and not including the signs "Butchers Hall" and "Custom House." It omits the moon which is in all previous designs, places nine columns in the steeple of the Church, and inserts a third smoking chimney at the right, perhaps to give symmetry. (See Plate no. 20.)

The third English printing of the Massacre plate is in *The Freeholder's Magazine* for May, 1770, London, printed for Isaac Fell, opposite page 136, accompanied by a six-page article giving an account of the massacre. The print, which is newly engraved, follows the Dilly print carefully. There are minor differences, such as capitalization and punctuation in the inscription below, and the drawing of eight instead of nine columns in the steeple of the Church. The outstanding difference is the omission of the nonchalant dog in the foreground, the only instance in contemporaneous prints where this prominent animal is omitted. The size of the print, to the border lines, is 5¾ inches high by 4¼ wide. There are copies in the American Antiquarian Society and many other libraries. (See Plate no. 21.)

The engraving in *The Freeholder's Magazine* of 1770 was reprinted in 1775, identically the same plate, as the frontispiece of a pamphlet entitled *Considerations on the Commencement of the Civil War in America; Addressed to the*

People of England, &c. by an American. Embellished with an elegant Engraving, exhibiting an exact Representation, of the inhuman and horrid Massacre, exercised without Distinction of Age, Sex, or Condition. It was printed at London for J. Williams, 39 Fleet Street, 1775, in a pamphlet paged [2], 46. Copies are in the New York Historical Society and the Boston Athenæum. (See Plate no. 21.)

The nineteenth-century reproductions and facsimiles of Revere's Massacre print are numerous, and except for the 1832 reprint and the 1835 woodcut are not reproduced in this volume. The 1832 facsimile is an interesting print. It copied the original Revere print as faithfully as any engraver could copy it, and is colored like the Revere coloring. The engraver honestly identified his print by inserting the line "Copy Right Secured" between the poem and the list of "Sufferers," and at the bottom he engraved the line "Boston, (Fac-Simile) Republished, at 15 Water St. March 5, 1832." If the lower line were cut off, and the words "Copy Right Secured" were scratched out, the facsimile could easily pass for an original Revere. There are minute differences, however, for instance in the drawing of the capital letters in the two lower lines of the print.

The plate, although unsigned in any way, was engraved by William F. Stratton, an excellent Boston engraver of his day. His name appears in the Boston Directory at various addresses from 1827 to 1834, but only in 1831 and 1832 is he at 15 Water Street. In the Directory for 1832, page 21, he has a long advertisement describing the nature of his work. The *Book of Strattons*, 1918, Volume 2, page 110, has a sketch of his life, with date of birth in 1803 and death in 1846. The size of the plate, to the edge of the text, is 9⅞ inches high by 8¾ wide, and to the edge of the cut, 7¾ high by 8¹¹⁄₁₆ wide. The American Antiquarian Society has two copies, one an early impression with margins of half an inch or slightly more, and the other a later and fainter impression, probably a restrike, with margins of from two to three inches. Strangely, although printed from the identically same plate, the width of the cut in the larger copy is ⅜ inch wider, presumably due to the quality of the paper. The American Antiquarian Society has the original pewter plate upon which the cut was engraved.

A woodcut reproduction appeared in the *American Magazine of Useful and Entertaining Knowledge* for 1835, Volume 1, page 221, published by the Boston

PLATE 20. DILLY REPRINT OF MASSACRE, 1770.

PLATE 21. FREEHOLDER'S MAGAZINE, 1770, REPRINT OF MASSACRE, AND 1775 CONSIDERATIONS ON CIVIL WAR.

Bewick Company. This was a woodcut completely redrawn, with some details omitted and several new figures inserted. Its size was 5 15/16 inches high by 5 13/16 wide, to the border lines. It was signed "H," the signature of Alonzo Hartwell, on the publishing staff of the magazine. When the Boston Bewick Company failed in 1836, their stock was taken over by other Boston publishers. The *Family Magazine* for June, 1838, Volume 6, page 5, published at New York by J. S. Redfield, used the same wood-block, taking the text from C. H. Snow's *History of Boston.* The *Boston Weekly Magazine* of May 11, 1839, Volume 1, page 281, published by John B. Hall, also used the same cut, copying the text from the *American Magazine* of 1835. During the next decade this woodcut was extensively printed on copy-book covers issued by the successors of the Boston Bewick Company, and sold to various booksellers in Boston and surrounding towns. It was also used on the back cover of *The Stranger's Guide, or Information about Boston and Vicinity*, an eight-page pamphlet published at Boston in 1844 by John B. Hall. Here it is erroneously called a "fac simile of a copperplate engraving issued by Paul Revere." The American Antiquarian Society has all of the items mentioned in this paragraph. Only the cut in the *American Magazine* is herewith reproduced.

In the Bostonian Society is a colored print, 7½ by 5½ inches, entitled *Boston Massacre*, and described as from an original painting by Alonzo Chappel, published by Johnson, Fry & Co., New York. It is an imaginative view, quite different from the eighteenth-century prints.

In *Ballou's Pictorial Drawing-Room Companion* of February 3, 1855, Volume 8, page 72, is a view of the Boston Massacre, entitled "State Street in 1770." It is an imaginative drawing by Samuel W. Rowse, with the background of buildings following Revere, but the grouping of soldiers and inhabitants completely changed. It carries an original text, measures 7¾ inches high by 9½ wide, and is not herewith reproduced.

Also not reproduced is the large colored lithograph of the Massacre drawn by W. Champney and lithographed by Bufford in 1856. Below the design it bears the title "Boston Massacre, March 5th 1770," and the imprint "Published by Henry Q. Smith 284 Washington St. Boston." Below the picture is: "Drawn by W. Champney. J. H. Bufford's Lith. 313. Washington St. Boston." Below the title is: "Entered according to act of Congress in the year 1856. by H. Q. Smith in the Clerk's Office of the District Court of Massachusetts." The background, with the design of the buildings, is the same as, or similar to, Revere's print, but the position of the soldiers and the inhabitants is entirely different. This part of the design was completely changed, apparently with the desire to make the scene more imaginative. The negro, Crispus Attucks, was the central figure of the design. Both the moon and the dog, prominent in Revere's print, are omitted, and guns are being fired from the balconies of the Custom House and the building opposite. The size of the print, to the margins of the lithograph, is 17⅞ inches high by 24 inches wide. A copy of this print was sold, and reproduced, in the American Art Association Sale of April 29, 1935, number 661. The American Antiquarian Society has the print, also a signed receipt from Henry Q. Smith, dated January 26, 1857, charging $6 for a picture of the Boston Massacre. Henry Q. Smith was a gilder and dealer in picture frames in Boston from 1854 to 1857.

There is another issue of the same print, identical in design and lettering except that in place of Henry Q. Smith as publisher, it bears the imprint "Published by Thomas A. Arms 270 Washington St. Boston." The size of the lithograph is 18 inches high by 24 inches wide. The American Antiquarian Society copy lacks the copyright line, which is the same as that in the print published by Henry Q. Smith. A copy of the print was sold at the Parke-Bernet Sale of October 25, 1949, number 600, where it was reproduced. Arms was a picture-frame maker in Boston from 1856 to 1866.

Later reproductions of Revere's print of the Boston Massacre, in historical works, society publications, auction catalogues, school-books, magazines, and newspapers are far too numerous to list. They are nearly always reduced, and often without the text. A crude photographic reproduction in exact size, but of the cut only, without text, appeared in a Boston publication of 1888 entitled *Boston in the Revolution. Illustrated. A Souvenir*, which was issued in newspaper form in sixteen pages. The best photographic reproduction, exact size and in color, is in the E. D. Church *Catalogue of Books relating to America*, 1907, Volume 2, page 2150. Other reproductions, much reduced but the first two in color, are in John Fiske's *American Revolution*, 1897, page 72; E. M. Avery's *History of the*

UnhappyBOSTON! ſee thy Sons deplore,
Thy hallow'd Walks beſmear'd with guiltleſs Gore.
While faithleſs P—n and his ſavage Bands,
With murd'rous Rancour ſtretch their bloody Hands;
Like fierce Barbarians grinning o'er their Prey,
Approve the Carnage, and enjoy the Day.

If ſcalding drops from Rage from Anguiſh Wrung
If ſpeechleſs Sorrows lab'ring for a Tongue,
Or if a weeping World can ought appeaſe
The plaintive Ghoſts of Victims ſuch as theſe;
The Patriot's copious Tears for each are ſhed,
A glorious Tribute which embalms the Dead.

But know FATE ſummons to that awful Goal,
Where JUSTICE ſtrips the Murd'rer of his Soul:
Should venal C—ts the ſcandal of the Land,
Snatch the relentleſs Villain from her Hand,
Keen Execrations on this Plate inſcrib'd,
Shall reach a JUDGE who never can be brib'd

Copy Right Secured.

The unhappy Sufferers were Meſs.ds SAML. GRAY, SAML. MAVERICK, JAMS. CALDWELL, CRISPUS ATTUCKS & PATK. CARR *Killed. Six wounded; two of them* (CHRISTR. MONK & JOHN CLARK) *Mortally*

Reproduced 1954

Boston, (Fac-Simile) Republished, at 15 Water St. March 5, 1832.

PLATE 22. BOSTON 1832 FACSIMILE OF MASSACRE.

PLATE 23. AMERICAN MAGAZINE, 1835, WOODCUT OF MASSACRE.

United States, 1908, Volume 5, page 108; Milton Waldman's *Americana*, 1925, frontispiece; G. F. Dow's *Arts & Crafts in New England*, 1927, page xvi; and M. B. Davidson's *Life in America*, 1951, Volume 1, page 132. Of all reproductions the most outstanding is that completely re-engraved by Sidney L. Smith for Charles E. Goodspeed in 1908, and colored by Mr. Smith's daughter, Amy, issued in an edition of seventy-five copies. Mr. Goodspeed also engaged Sidney Smith, in 1904, to make a personal bookplate reproducing the Massacre on a minute scale.

Original prints of Revere's Boston Massacre are fairly common for a supposedly rare pre-Revolutionary engraving. A striking fact is that about half of the prints discovered are in early, or original, frames, apparently showing that Revere sold many prints in his own frames, which may well account for so many copies having been preserved. I will not attempt to list all the copies which might be found, as I have made no effort to locate the copies sold at auction, nor have I canvassed libraries and private collectors. Those copies which I have seen in institutions are as follows: American Antiquarian Society, Boston Museum of Fine Arts, Boston Public Library, Bostonian Society, Connecticut Historical Society, Essex Institute, Harvard, Huntington Library, Library of Congress, Massachusetts Charitable Mechanics Association, Massachusetts Historical Society, Metropolitan Museum, New York Historical Society, New York Public Library, Petersham Memorial Library, Philadelphia Free Library, Williams College, Winterthur Museum, Worcester Art Museum, and Yale Gallery of Fine Arts. Collectors whose copies I have seen or located are as follows: Mrs. John Nicholas Brown, Monroe F. Dreher, Dr. J. E. Fields, Henry N. Flynt, Mrs. Schofield B. Gross, Jr., Amor Hollingsworth, Caroline C. Hollingsworth, Josiah K. Lilly, Clarence C. Little, Mrs. Laird U. Park, Edward H. R. Revere, Carleton R. Richmond, Charles F. Rowley, Lessing J. Rosenwald, Society of the Cincinnati in New Hampshire, and Mrs. Louise L. Sturgis.

Landing of the Troops, 1770

REVERE'S View of Boston and the Landing of the Troops in 1768 is one of the largest, rarest, and most interesting of his prints. It shows in the foreground a view of the north part of the town from the water side, with eight British ships of war and several smaller vessels, Long Wharf and Hancock's Wharf jutting out into the harbour, and in the background the houses of the town with the spires of Fanueil Hall, the old State House, and seven churches showing against the horizon. The title on a ribbon above is "A View of Part of the Town of Boston in New-England and Brittish Ships of War Landing their Troops! 1768." At the lower right is a shield bearing this dedication: "To the Earl of Hillsborough, His Majests. Secy. of State for America. This View of the only well Plan'd Expedition, formed for supporting ye dignity of Britain & chastising ye insolence of America, is hum'y Inscrib'd." Under the print are recorded the names of the eight ships of war, the two wharves, and the North Battery, and the following description of the event: "On fryday Septr. 30th 1768, the Ships of War, armed Schooners, Transports, &c. Came up the Harbour and Anchored round the Town: their Cannon loaded, a Spring on their Cables, as for a regular Siege. At noon on Saturday October the 1st the fourteenth & twenty-ninth Regiments, a detachment from the 59th Regt. and Train of Artillery, with two peices of Cannon, landed on the Long Wharf; there Formed and Marched with insolent Parade, Drums beating, Fifes playing, and Colours flying, up King Street. Each Soldier having received 16 rounds of Powder and Ball." In the lower right corner are the words: "Engraved, Printed, & Sold by Paul Revere. Boston." The details of the view and the inscriptions are shown in the reproduction, Plate no. 24.

The size of the print is 9¾ inches high by 15½ inches wide. The coloring is a light blue for the sky and the distant hills, a pale red for the houses and buildings, and a deep red for the uniforms of the troops. The color of the flags on the vessels varies in different prints. In the American Antiquarian Society copy the stern flags on the ships of war are blue with a red cross in the canton, but in most copies the field is red, with the canton in blue. The bow flag, or Union Jack, has generally a blue field, with the red and white cross. Christian Remick unquestionably colored these prints. In fact, the copy owned by the late Valentine Hollingsworth carries the manuscript signature "Cold. by Chn. Remich," apparently contemporaneous and in Christian Remick's own hand. The water-mark, at least in the American Antiquarian Society copy, is that of "J. Whatman."

Christian Remick probably designed and drew this view. In the *Boston Gazette* of October 16, 1769, is the following advertisement: "Christian Remick, lately from Spain, Begs Leave to inform the Public, That he performs all sorts of Drawing in Water Colours, such as Sea Pieces, Perspective Views, Geographical Plans of Harbours, Sea-Coasts, &c. Also, Colours Pictures to the Life, and Draws Coats of Arms at the most reasonable Rates. Specimens of his Performances, particularly an accurate View of the Blockade of Boston, with the landing the British Troops on the first of October 1768, may be seen." Further details about Remick are given in the chapter on the Boston Massacre. Revere could not miss the opportunity to engrave and publish this view at a time when the town was seething with the excitement of the Boston Massacre of March 5 previous. In the *Boston Gazette* of April 16, 1770, he inserted this advertisement: "Just Published, and to be Sold by Paul Revere, Opposite Dr. Clark's at the North-End, And by the Printers hereof, A Copper-Plate Print, containing a View of Part of the Town of Boston in New-England, and British Ships of War landing their Troops in the Year 1768. Dedicated to the Earl of Hillsborough."

The expression of loyalty in the dedication, contrasted with the patriotic sentiment in the inscription, is noticeable. The dedication to the Earl of Hillsborough terms the expedition of 1768 not only well planned, but formed "for supporting the dignity of Britain and chastising the insolence of America." The inscription gives the detail of the landing of the troops and states that they marched into town "with insolent parade." Revere evidently wished to impress the Earl with the humility of his loyalty, but could not refrain from referring to the "insolence" of the British troops as they entered Boston. Perhaps he knew that the British parliament had under consideration the question of reconciliation with America. Per-

PLATE 24. LANDING OF T

open out

…he Troops, 1770.

haps his dig at the British was only another expression of his sly humor, a characteristic with him not unusual.

Just about two months earlier, on February 19, 1770, Edes & Gill had announced in their *Boston Gazette* that on "Thursday next [February 22] will be published Edes & Gill's North-American Almanack for 1770 . . . containing A Prospective View of the Town of Boston . . . and of the Landing of Troops in 1768." This almanac includes as a frontispiece, cut on type-metal, "A Prospective View of the Town of Boston, the Capital of New-England, and of the Landing of Troops in the Year 1768." It is signed "P Revere." and differs considerably from the later engraved view. The ships are placed differently — the *Beaver*, for instance, which is on the right in the engraved view, is at the extreme left in the woodcut. Whereas the engraved view extends south only to include Long Wharf, the woodcut shows the South Battery, Fort Hill, and three additional spires of churches. If Revere used as his model Christian Remick's view of the Landing of the Troops, advertised in October, 1769, this woodcut might show that the Remick water-color covered a more extensive portion of the water front than Revere showed in his engraved view. The almanac view is discussed more at length in the chapter on Revere's Metal Cuts.

Copies of Revere's original 1770 engraved view of Boston and the Landing of the Troops have been located by me as follows:

American Antiquarian Society. Has two small mutilations in the left margin which, however, have been repaired. Long owned by the Society, at least fifty years to my personal knowledge, and source not known to me.

Valentine Hollingsworth, Jr., Manchester, Massachusetts. This was the copy received by bequest from his father, Valentine Hollingsworth of Boston, who died in 1942. Mr. Hollingsworth obtained it in 1931 from Goodspeed's, who acquired it from Harold Murdock. Below the print is "Cold. by Chn. Remich," apparently in Remick's own hand. It is the copy here reproduced.

Amor Hollingsworth, Boston, Massachusetts. Inherited from his father, Zachary Hollingsworth, an excellent impression now at the Paul Revere Life Insurance Company, Worcester.

DuPont Winterthur Museum. Purchased from Harry M. Bland, who acquired it from Cornelius Michaelson, who obtained it from Brooks Adams of Boston. It is a good impression, in a fine original frame.

Henry L. Shattuck, Boston, Massachusetts. A good impression purchased from Goodspeed's in 1935.

Mrs. Charles L. Bybee. A copy bought from a dealer nearly twenty years ago for $2,000, but imperfect in the lower right corner.

James Lawrence, Boston, Mass. An excellent impression, inherited in the family. This copy also has the manuscript signature, "Cold. by Chn. Remich," in the colorist's hand.

Philadelphia Free Library. The copy received through bequest from William M. Elkins, who purchased it at Anderson's (the George R. Barrett copy), January 3, 1924. It is a good impression, in an early black frame.

Boston Athenæum. A fairly good impression purchased from Charles D. Childs in 1955.

New York Public Library. This copy, which is in the Emmet Collection, although complete, is not in perfect condition, being worn and much of the coloring rubbed.

At least three copies have been sold at auction:

Merwin-Clayton Sales Co., December 6, 1910, number 219. Described as having one or two small holes in centre and surface somewhat discolored.

Hudson's, October 20, 1914, number 493. Perfect and in contemporary black frame, and reproduced at page 52. Sold to "Order" for $112.50.

Anderson Galleries (George R. Barrett Sale), January 3, 1924, number 364. Described as stained near right side and with a few imperfections in margin and reproduced at page 68. Bought by William M. Elkins for $1050.

The original copper-plate of the Landing of the Troops is now in the Massachusetts Archives office. It was used by Revere to engrave the reverse of the 10, 14, 16, 22, 28, 36, 42, and 48 shilling bills of December 7, 1775. To make the plate of the proper size for the currency printing, he cut off nearly three inches from the left edge and nearly two inches from the bottom of the plate, so that the currency plate measured 7⅞ by 12¼ inches. This reverse showed a soldier with drawn sword in his right hand and in his left a scroll with the words "Magna

Charta," and with appropriate mottoes above and below. He used the plate again to engrave the same denominations for the bills of September 17, 1776, where he had to alter only the date. Again for the bills of November 17, 1776, he altered the plate by changing the date and inserting the word "Independence" in place of "Magna Charta." These alterations were accomplished by pounding out the surface of the reverse, smoothing and polishing the copper and re-engraving the changed words. As a result, the reverse of the plate, which of course was the Landing of the Troops, still shows the marks of the punched-out surface. Many restrikes have been made at different times from the copper. The American Antiquarian Society has at least four, all with the left and bottom margins cut off. Although they have little commercial value, it is a fact that in the Whitmore Sale of November 11, 1902, lot number 2797, a copy of the restrike sold for $100 and is now in the Boston Public Library. Apparently two buyers were anxious to acquire it, not realizing that anyone could get a restrike from the original copper in the State Archives and have it printed on old paper. Occasional restrikes have been made from the copper showing the reverse of the currency engraving, and there are copies in the American Antiquarian Society and the Massachusetts Historical Society. Also it is reproduced in Harriet E. O'Brien's *Paul Revere's Own Story*, 1929, page 41.

A facsimile of Revere's engraving was made in 1868 which has caused trouble for collectors even since. Alfred L. Sewell published a magazine in Chicago called *The Little Corporal*. He frequently gave prizes in connection with his magazine, and in the issue of June, 1868, page 93, he announced that he had acquired an original of Revere's engraving of the Landing of the Troops for $50, and had made a facsimile of the same size, and as nearly like it in design and color as lithography could make it. He offered to send a copy free to every subscriber who renewed his subscription, or he would sell prints at $1 each. The facsimile was circulated freely. It was marvellously executed, and even with the aid of a microscope it is difficult to find variations from the original. There are of course many variations. In the vignette at the lower right, in the eighth line, the letter "n" in "Britain" in the facsimile barely touches the mantling of the border, whereas in the original it overlaps the mantling. In the second line of the inscription underneath, the words "on Saturday" are separated in the facsimile, whereas they touch in the original. The further pair of soldiers on Long Wharf have the bayonets of their guns well below the second tier of windows in the facsimile, whereas the bayonets touch the windows in the original.

Sewell cleared himself of blame in palming off a facsimile for an original by printing clearly in the bottom margin: "This Fac-Simile of Paul Revere's Picture of One Hundred Years Ago is issued by Alfred L. Sewell, Publisher of The 'Little Corporal' Chicago Ill.," and at the right "Western Bank Note & Engraving Co. Chicago." If the line of imprint under the border is cut off, it is difficult to distinguish the facsimile from the original. The coloring is excellent, although the red in the flags and the soldiers' uniforms is fresher and more brilliant. There is little tinting of color on the houses, and the blue in the sky and water is fainter. The size of the print, to the border lines, is exactly the same as the original, 9 by 15½ inches.

But a more serious facsimile problem arose in 1882. In that year James H. Stark, in his *Antique Views of Boston*, reproduced, at page 202, Revere's Landing of the Troops in exact size, in a print made by the Photo-Electrotype Engraving Company of Boston. He stated that it was an exact reproduction of Revere's original engraving, but instead it was a photographic reproduction of Alfred Sewell's 1868 facsimile, with the lower line of imprint cut off. He said that copies of the prints in his book could be separately procured from the publishers, which accounts for the numerous copies to be found. The print, however, was not colored. Stark reissued his book in 1901 and 1907, although the prints were the same.

A curious facsimile is shown in a sixteen-page folio published in 1888, entitled *Boston in the Revolution. Illustrated. A Souvenir.* This contains, on page 4, a photographic reproduction of the plate in Stark's *Antique Views of Boston*, but since the Stark plate was slightly too wide, the photographer cut off half an inch, rearranged the printing below the plate, and re-photographed it for his shortened reproduction.

Many libraries and collectors have the colored Sewell facsimile of 1868 or the Stark reproduction of 1882 (often recently colored), believing them to be original. Also many of the reproduced reproductions in various books of history are from the Sewell or Stark prints. Among them are the reproductions in the *Bunker Hill Centennial*, eight-page folio newspaper published by Rand, Avery & Company, Boston, 1875 (only slightly reduced); *Celebration of the Centennial Anniversary of the Evacuation of Boston*, 1876, page 18; Bryant and Gay's *Popular History of the United States*, 1879, Volume 3, page 356; Justin Winsor's *Memorial History of Boston*, 1881, Volume 5, page 532; E. H. Goss's *Life of Paul Revere*, 1891, Volume 1, page 81; the Bostonian Society *Proceedings* for 1902 and for 1928; E. M. Avery's *History of the United States*, 1908, Volume 5, page 96; A. W. Mann's *Walks about Historic Boston*, 1917, page 80; the Stokes-Haskell *American Historical Prints*, 1932, plate 21; and Marshall B. Davidson's *Life in America*, 1951, Volume 1, page 131.

Reproductions of the original engraving, again much reduced, are shown in the Hudson Sale Catalogue of October 20, 1914, lot number 493, page 52; and the Anderson Sale Catalogue, January 3, 1924, lot number 364, reproduced at page 68.

Revere engraved another view of Boston and the ships of war in the harbor for *The Royal American Magazine* of January, 1774, published by Isaiah Thomas. The plate appears as the frontispiece of the issue of January, 1774, and is titled in a scroll at the top: "A View of the Town of Boston with several Ships of War in the Harbour." It is unsigned, but characteristically Revere's work. In his manuscript Day Book under date of February 6, 1774, Revere charges I. Thomas with "Engraving two plates for Magazine 6–0–0." The two plates in the January issue were the View of Boston and "The Thunder Storm," which is signed by Revere. The Boston view is similar to the 1770 engraving, in the drawing of the ships and of the town, but follows rather the viewpoint of the woodcut view in *Edes & Gill's North-American Almanack* for 1770, since it shows the shore front of Boston to the left of Long Wharf, including the South Battery and Fort Hill which were not included in the 1770 print. This plate is more carefully treated in the chapter on the *Royal American Magazine*.

The New-England Psalm-Singer, 1770

REVERE'S engraving for William Billings's *New-England Psalm-Singer* in 1770 was his largest undertaking. It consisted of an engraved frontispiece and a total of 116 pages of engraved music. The title-page of the book, enclosed in a border of type ornaments, is as follows:

> The/ New-England Psalm-Singer:/ or,/ American Chorister./ Containing/ A Number of Psalm-Tunes, Anthems and Canons./ In Four and Five Parts./ [Never before Published.]/ Composed by William Billings,/ A Native of Boston, in New-England./ [Four lines of quotations.] Boston: New-England. Printed by Edes and Gill./ And to be Sold by them at their Printing-Office in Queen-Street; by Deacon Elliot, under Liberty-Tree;/ by Josiah Flagg, in Fish-Street; by Gillam Bass, the Corner of Ann-Street, and by the Author./ [Price Eight Shillings, L.M.].

The size of the volume is 6¼ high by 8½ inches wide. The collation is as follows:

Frontispiece
Title-page
Page 2, Preface
Pages 3–9, Essay on Sound
Page 10, poem "On Music," by Rev. Dr. Byles
Blank page
Pages 1–8, engraved music
Page 8 reverse, blank
Pages 9–21, text of Introduction to Rules of Music
Page 22, New-England Hymn, by Rev. Dr. Byles
Pages 1–108, engraved music
Page 109, text of explanation
Page [110], Hymn by Rev. Mr. Whitefield
Page [111], Alphabetical List of Tunes (generally pasted on back cover)

William Billings's preface is dated October 7, 1770. On page 21 of the Introduction is inserted the following Advertisement: "To the generous Subscribers for this Book. The Author having to his great Loss deferred the Publication of these Sheets for Eighteen Months, to have them put upon American Paper, hopes the Delay will be pardoned; and the good Ladies, Heads of the Families, into whose Hands they may fall, will zealously endeavour to furnish the Paper Mills with all the Fragments of Linnen they can possibly afford: Paper being the Vehicle of Literature, and Literature the Spring and Security of human Happiness."

Edes and Gill, in their *Boston Gazette* of December 10, 1770, announce the publication as follows:

> William Billings
>
> Takes this Method to inform the Public, that his Composition of Church-Musick intitled, The New England PSALM SINGER, is published, and to be had at Edes and Gill's Printing Office in Queen Street; at Deacon Elliot's under Liberty-Tree; at Mr. Josiah Flagg's in Fish-Street; and at Mr. Gillam Bass's, near the Flat Conduit — where Subscribers and other Purchasers may apply for Books. — Those Persons that have Subscription Papers in their Hands, are desired to leave them at Edes and Gill's Office; and in so doing, they will oblige their humble Servant,
>
> William Billings,
>
> P. S. Any Gentlemen Subscribers, or others that incline to purchase, who reside in the County of Plymouth, may be supply'd by applying to Capt. Joseph Cushing in Hanover, rear North-River Bridge.

This advertisement was occasionally repeated in subsequent issues until the spring of 1771. Deacon John Eliot was a bookseller, whose place of business was next to the Tree of Liberty. He was a deacon of the Hollis Street Church, and died November 14, 1771, aged eighty-one (Thomas's *History of Printing*, 1874 edition, Volume 2, page 223). Josiah Flagg, in addition to his early trade of jeweller, was a composer of church music and it was he who had compiled the *Collection of the best Psalm Tunes*, published at Boston in 1764, for which Revere had engraved the plates. He was later a concert manager and in 1773 established a band which gave several concerts in Faneuil Hall (see F. L. Ritter's *Music in America*, 1883, page 44, and J. T. Howard's *Our American Music*, third edition, 1946,

PLATE 25. NEW ENGLAND PSALM SINGER, 1770.

page 64). Gillam Bass, born 1746 and died 1816, was a prominent patriot and a member of the Committee of Correspondence.

William Billings, author of the book, was the pioneer American composer. Born in Boston, October 7, 1746, and died September 29, 1800, he was a tanner by trade and a self-taught musician. He published six collections of music, became a music teacher and choir-master, and influenced music in New England more than anyone of the eighteenth century (see N. D. Gould's *Church Music in America*, 1853, pages 42–51; F. L. Ritter's *Music in America*, 1883, pages 56–68; F. J. Metcalf's *American Writers of Sacred Music*, 1925, pages 51–64; L. C. Elson's *History of American Music*, 1925, pages 12–19; J. T. Howard's *Our American Music*, third edition, 1946, pages 49–57; Raymond Morin's "William Billings" in *New England Quarterly*, Volume 14, page 30).

Revere's frontispiece shows seven men seated around a table, with singing-books before them. Around the scene is a staff of music, engraved in an oval and consisting of a canon in six parts. The words are not here repeated, as they are shown in Plate number 25. The plate is signed "P Revere sculp." The size of the print to the outside of the engraving is 5¾ inches high, by 6⅝ inches wide. There is every reason to believe that Revere designed as well as engraved the plate, as the drawing is crude and no English original is known. Revere engraved all of the music for the book, both staff and words, one hundred and sixteen pages in all. No charge for the engraving appears in Revere's Day Book, nor is any bill for the work known. A comparison to show the approximate cost of the engraving can be made from Revere's charge of £150 for one half of engraving the copper plates for Josiah Flagg's *Collection of Psalm Tunes* published in 1765, a book of sixty-six pages.

The known copies of *The New-England Psalm-Singer* are as follows:

American Antiquarian Society. Two copies. One is perfect, in original binding, and the frontispiece, which has wide margins, is here reproduced. It was purchased from C. F. Heartman, April 4, 1925. The second copy was bought by Perry Walton from Thomas J. Taylor of Taunton in 1928, sold to Mrs. Nathaniel Thayer in 1929, and came to Edward H. R. Revere after Mrs. Thayer's death in 1934. In June, 1951, Mr. Revere presented the volume to the American Antiquarian Society in memory of Pauline Revere Thayer. It is perfect, in original binding, except that the lower line of the frontispiece is slightly shaved.

William L. Clements Library. Two copies. One is complete, in original binding, but modern marbled paper on the boards, containing the inscription "Poley Pitcher, Her Book; Peter Read Singing Master of Attleborough 1778," received as a gift from Fannie Read Cook in 1937. The other copy lacks only pages 97–108, and is in original binding — source untraced.

John Carter Brown Library. Complete copy. Bought in 1944 from Goodspeed's Book Shop. Although perfect and in original covers, the lower line on the frontispiece is worn, affecting a few letters.

Boston Public Library. Complete. Purchased at E. B. Holden Sale at American Art Association, April 21, 1910. The Holden copy lacked pages 97–108 which, however, were supplied in 1940 from an imperfect copy.

Library of Congress. Two imperfect copies. One, lacking only pages 97–108, was the Manson-Appleton copy bought at Libbie's, May 15, 1906. The other, lacking only pages 109–[110], was bought at the Fabyan Sale at the American Art Association, February 17, 1920. The two, if put together, would form a perfect copy.

Massachusetts Historical Society. Two imperfect copies. One lacks the frontispiece, pages 109 and [110] at the end of the book, and has the final leaf of Index mutilated. The other copy is only a fragment, but it includes the frontispiece with the lower line shaved at the lower left corner, and the three final pages. The two, if combined, would constitute a perfect copy, except for the slightly imperfect frontispiece.

Huntington Library. Lacks pages 109–[110]. The F. R. Halsey copy acquired in 1915. Mr. Halsey bought it at the M. Stickney Sale at Libbie's, November 25, 1907.

Watkinson Library. Lacks pages 89–96, 99–102, 109–[111]. Obtained many years ago from Charles Wells of Hartford.

Yale University. Lacks title-page, pages 1, 6–7, of the first section of engraved music, and pages 109–[110] of the final text. It was the Lowell Mason copy, which went to Yale in 1873.

New York Public Library. Two copies, both imperfect. One, acquired from the stock of Thomas J. Taylor of Taunton in 1934, lacks the frontispiece, pages 1–8 of preliminary text, pages 1–8, 13–14 of the second paging, and pages 81–88 of the engraved music. The other copy, bought at a Henkels Sale, April 24, 1928, lacks frontispiece, page 1, 6–7 of the second paging, pages 81–82, 87–88, 99–102 of the engraved music, and pages 109–[110] of the final text.

At least seventeen copies of the *New-England Psalm-Singer* have been sold at auction, although some are the same copies sold twice. The collations are frequently misleading, as the cataloguers did not know what constituted a perfect copy. The list of auction sales follows:

Libbie (Thayer Sale) February 8, 1898 (number 175) $19. Lacks 8 leaves after page 80.

Libbie (Manson Sale) March 14, 1899 (number 2811) $85. Lacks pages 97–108. The copy noted by Goss.

Libbie (Whipple Sale) April 7, 1903 (number 1250) $105. Lacks pages at end. 4 pages misbound. Pages 97–108 irregular. *Frontispiece reproduced.*

Libbie (Bartlett Sale) May 19, 1903 (number 1244) $226. Complete. Bought by Hartranft. *Frontispiece reproduced.*

Libbie (Appleton Sale) May 15, 1906 (number 1945) $135. Contains only 96 pages of engraved music and 3 pages of text at end. Bought by Library of Congress. *Frontispiece reproduced.*

Libbie (M. Stickney Sale) November 25, 1907 (number 1618) $140. Lacks pages 109–[110]. Bought by Dodd, Mead Company for F. R. Halsey. *Frontispiece reproduced.*

Libbie (J. Stickney Sale) March 22, 1910 (number 1440) $26. Lacks frontispiece and pages 109–[111].

American Art (Holden Sale) April 21, 1910 (number 2992) $101. Lacks pages 97–108. Bought by R. Fridenberg.

Scott & O'Shaughnessy April 22, 1915 (number 490) $15. Lacks frontispiece, 8 leaves of music and apparently pages 109–[111].

Scott & O'Shaughnessy December 8, 1916 (number 31) $240. Bought by G. D. Smith. *Frontispiece reproduced.*

American Art (Fabyan Sale) February 17, 1920 (number 104) $210. Complete. Bought by F. Morris for Library of Congress. *Frontispiece reproduced.*

Heartman April 4, 1925 (number 151) $203. Apparently the Scott & O'Shaughnessy, 1916, copy.

Henkels April 24, 1928 (number 852) $10.50. Lacks frontispiece and pages 81, 87, 99–102. Bought by New York Public Library.

Ritter March 11, 1931 (number 24) $95. Lacks frontispiece, pages 65, 109–[110].

Parke-Bernet December 8, 1939 (number 303) $45. Lacks leaf I. Autograph of Asa Dyer. Bought by Goodspeed.

G. A. Baker March 31, 1942 (number 109) $6. Lacks 4 pages and has other defects. Bought by Aldine Book Company.

Parke-Bernet November 18, 1946 (number 503) $150. Plate slightly defective at outer side. Title-page torn. Lacks page [111]. Bought by Goodspeed.

Revere's engraved frontispiece has been reproduced many times, including E. H. Goss's *Life of Paul Revere*, 1891, Volume 1, page 56; W. L. Andrews's *Paul Revere*, 1901, page 61; A. W. H. Eaton's *The Famous Mather Byles*, 1914, page 110; and at least six auction catalogues as noted in the checklist of auction sales. These reproductions were all shown in much reduced form. The only reproduction in exact size was in Raymond Morin's article on William Billings in the *New England Quarterly*, 1941, Volume 14, page 30, and only slightly reduced in Harriet E. O'Brien's *Paul Revere's Own Story*, 1929, page 33.

PLATE 26. PORTRAIT OF WILLIAM PITT, 1771.

Portrait of William Pitt, 1771

A PORTRAIT of William Pitt, signed by Revere, is represented by an unique example in the American Antiquarian Society. It appears on a broadside entitled "A Speech of the Rt. Hon. the Earl of Chatham," with the imprint "Printed by Edes & Gill, 1771." The broadside is 16¼ inches high by 11¾ wide, to the outside of the print. The oval portrait at the top is 3⁹⁄₁₆ by 3¼ inches, with the inscription "The Right Honble. William Pitt. Esqr.," and signed "P Revere sculp." (See Plate no. 26.)

Pitt's speech, reprinted in four columns, was delivered in the House of Lords on November 22, 1770, and the news of it reached Boston so that it was printed by Edes & Gill in the *Boston Gazette* of February 4, 1771. In the same issue is this announcement: "At the Desire of a Number of our Readers, we shall publish Lord Chatham's Speech in a separate Sheet on Wednesday next, with an elegant Copper Plate Print of that great Patriot at the Head of it."

Revere undoubtedly copied the print from some English magazine, but not as yet located by me. There was a similar print in the *Gentleman's Magazine* of March, 1770, but quite different in design.

Susannah Carter's *Frugal Housewife* Boston, 1772

IN 1772 Edes and Gill of Boston published an edition of Susannah Carter's *Frugal Housewife, or Complete Woman Cook.* It has a lengthy title-page which is shown in the accompanying reproduction. The imprint is "London. Printed for F. Newbery, at the Corner of St. Paul's Church-Yard. Boston: Re-Printed and Sold by Edes and Gill, in Queenstreet." Edes & Gill, in their *Boston Gazette* of March 2, 1772, advertised this book as "This day published," and quoted the title in full. They added that it was "Sold also by Cox & Berry in King-Street." The *Massachusetts Spy*, in the Supplement of February 27, 1772, carried the same advertisement, also the *Boston Evening Post* on March 2, 1772, and the *Massachusetts Gazette and Boston News-Letter* on March 12, 1772. In Cox & Berry's printed *Catalogue of Books*, undated, but printed at Boston in 1772 (copy in American Antiquarian Society), the last page is given over to an advertisement of *The Frugal Housewife*, quoting the title in full.

That Edes and Gill copied an English book is proved by the Newbery edition in the possession of Mrs. Thomas M. Scruggs, of Richmond Heights, Missouri. It bears the title of *The Frugal Housewife, or Complete Woman Cook*, by Susannah Carter, London: Printed for F. Newbery, at the Corner of St. Paul's Church-Yard, no date, but presumably 1772. The Boston edition faithfully copied the London title-page for the upper two-thirds. But the English title states that to the text are added twelve new prints, exhibiting a proper arrangement of dinners. The Boston title omits reference to the twelve prints and states that prefixed to the text are various bills of fare. Both titles are herewith reproduced. The pagination of the London edition is xii, 180, 12, and of the Boston edition [xii], 168, due to the fact that Edes and Gill omitted the last fourteen wine receipts on

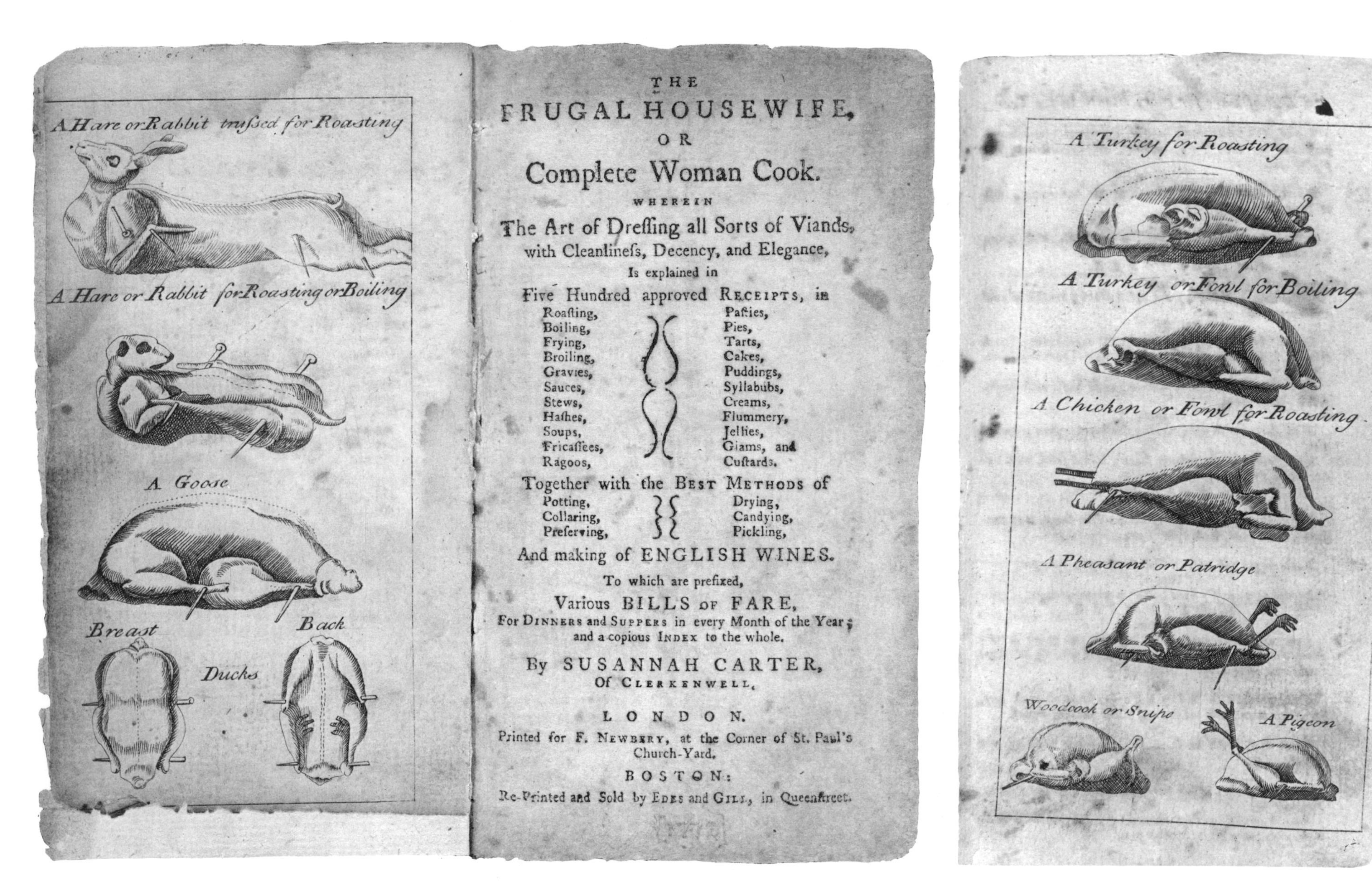

THE
FRUGAL HOUSEWIFE,
OR
Complete Woman Cook.
WHEREIN
The Art of Dreſſing all Sorts of Viands,
with Cleanlineſs, Decency, and Elegance,
Is explained in
Five Hundred approved RECEIPTS, in

Roaſting,	Paſties,
Boiling,	Pies,
Frying,	Tarts,
Broiling,	Cakes,
Gravies,	Puddings,
Sauces,	Syllabubs,
Stews,	Creams,
Haſhes,	Flummery,
Soups,	Jellies,
Fricaſſees,	Giams, and
Ragoos,	Cuſtards.

Together with the BEST METHODS of

Potting,	Drying,
Collaring,	Candying,
Preſerving,	Pickling,

And making of ENGLISH WINES.
To which are prefixed,
Various BILLS OF FARE,
For DINNERS and SUPPERS in every Month of the Year;
and a copious INDEX to the whole.
By SUSANNAH CARTER,
Of CLERKENWELL.
LONDON.
Printed for F. NEWBERY, at the Corner of St. Paul's Church-Yard.
BOSTON:
Re-Printed and Sold by EDES and GILL, in Queenſtreet.

PLATE 27. FRUGAL HOUSEWIFE, BOSTON, 1772, WITH SECOND CUT.

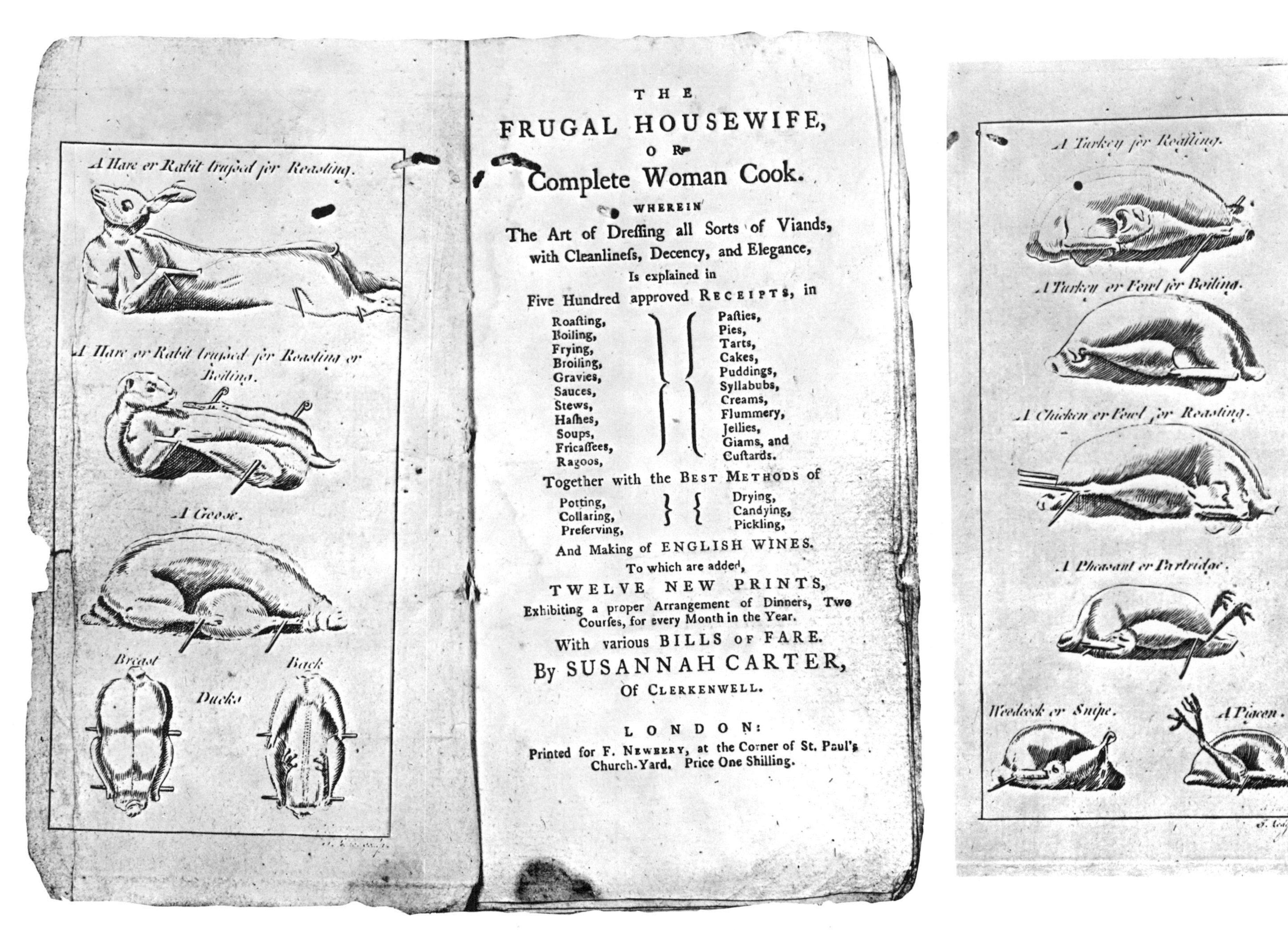

THE

FRUGAL HOUSEWIFE,

OR

Complete Woman Cook.

WHEREIN

The Art of Dreſſing all Sorts of Viands,
with Cleanlineſs, Decency, and Elegance,
Is explained in
Five Hundred approved RECEIPTS, in

Roaſting, Boiling, Frying, Broiling, Gravies, Sauces, Stews, Haſhes, Soups, Fricaſſees, Ragoos,	Paſties, Pies, Tarts, Cakes, Puddings, Syllabubs, Creams, Flummery, Jellies, Giams, and Cuſtards.

Together with the BEST METHODS of

Potting, Collaring, Preſerving,	Drying, Candying, Pickling,

And Making of ENGLISH WINES.

To which are added,

TWELVE NEW PRINTS,

Exhibiting a proper Arrangement of Dinners, Two Courſes, for every Month in the Year.

With various BILLS OF FARE.

By SUSANNAH CARTER,

Of CLERKENWELL.

LONDON:

Printed for F. NEWBERY, at the Corner of St. Paul's Church-Yard. Price One Shilling.

Plate 28. Frugal Housewife, London, 1772, with Second Cut.

pages 173–180 of the English edition and also the twelve pages containing the twelve woodcut prints. In the English edition the frontispiece plate and the plate before page 1 are signed "I. Lodge sculp." Revere copied these two plates with faithful exactness. In the Boston edition, in original binding, the two plates are inserted as a frontispiece and opposite page [xii]. The prints in both editions are reproduced on Plates 27 and 28.

That Revere made these plates is shown by the entry in his Day Book, under date of January 20, 1772, as follows: "Mesr Edes & Gill Dr. To Engraving a Copper plate for coocrey Book & 500 prints 2–14–0." The plates bear Revere's characteristic style of lettering. The existence of two plates in the volume, whereas Revere charged the publishers for one, is presumably explained by the fact that he engraved both small plates on one copper.

Two perfect copies of the book are known, in the American Antiquarian Society and Harvard. The Library of Congress copy lacks the frontispiece plate and the John Carter Brown Library has the frontispiece plate slightly imperfect. The Ross County Historical Society, Chillicothe, Ohio, has a copy lacking only the left-hand corner of the title-page, affecting four or five words. The American Antiquarian Society also has copies of the New York undated edition of 1792, the Philadelphia edition of 1796, and the Philadelphia edition of 1802. The plates in these editions follow the plates of the Boston edition, or possibly the London edition, but distinctly vary.

History of King Philip's War, 1772

REVERE'S two plates appeared in the second edition of *The Entertaining History of King Philip's War*, by Thomas Church, Newport, 1772. His contribution consisted of two portraits, one inscribed "Philip King of Mount Hope. P Revere sc," and the other "Col. Benjamin Church. P Revere sc." The former is a grotesque effigy of what Revere supposed the celebrated Indian chief looked like. The latter, as Charles Deane has shown (Massachusetts Historical Society *Proceedings*, 1882, Series 1, Volume 19, page 244), is an almost exact replica of the portrait of Charles Churchill, the poet, as it appeared in the *Court Miscellany and Gentleman and Lady's Magazine* for September, 1768, Volume 4, page 457 (which in turn was copied from Smollett's *Continuation of the History of England*, 1765, Volume 5, page 118), the only differences being the name and the insertion of a powder-horn around the neck of the Puritan warrior. This is another example of how Revere used English originals for his models. The Church-Churchill portraits are reproduced in the Historical Society *Proceedings* noted above, and also in W. L. Andrews's *Essay on the Portraiture of the American Revolutionary War*, 1896, page 5.

Henry M. Dexter, in his introduction to the 1865 edition of Church's *History of King Philip's War*, page xliii, refers to the similarity between the portraits of Benjamin Church and Charles Churchill, and says: "I imagine that Benjamin, the 'vendue-master,' who had some literary culture, and who busied himself in regard to the getting up of Dr. Stiles's edition, to the extent, at least, of writing the 'Ode Heroica,' remembering the face of his grandfather, and being struck with some decided resemblance between it and this picture of Churchill, engaged Revere to furnish a likeness of the Colonel based upon that of the poet. And the fact that there is a look to this day retained by many of the descendants of the

Plate 29. Church's King Philip's War, 1772.

Church family very far from being unlike to the general character of this picture, strengthens this supposition in my own mind to a strong probability."

The Newport, 1772, edition of Church is a reasonably common book, and at least two dozen copies can be located in American libraries. The frontispiece portrait of Colonel Benjamin Church measures 3⅞ by 3 inches to the edge of the medallion and 4¼ inches to the bottom of the title. The picture of King Philip, facing page 88, measures 6¼ by 3$^{15}/_{16}$ inches. (See reproductions, Plate no. 29, and see Bradford Swan, *An Indian's an Indian*, Publication 44 of the Society of Colonial Wars in Rhode Island, for the sources of this portrait of King Philip.)

Captain Cook's New Voyage, 1774

IN 1774 James Rivington of New York published a work in two volumes, *A New Voyage, round the World, In the Years 1768, 1769, 1770, and 1771; Undertaken by Order of his present Majesty. Performed by Captain James Cook. . . . By John Hawkesworth, L.L.D. and late Director of the East-India Company. In two volumes: With Cutts and a Map of the whole Navigation.* Volume 1. New-York: Printed by James Rivington, 1774.

Volume I has pages [2], 17, [1], 4, [2], 260; and Volume II contains pages [2], 250. The first volume includes seventeen pages of a list of Subscribers, covering the several colonies, Canada and the West Indies, and containing six hundred and sixty-eight names, one of the longest lists in any American book before the Revolution. A varying issue, otherwise identical throughout, contains an additional list of forty-seven subscribers on the reverse of page 17. A third issue omits the entire list of subscribers and bears the imprint: "Printed for William Aikman, Bookseller and Stationer, at Annapolis, 1774." There was no Maryland list in the earliest issue and Aikman evidently thought that he could sell enough copies to justify Rivington putting Aikman's name in the imprint. The American Antiquarian Society has all three issues, and one or more editions are in many libraries.

There are three engraved plates in the two volumes. The frontispiece of Volume I is entitled: "Dramatic Interlude & Dance given by the Indians of Ulietea performed by two Women & Six Men with three Drums." The plate is headed "to front the title of Cooks Voyage Vol Ist," and is signed in lower right corner "P Revere scp." The size of the print is 4 15/16 by 6 5/8 inches. Opposite the first page of the text is a long folding map of the world, which is signed at the lower right corner "Protracted by B. Romans," and presumably engraved by him. The frontispiece of Volume II shows "A New Zealand Warriour" and "Two Natives of New Holland." It is unsigned. Neither the map nor the second plate is in Revere's style, in design, or in lettering.

PLATE 30. COOK'S VOYAGE, 1774, AND ENGLISH PRINT, 1773.

Rivington, who published the work, took good care to announce it in his newspaper, *Rivington's New-York Gazetteer*, during the year 1774 (file in American Antiquarian Society). He made a preliminary announcement in the issue of February 3, 1774. In the issue of February 24, he elaborately described the prospective publication and said: "The principal Copper Plate Cutts, expressive of the Persons, Habits, Ceremonies, Pastimes, &c. &c. of the Inhabitants are engraving, and will be delivered with the Book; the utmost Price of which shall not exceed One Dollar and an Half." On October 20, 1774, he advertised the work as "This Day is published," and said: "These books are printed upon a paper fabricated by Mr. Christopher Leffingwell, of Norwich in Connecticut, with ink made at Boston, and every part of the labour effected by inhabitants of the city of New-York." The price was announced as twelve shillings half bound, and sixteen shillings full bound and lettered, for the two volumes. In all the announcements it was mentioned that Henry Knox of Boston was taking subscriptions.

In some Henry Knox correspondence of 1772–1774, published in the Massachusetts Historical Society *Proceedings* for 1928, Volume 61, several letters from James Rivington to Knox are included. One letter (page 279) dated April 8, 1774, says: "Enclosed is a Print which I desire you will immediately employ Mr. Riviere to engrave with all the ability in his power and to let it be done as soon as possible, be pleased to acquaint him that the Plate must be of such a size as will be adapted to a very large Duodecimo which you know is the size of Cook's Voyage and that it is to fold out Length ways as it lies now enclosed. I beg his best Execution and speedy dispatch of it."

In Revere's Day Book, under date of May 3, 1774, is the following charge: "Mr Henery Knox Dr/ To Engraving a Copper plate for Rivington/ 4–0–0." There is only this one charge for one plate.

The origin of this plate can be traced, as is usual with most of Revere's designs. The engraving of the Dance at Ulietea appeared in John Hawkesworth's *Account of the Voyages . . . by Commodore Byron, Captain Wallis, Captain Carteret, and Captain Cook*, London, 1773, in Volume 2, page 265. The plate measured 13 inches in width, and was designed by J. B. Cipriani and engraved by F. Bartolozzi. In the review of this work in *The Town and Country Magazine* for June,

1773, Volume 5, page 313, the plate is re-engraved in reverse and is entitled "Representation of a Dance, in the Island of Ulietea, to the Music of that Country." It is effectively engraved, but is reduced in width to 6¾ inches. Revere followed this as his model, rather than the original in the volume of *Voyages*. He changed the title, furthermore, as will be shown in Plate number 30. The engraving, although a reasonably faithful copy, is much more crude than the plate which he copied.

Royal American Magazine, 1774-1775

THE plates which Revere made for the *Royal American Magazine* in 1774–1775 constituted one of his most important undertakings in the field of engraving. The magazine had a wide circulation, about a thousand copies, and Revere's name was carried to places where he was hitherto unknown. It is true that the designs were copied mostly from English originals, but Revere never professed to be an artist. He was only an engraver and in that respect exceedingly proficient. The copies which he made from English originals were faithfully and attractively done, losing none of the beauty of the initial designs.

The *Royal American Magazine* was established by Isaiah Thomas with the issue of January, 1774, and continued by him through the issue of June, 1774. Perplexed by the condition of affairs in the colonies, and by the lack of funds, he ceased publication in June and was immediately followed by Joseph Greenleaf, who published the magazine from July, 1774 to its final issue in March, 1775.

The fifteen numbers contained twenty-two full-page engraved plates, thirteen signed by Revere, and three by Callender. Of the six unsigned plates, internal evidence or documentary proof show that four were by Revere and two by Callender.

In common with the practice of the times, the text was largely taken from London magazines, and the plates were nearly all based on English originals. In the first two issues there was some attempt made to give the title of the magazine from which the text was taken, but thereafter the material was generally lifted bodily from London periodicals without credit. Of course a fair share of the text was of American authorship, but American writers were increasingly difficult to obtain. There were copyright laws in England to protect the publisher, print-seller, or engraver. The so-called "Hogarth Act" of 1735 protected an engraver for fourteen years against piracy of his print, except with permission of the publisher. The Act was amended in 1767 and again in 1777. But it was neither enforced nor observed. English magazines frequently copied each other's prints. In the far-away colonies there was never a thought that it was illegal or improper to copy a print. Therefore Revere, like all other American engravers, felt entirely free to copy any plate that his publisher gave him to engrave. The source of his prints, however, is historically and bibliographically interesting. Fortunately most of the originals have been discovered, as will be shown in the list that follows.

The initial issue of the *Royal American Magazine* was that for January, 1774. It included two plates. The frontispiece was "A View of the Town of Boston with several Ships of War in the Harbour," size 6 9/16 by 10 3/8 inches, to the border lines. Above the plate, at the upper left, is engraved the words "Vol. I. No I." There is no signature or lettering below. In Revere's Day Book, under date of February 6, 1774, is the charge against Isaiah Thomas "To Engraving two plates for Magazine 6–0–0." This included the charge for the plate of "The Thunder Storm," also in the January issue. The View of Boston is characteristically Revere's work and is very similar to his earlier views of Boston. It follows in size, design, and general appearance his large view separately issued in 1770, except that it extends the shore line of Boston further to the left of Long Wharf, showing the South Battery and Fort Hill, as he had done in the small woodcut view of Boston in *Edes & Gill's North-American Almanack* for 1770. In the Royal American engraving the ships-of-war are numbered and the shore locations are lettered to correspond to a key, which is printed on page 40 of the magazine. For the supposition that Revere based all these views of Boston on a water-color by Christian Remick, made in 1769, see my chapter on the 1770 Landing of the Troops. The print is reproduced, in reduced form, in Justin Winsor's *Memorial History of Boston*, 1881, Volume 2, page 411, and in W. L. Andrews's *Paul Revere and his Engraving*, 1901, page 43. A copy of this print was sold in the William H. Whitmore Sale at Libbie's, November 11, 1902, number 2798, for $95. (See reproduction, Plate no. 31.)

In addition to charging Isaiah Thomas for two plates for the January magazine, Revere under the same date of February 6, 1774, also charged him "To Engraving a Leading Cutt for Magazine 0–16–0." This was the vignette which appeared on the title-page of each issue. It is discussed under the heading of "Revere's Metal Cuts."

PLATE 31. VIEW OF BOSTON, ROYAL AMERICAN MAGAZINE, 1774.

PLATE 32. THUNDER STORM, ROYAL AMERICAN MAGAZINE, 1774, AND ENGLISH PRINT, 1773.

The second engraved plate in the January issue is "The Thunder Storm," opposite page 26, size 5¾ by 3½ inches, to the border lines. Above the border line is "Vol. I No. II," and below is "P. Revere sculp" and the title. For Revere's charge in his Day Book see the entry under the "View of the Town of Boston." The engraving of "The Thunder Storm" was a faithful copy of a plate, with the same title, in the *Town and Country Magazine*, London, September, 1773, Volume 5, page 473. (See reproductions, Plate no. 32.)

The February issue contained two plates. The first, used as a frontispiece, was entitled "Sir Wilbraham Wentworth." The size to the border lines is 6⅜ by 4½ inches. Above the border line is "Vol. I. No. III.," and below is 'P Revere sculp" and the title. Revere's charge in the Day Book, under date of March 5, 1774, reads "Mr Isaiah Thomas/ To Engraving a plate for Feby Magzin 3–0–0/ To Printing 1000 at 2–8 1–6–8." The article accompanying the print begins on page 53, credits the original printing to "a London Magazine," and adds "Illustrated with an elegant Engraving, not in the London Edition." The English Magazine was *The London Magazine* for May, 1768, where the article began on page 236 of Volume 37, but with no engraving either shown or mentioned. The American Antiquarian Society has an engraving identical with Revere's print, but without name of subject. It is very slightly larger then the Revere copy, being 6¾ by 4¾ inches, to the edge of the engraved surface. Above is the number "14," and below is "Collet invt et del." and "R. Pranker sculp.," and at the bottom of the print, "London, printed for Robt. Sayer N. 53 Fleet Street, as the Act directs." What the number means above the engraving or why it does not have the name of the subject, I have not found, although I have searched at the British Museum and elsewhere. Presumably it must have been a portrait of Sir Wilbraham Wentworth, or Revere would not have so used it. Perhaps our copy is a proof before letters. There are other similar engravings by Pranker after Collet. The Revere print and the English original are reproduced (Plate no. 33), as in the case of all the engravings in the *Royal American Magazine*, where the English originals are known.

The second plate in the February issue, at page 57, is "The Night Scene," signed "J. Callender Spt." Although this chapter primarily lists Revere's engravings, it can be noted that the original of this plate is in *The Royal Female Maga-*

zine for July, 1760, Volume 2, page 17, a copy of which is in the American Antiquarian Society.

The March issue contains two plates. The first, used as a frontispiece, was entitled "The Honble. John Hancock, Esqr.," is signed "P Revere sc," and has a line at the top "No. V Engraved for Royl. American Magazine Vol. I." The measurements, including the lines of print, are 5 1/16 by 3 5/8 inches. The description of the engraving on the title-page refers to it as "The Bust of the Hon. John Hancock, Esq; supported by the Goddess of Liberty and an ancient Briton." The portrait is presumably Revere's own design, based on Copley's portrait of John Hancock painted in 1765. The supporting frame follows, with some variations, the emblematic vignette bust portrait of Richard, Earl Temple, in *The Scots Scourge, being a Compleat Supplement to the British Antidote to Caledonian Poison*, Volume 1, third edition, [1765], plate following title-page. The same plate, apparently the same copper, appears in *The North Briton Extraordinary. No 1763. Or, a Peep into Futurity* [caption title], no date, opposite page 48. Both books are in the American Antiquarian Society, as well as a separate print in red instead of black. (See reproductions, Plate no. 34.)

The English print, as is shown in the reproduction, has the portrait of Richard, Earl Temple, in a different type of medallion, with mantling and decoration. At the left stands the figure of Liberty with liberty cap and staff, and leaning against her a lion with his paw clutching the shoulder of Lord Bute. At the right is a soldier in armor with spear and shield. Above is the angel of Fame sounding her trumpet and facing to the left. Below is a scroll with the words "Magna Charta." The print is described, with its political significance, in the British Museum *Catalogue of Political and Personal Satires*, 1883, Volume 4, page 247, where it is dated in 1763. Revere copied the design of the English plate, but reversing right to left all of the figures. The figure clutched by the lion is labelled "G R XXIX," signifying a soldier of the "infamous" twenty-ninth regiment which had taken part in the Boston Massacre.

In his Day Book Revere, under date of April 11, 1774, has the following entry: "Mr Isaiah Thomas Dr/ To 1000 prints for March Magazine 6–0–0." His charge for engraving a print for the magazine was usually £3. Therefore

PLATE 33. SIR WILBRAHAM WENTWORTH, ROYAL AMERICAN MAGAZINE, 1774, AND ENGLISH PRINT.

this undoubtedly meant that he charged at the same time for the similar Samuel Adams print, which did not appear until the April issue.

The John Hancock print is reproduced in E. H. Goss's *Life of Paul Revere*, 1891, page 89, in W. L. Andrews's *Essay on the Portraiture of the American Revolutionary War*, 1896, page 75, and in the American Art Association Catalogue of the John C. Williams Sale, November 6, 1929, page 31.

In the Hampton L. Carson Sale of Engraved Portraits, conducted by Henkels, December 16, 1904, Catalogue Number 906, Part III, Lot #3186, there is described a bust portrait of John Hancock in an oval between laurel branches, and over the oval a liberty cap and diverging rays. The size is given as 4⅛ inches high by 3⅝ wide. The statement is plainly made that the engraving was "engraved by Paul Revere." There is a full size reproduction used as a frontispiece to the Catalogue. According to our annotated copy of the Catalogue, this engraving was bought by a buyer under the name of "Buck" for $85. The buyer I cannot identify.

In the *Antiquarian* for October, 1925, Volume 5, page 27, is an article by Russell W. Thorpe on the Portraits of John Hancock, in which this engraving, called unique, is reproduced in reduced size and the ownership ascribed to a private collection.

I can see no reason whatever for assigning this portrait to Revere. It is not characteristic of his work and resembles the portrait credited to Littleford and reproduced at several times in 1775 and afterwards. Revere had engraved his portrait of John Hancock for the *Royal American Magazine* in March, 1774, Volume 1, opposite page 80. He followed for his model Copley's portrait of Hancock which had been painted in 1765, although he used an English engraving for the framework around the oval portrait. This portrait was signed by him. I believe that the statement in the Carson Catalogue is erroneous.

The same portrait of Hancock was used on a broadside Declaration of Independence, in fact it is apparently from the same copper as the print in the Carson Sale. The original is in the John Carter Brown Library and is described in M. J. Walsh's *Contemporary Broadside Editions of the Declaration of Independence*, 1949, number 17. This broadside Mr. Walsh believes to have been printed in

England. The Carson print, failing an examination of the original, may well have been cut from the top of the broadside Declaration.

The second plate in the March issue, at page 101, is "The Fortune Hunter," signed "J. Callender sculp." The original of this plate is in *The Royal Female Magazine* for August, 1760, Volume 2, page 53, a copy of which is in the American Antiquarian Society.

The April issue contains two plates. The first, used as a frontispiece, was entitled "Mr. Samuel Adams," is signed "P Revere Scp." and has a line at the top "No VII Engravd. for Royal American Magazine Vol. I." The measurements, including the lines of print, are 5⅛ by 4⅛ inches. The portrait itself, in an oval frame, is apparently Revere's own design, based upon Copley's portrait of Adams, at that time owned by John Hancock, and painted in 1770 or soon afterward (see Parker and Wheeler's *John Singleton Copley*, 1938, page 18). Revere again used the Earl Temple design for his model of the framework, placing the figure of Liberty at the left, substituting for the soldier a female figure, with a shield and spear on the right, and having the Angel with the trumpet above facing the left. The figure of Liberty stands upon a large book lettered "Laws to Enslave America," the figure of the woman on the right is holding her spear upon the shoulder of the soldier of the twenty-ninth regiment, and below is the scroll of "Magna Charta." Revere's charge for the engraving is noted in the description of the Hancock print. The Adams engraving is reproduced in E. H. Goss's *Life of Paul Revere*, 1891, page 88. (See reproduction, Plate no. 34.)

The second plate in the April issue, at page 152, is "The Hill Tops, A New Hunting Song," signed "J. C. sp." I cannot find the original of Callender's design in an English magazine.

The May issue contains but one plate, at page 185, "An Indian Gazette," size 6⅝ by 7³⁄₁₆ inches. Although unsigned, the style of the lettering and the method of design show it to be Callender's work. There is no entry in Revere's Day Book for the May magazine. The print was copied, both text and plate, from the *Royal Female Magazine* for May, 1760, Volume 1, page 219. The text states: "This print is engraved from an authentic copy, drawn by a French engineer, from the American original." In smaller form this plate had previously appeared in

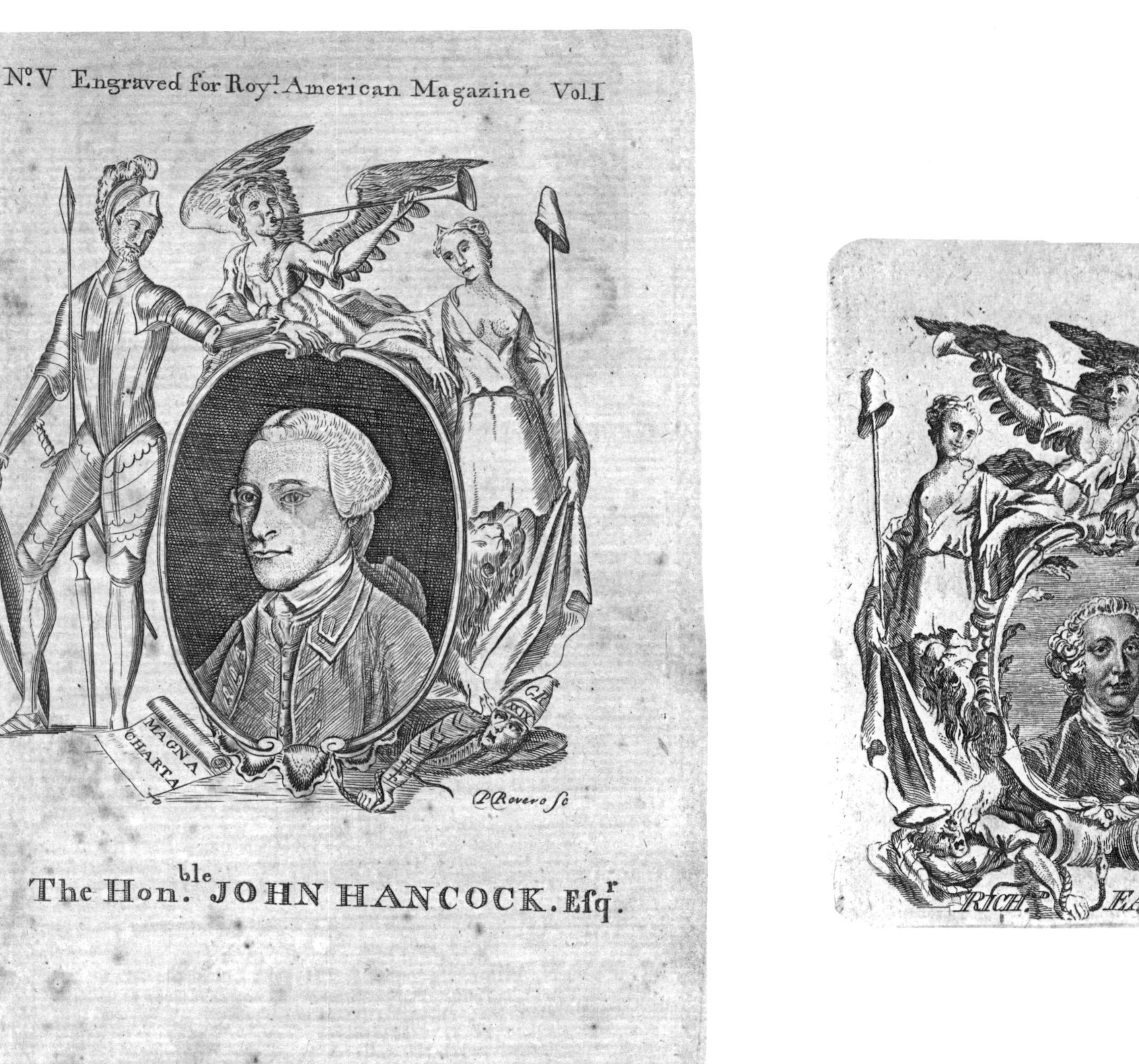

PLATE 34. JOHN HANCOCK, ROYAL AMERICAN MAGAZINE, 1774, AND ENGLISH PRINT.

Plate 34a. Samuel Adams, Royal American Magazine, 1774.

LaHontan's *New Voyages*, in both the French and English editions, from 1703 to 1741 — for instance, in the English edition, London, 1703, page 86. But in all the editions of LaHontan the ten sets of hieroglyphics are placed in a narrow print, 7¼ inches high, and about 3 inches wide, slightly narrower at the top than at the bottom. The text of LaHontan is different from that of the *Royal American Magazine*. Between 1770 and 1774, John Dunlap of Philadelphia published the Indian Gazette as a broadside, with the full text below, and the plate, which is 6½ by 6 15/16 inches, above. The full size of the broadside is 14½ by 7¼ inches. Dunlap presumably copied it from the *Royal Female Magazine*. The broadside first appeared in a Rosenbach Catalogue priced at $80. It was bought by C. F. Heartman who put it in an auction sale of April 21, 1923, from which it was purchased by the American Antiquarian Society for $100. The Society files it in its broadsides under 1774. Isaiah Thomas included both the text and the plate in his *History of Printing in America*, 1810, Volume 2, page 184. He says: "Annexed is an engraving of a copy of an Indian Gazette taken many years since, by a French officer, from the American original, and an explanation of the same. It relates to an expedition of a body of Canadian warriors, who, soon after the settlement of this part of America, took up the hatchet in favor of the French, against a hostile tribe that adhered to the English. It was communicated to me about forty years ago, and soon after I had it engraved for the Royal American Magazine. It had previously appeared in several works published in Europe." The size of his plate is 6⅝ by 7¼ inches, and it is apparently from the original copper which Thomas of course could have retained. All of the items noted above are in the American Antiquarian Society. The print is reproduced, in reduced form, in W. L. Andrews's *Paul Revere and his Engraving*, 1901, page 144.

The June issue contains two plates. The first, used as a frontispiece, was entitled "The able Doctor, or America Swallowing the Bitter Draught," is signed "P Revere Sculp," and has a line at the top "No X Engraved for Royal American Magazine. Vol. I." The measurements, to the border lines, are 3⅝ by 5 13/16 inches. In his Day Book, under date of August 8, 1774, Revere has the following entry: "Mr Isaiah Thomas Dr/ To Engraving plate for June Magazine 2–0–0/ To Engraving Dito for Dito 0–16–0/ To printing 1000 impressions at 2–8

1–6–8." The plate is a faithful copy of the cut in the *London Magazine* for April 1774, Volume 43, page 185, which has the same measurements. The only change Revere inserted was to letter "TEA" on the tea-pot used in the London print. (See Plate no. 35 of both prints.) The *Hibernian Magazine*, published at Dublin, in its issue of May, 1774, Volume 4, page 251, copied the plate from the *London Magazine*, although reversing it. The British Museum *Catalogue of Satires*, 1935, Volume 5, page 165, describes in detail the English engraving, dating it May 1, 1774, and explaining all of the characters shown in the print. In Philadelphia in August, 1774, the print was re-engraved from the *London Magazine*, but reversed, in much larger form, and entitled "The Persevering Americans or the Bitter Draught Return'd." It bears the imprint "Phila Published Augt 8 1774." The size to the border lines is 6¼ by 9¾ inches. This rare print was acquired by Matt B. Jones in 1939 and went with most of his library to the Harvard College Library. The American Antiquarian Society has an original copper-plate, which on the obverse side has an engraving, copied from the *London Magazine*, of the "Able Doctor" print, but in addition has the figures numbered from 1 to 10, evidently a key to some unidentified text. On the reverse of the copper is cut the elaborate advertising card of William Putnam, whose shop was "at the Sign of the Crown and Cushion opposite the Rev. Mr Barnards Meeting-House in Salem." This was a larger plate which had been cut down, as several of the words in the Putnam advertisement are cut off at the bottom of the plate. Presumably it was a reproduction of the "Able Doctor" print made in Salem, accompanying a text not yet identified. Revere's print is reproduced in E. H. Goss's *Life of Paul Revere*, 1891, page 151; W. L. Andrews's *Paul Revere*, 1901, page 33; and the Old Print Shop *Portfolio*, July, 1946, page 236.

The second plate in the June issue is "The Hooded Serpent," appearing at page 224. The lettering underneath is "Engraved for Royl. American Magazine," and above, "Vol. I The Hooded Serpent No XI." The measurements, to the outside edges of the printing, are 6¾ by 4 5/16 inches. The plate is unsigned, but it is characteristically Revere's work. In addition, in his Day Book, under date of August 8, 1774, Revere charges for a second plate in the June issue, as will be seen from the copy of the charge under the account of the first plate. Why he

PLATE 35. ABLE DOCTOR, ROYAL AMERICAN MAGAZINE, 1774, AND ENGLISH PRINT.

PLATE 36. HOODED SERPENT, ROYAL AMERICAN MAGAZINE, 1774, AND ENGLISH PRINT, 1771.

PLATE 37. SPANISH TREATMENT, ROYAL AMERICAN MAGAZINE, 1774, AND ENGLISH PRINT, 1771.

PLATE 38. SALT-PETRE, ROYAL AMERICAN MAGAZINE, 1774.

charged only sixteen shillings for engraving is not clear, when he generally charged £1–16–0 for a simple plate without much engraving. Thomas copied the plate and the text from the *Gentleman's Museum and Grand Imperial Magazine* for February, 1771, Volume 1, page 344, a copy of which is in the American Antiquarian Society. (See Plate no. 36.) The same print had previously been published in the *Royal Magazine* for April, 1766, Volume 14, page 176.

The only plate in the July issue, appearing at page 235, is "Spanish treatment at Carthagena." At the top of the engraving is "No XII. Engrav'd for Royal American Magazine. Vol. I," and at the lower right corner is "P Revere, sc." The measurements, to the border lines, are 3⅞ by 6$\frac{5}{16}$. Revere in his Day Book, under date of September 10, 1774, has the following entry: "Joseph Greenleaf Esqr Dr/ To Engraving a Plate for July Magazine 2–8–0/ To Dito for August Magazine 1–16–0." This was Greenleaf's first issue and he apologizes in a preface for bringing out the July number in September. Revere copied the plate from the *London Magazine* for December, 1771, Volume 40, page 610, but the source of the text I have not located. (See reproductions, Plate no. 37.)

The only plate in the August issue, at page 285, is "The Method of Refining Salt-Petre." At the top is "No. XIII Engrav'd for Royal American Magazine. Vol. I." The plate, although unsigned, is characteristically Revere's work, and in addition he charges Greenleaf in his Day Book for engraving the plate, at £1–16–0 (see entry in account of previous plate). The measurements are 3$\frac{13}{16}$ by 6$\frac{9}{16}$ inches. Revere undoubtedly copied the plate from an earlier English engraving, but so far I have not found the source. (See reproduction, Plate no. 38.)

The only plate in the September issue, at page 341, is an engraving of a Water-Spout. It carries no title, but in the text on the page opposite is the line "Exhibiting an Elegant Engraving of a Water-Spout." Above the engraving is the line: "No. XIV. Engraved for the Royal American Magazine. page 341. Vol: I." The plate is unsigned but was unquestionably engraved by Callender. The text and plate were taken from Benjamin Franklin's *Experiments and Observations on Electricity*, Fifth Edition, London, 1774, pages 224–241 (the same plate is in the London, 1769, edition). The plate in Franklin's book, at page 232, contains three figures — No. I, the ground plan of a whirlwind; No. II, the elevation of a water-spout; and No. III, the figures of a "magic square," which is a later study on a different subject by Franklin and noted in his *Experiments* at page 360. Also in the water-spout article, Franklin inserted on page 237 the line-cut of a section of the water-spout, showing the vacuum. Greenleaf, in executing his plate, omitted the "magic square," Figure III, and substituted the vacuum plate. He also changed the wording in Franklin's article from "by inspection of this figure in the margin" to "by inspection of Fig. III." Sparks, in his edition of Franklin's *Works*, 1838, Volume 6, page 156, reproduced the plate, but followed the plate and text shown in the *Royal American Magazine* rather than the design engraved for Franklin's *Experiments*. Bigelow's edition of Franklin's *Works*, 1904, Volume 2, page 392, follows Sparks. Or perhaps Greenleaf, Sparks, and Bigelow all copied the plate from some early magazine publication which I have not discovered.

The only plate in the October issue, at page 365, is "The Mitred Minuet." At the top is "No XV. Engrav'd for Royal American Magazine. Vol. I," and at the lower right corner is "P Revere sc." The measurements, to the border line, are 3⅝ by 6⅜ inches. Revere in his Day Book, under date of November 7, 1774, has the following entry: "Joseph Greenleaf Esqr Dr/ To Engraving a Plate for October Magazine 2–8–0." Revere copied the plate from the *London Magazine* for July, 1774, Volume 43, page 312, which has the same measurements. (See Plate no. 39.) The *Hibernian Magazine*, of Dublin, for November, 1774, Volume 4, page 680, copied the plate from the *London Magazine*, although reversing it. The British Museum *Catalogue of Satires*, 1935, Volume 5, page 166, describes in detail the meaning and characters of the English print. Revere's print is reproduced in W. L. Andrews's *Paul Revere*, 1901, page 72.

There are two plates in the November issue. The first, at page 407, is "The Gerbua or Yerboa," signed "P Revere Sc." Above the top border line is "Vol I. Engrav'd for Royal American Mag. No XVI." The measurements, to the border lines, are 5 13/16 by 3 11/16 inches. Revere in his Day Book, under date of December 5, 1774, has the following entry: "Joseph Greenleaf Esq Dr/ To Engraving a Plate for Novr Magze 1–12–0/ To Engravg Dito for Novr Magazine 3–6–8." The second charge was for the plate of "Mademoiselle Clairon" and the disparity between the charges undoubtedly represented the difference in the amount of en-

PLATE 39. MITRED MINUET, ROYAL AMERICAN MAGAZINE, 1774, AND ENGLISH PRINT.

PLATE 40. GERBUA, ROYAL AMERICAN MAGAZINE, 1774,

PLATE 41. MME. CLAIRON, ROYAL AMERICAN MAGAZINE, 1774,
AND ENGLISH PRINT, 1765.

Plate 42. Colonel Bouquet, Royal American Magazine, 1774,
and English Print, 1766.

graving. The Gerbua plate was copied from "The Gerbua or Yerboa" in the *Gentleman's Magazine* for April, 1768, Volume 38, page 151, following the cut, the text, and the size. The London plate, however, included the front and reverse of a Russian coin, which Revere omitted. (See Plate no. 40.)

The second plate in the November issue, at page 421, is "Mademoiselle Clairon," signed "P Revere Sc." At the top of the plate is "Engd for Royl Ameri Mag" and under the top line, "Vol. I" and No XVII." The measurements, to the edge of the engraving, omitting line of title, are 6¼ by 3½ inches. Revere's charge of £3–6–8 for the engraving is shown in the entry above. The plate was copied, for cut, text, and size, from the *Court Miscellany* for October, 1765, Volume 1, page 169. (See Plate no. 41.)

There are two plates in the December issue. The first, at page 449, is "A Conference held between some Indian Chiefs and Colonel Bouquet, in the Year 1764," and is signed "P Revere Sc." At the top, in two lines, is "Engd. for Royl Amer'n Mag" and "Vol. I No XIX." Revere in his Day Book, under date of January 5, 1775, has the following entry: "Joseph Greenleaf Esq D/ To Engraving plate for Decmr Magazine 2–8–0/ To Engraving Dito for Dito No 19 3–0–0." Revere entered the plates Numbers 18 and 19 in that order, but Greenleaf placed Number 19 at page 449 and Number 18 at page 465. The measurements of the Bouquet plate, including all of the frame and the lettering underneath, are 6⁹⁄₁₆ by 3½ inches. The plate and text were copied from the *Court Miscellany* for November, 1766, Volume 2, page 606. This, in turn, was copied, although somewhat reduced, from an engraving, 8 by 6⅛ inches, by Grignion of a painting by Benjamin West, facing page 14 of the London, 1766, edition of Bouquet's *Historical Account of the Expedition against the Ohio Indians.* The American Antiquarian Society has an impression from the original Revere copperplate on a copy-book cover, which was used for early nineteenth-century manuscript entries. Evidently Greenleaf preserved the copper and used it on a copybook, a custom which seems to have been prevalent with publishers of the period. At least one other Revere copper was so used. The Revere engraving is reproduced in W. L. Andrews's *Paul Revere*, 1901, page 75. (See reproductions, Plate no. 42.)

The second plate in the December issue, at page 465, has no title underneath, but is described on the title-page of the issue as "The manner that Bees take their repose, &c." The text which relates to the plate covers pages 465 to 471. The measurements of the plate, to the border lines, are 6⅞ by 4⅜, of such length as to preclude lettering underneath. At the top is "Vol. I. Engrav'd for Royal American Magazine. No XVIII." The plate is not signed but is unquestionably by Revere. Also in his Day Book, as will be seen from the previous entry, Revere charges Greenleaf £2–8–0 for engraving the plate. It was copied, both plate and text, from the *Universal Magazine* for June, 1768, Volume 42, pages 356–359. (See reproductions, Plate no. 43.)

There is one plate in the issue of January, 1775, placed as a frontispiece, opposite title-page entitled "A Certain Cabinet Junto." At the top is "Vol. II. Engraved for Royal American Magazine. No. I." and it is signed "P Revere Sc." The measurements of the plate, to the border lines only, are 3 15/16 by 6½ inches. Apparently there is no text accompanying the plate. Revere in his Day Book, under date of February 12, 1775, has the following entry: "Joseph Greenleaf Esqr Dr/ To Engraving a copper plate for/ Jany Magazine 3–0." I have not located any plate in an English magazine exactly like Revere's cut. Apparently he adapted it from a plate in the *Oxford Magazine* for May, 1773, Volume 10, page 182, entitled "A retrospective View of a Certain Cabinet Junto," size, to border lines, 5¾ by 3½ inches. This shows a scene in which King George III, seated at the right, is conversing with Lord North, seated opposite. There are three other figures in the scene. There is a paper sticking out of North's pocket reading "Treaty of Alli[ance] with France & Spa[in]." The cartoon concerns the desire of the Junto to obtain a subsidy from France while at the same time shamming war with that nation (see British Museum *Catalogue of Satires*, 1935, Volume 5, page 122). Revere faithfully copied the two seated figures and the paper in North's pocket, but omitted the other figures and the sentiments expressed in the English engraving. He finished out his scene with figures of his own composition or drawn by some American artist. The balloons in Revere's engraving express highly patriotic American sentiments, which probably would not have been published in England. (See Plate no. 44.)

In the February issue, at page 49, there is one plate, entitled "History of

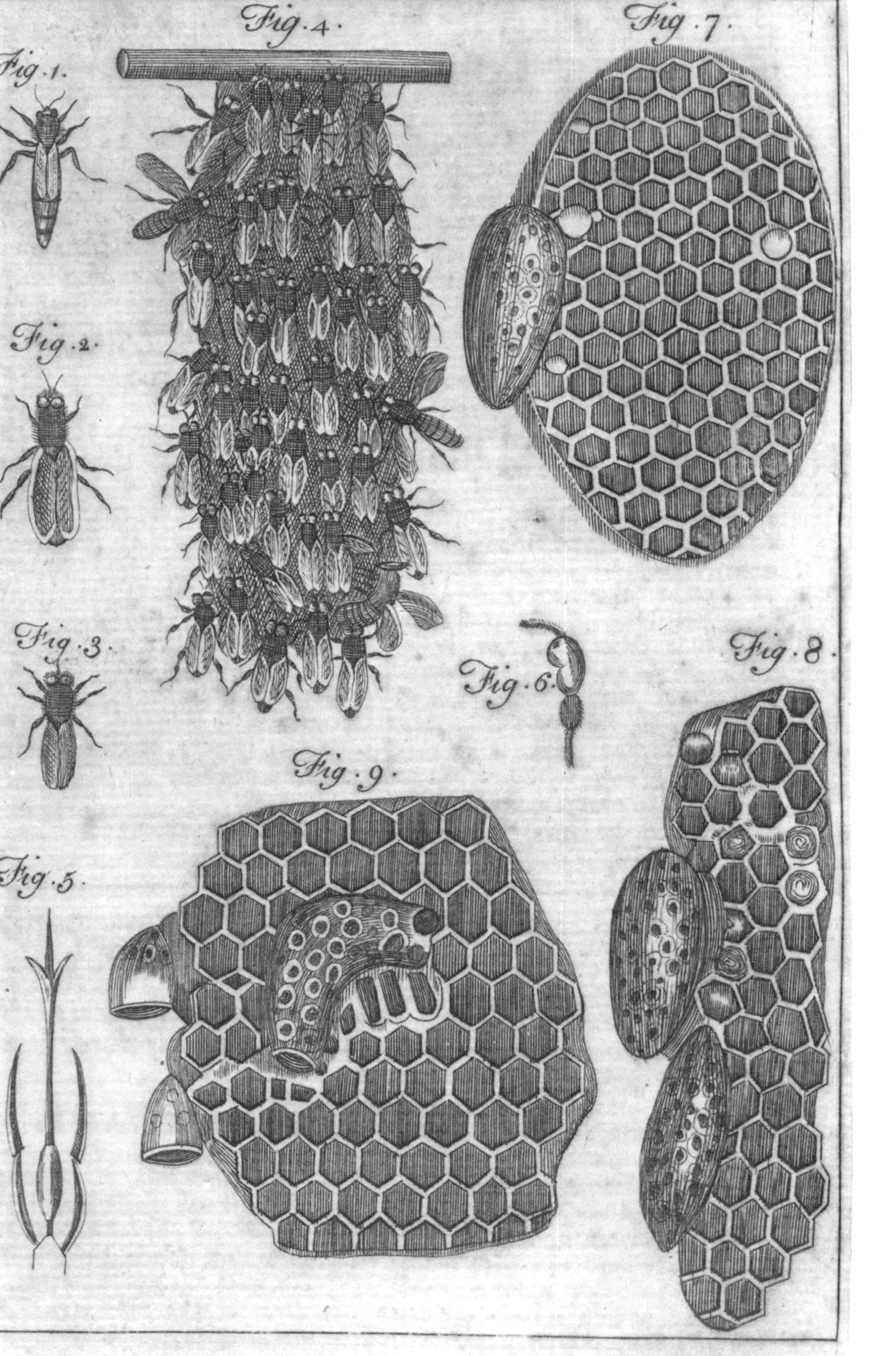

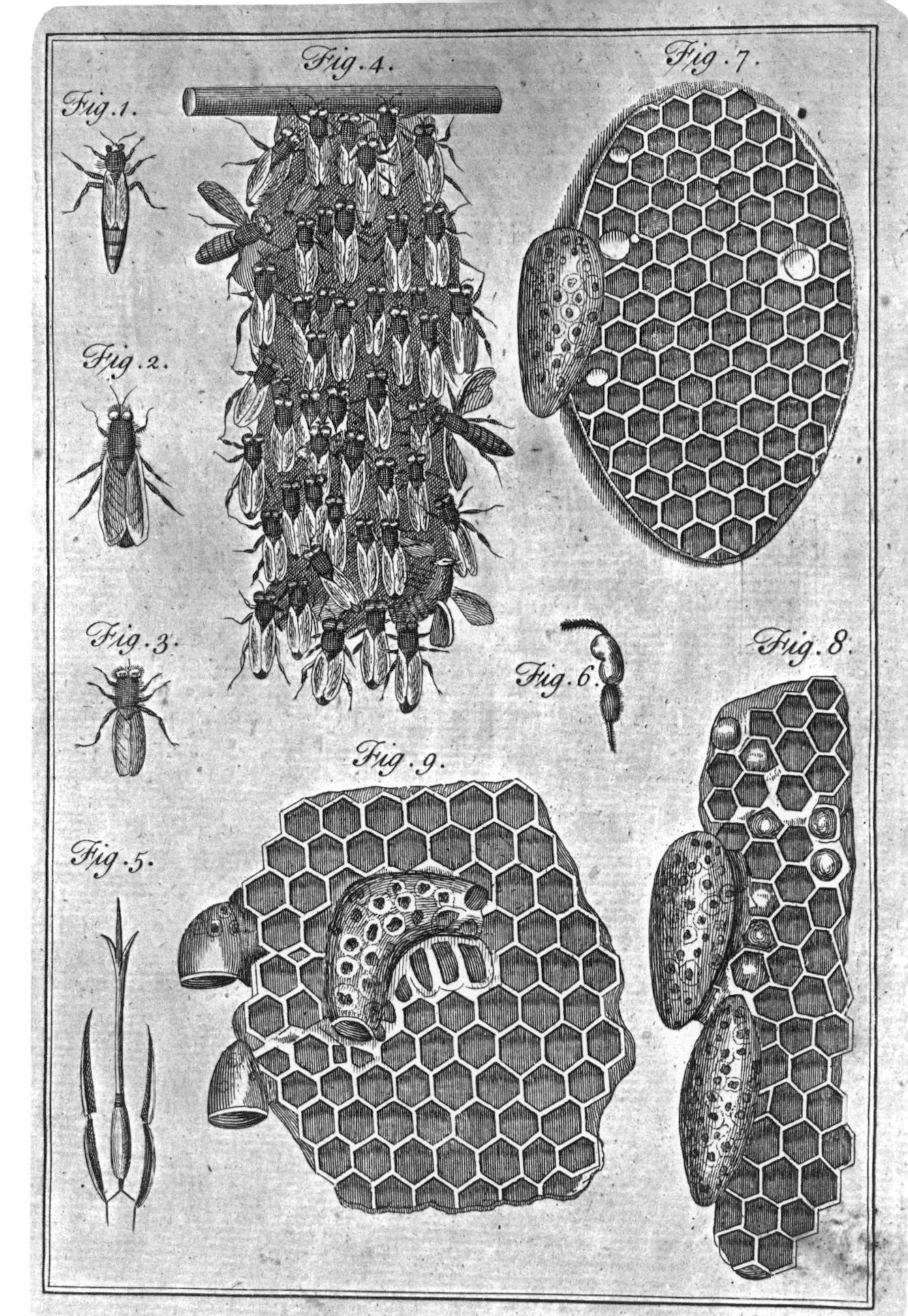

Plate 43. Bees, Royal American Magazine, 1774, and English Print, 1768.

PLATE 44. CABINET JUNTO, ROYAL AMERICAN MAGAZINE, 1775, AND ENGLISH PRINT, 1773.

PLATE 45. LAURETTA, ROYAL AMERICAN MAGAZINE, 1775, AND ENGLISH PRINT, 1773.

PLATE 46. AMERICA IN DISTRESS, ROYAL AMERICAN MAGAZINE, 1775, AND ENGLISH PRINT, 1770.

Lauretta." Above in two lines is "Eng'd for Royal Americ'n Mag.," and "No II Vol. II." Below is the signature "P Revere Sc." The measurements of the plate to the edges of the frame, omitting only the lettering underneath, are 6$\frac{5}{16}$ by 3$\frac{1}{2}$ inches. In his Day Book, under date of March 9, 1775, Revere has the following entry: "Joseph Greenleaf Esqr Dr/ To Engraving a plate for Feby Mag" 3–0–0." The text of the "History of Lauretta. A Moral Tale" occupies pages 49 to 54, which is the concluding installment of a story which had appeared in several preceding issues. The plate and text were copied from the *Court Miscellany* for September, 1765, Volume 1, page 152, where the cut is the same size as Revere's. (See Plate no. 45.) The American Antiquarian Society has a restrike from the original copper on a copy-book cover used by Samuel Hodges as a letter-book in 1816. Evidently Greenleaf, or his successors, preserved their coppers and used them to advantage later.

In the issue of March, 1775, the final issue, there is one plate, placed as a frontispiece, opposite the title-page, entitled "America in Distress." The measurements, to the border lines, are 6$\frac{1}{4}$ by 4$\frac{1}{8}$ inches. At the top is "Vol. II. Engraved for Royal American Magazine. No III," and at the lower right is the signature "P Revere Sc." In his Day Book, under date of April 1, 1775, Revere has the following entry: "Joseph Greenleaf Esqr Dr/ To Engraving plate for March Mag. 3–0–0." The plate was copied, with a few variations, chiefly in the sentiments expressed in the balloons, from "Britannia in Distress" in the *Oxford Magazine* for February, 1770, Volume 4, page 64, size 6$\frac{1}{4}$ by 4$\frac{3}{16}$ inches. A comparison of the two plates, which are reproduced, will show how the sentiments were altered to suit American consumption. The English plate was rather crudely drawn, and this is one of the few occasions when Revere was able to improve upon the original. (See reproductions, Plate no. 46.)

Complete files of the *Royal American Magazine* are indeed scarce, as I have found by canvassing the holdings of over thirty libraries. There are only four sets complete for both text and plates. The file in the American Antiquarian Society is the most desirable as it is complete for text and plates, and nearly all the numbers are as issued, uncut, and with front and back covers. The covers are interesting because of the announcements and the advertisements. The three other complete files are in the New York Public Library, Yale, and the Boston Athenæum. Sets which are nearly complete are in the Boston Public Library which lacks one plate, the Massachusetts Historical Society which lacks the final issue and two plates, and the John Carter Brown Library which lacks a few pages and two plates. All other files checked lack text and from four to twenty plates. I have a detailed list of the plates missing in the several files.

I also have a record of all sales of the *Royal American Magazine* at auction, from 1879 to date. Most of the files so offered were very incomplete. The best file to appear at auction was in the John C. Williams Sale at the American Art Association, November 6, 1929, which had all the plates and lacked only the pages of Hutchinson's *History* in Volume I and four pages in Volume 2. It brought $1850, and was acquired by Francis P. Garvan, later given to Yale.

Maps for Romans's East Florida, 1775

TO what extent Revere engraved the large maps issued to accompany Bernard Romans's *Concise Natural History of East and West Florida*, New York, 1775, is a problem which is difficult to solve. In fact, the entire question of the publication of the book, its printer, the number of its plates, and the format of the "sheet maps" is fraught with numerous bibliographical uncertainties.

The book was completed and printed at New York in 1775. Its title was as follows: *A Concise Natural History of East and West Florida: containing* [17 lines describing the contents]. *By Captain Bernard Romans. Illustrated with twelve Copper Plates, And Two whole sheet Maps. Vol. I. New-York: Printed for the Author, M,DCC, LXXV.* Pages [1–2], 3–4, i–viii, [1]–342, [343–344], i–lxxxix, [xc–xciii]. The E. D. Church *Catalogue*, 1907, Volume 5, pages 2228–2232, reproduces the title-page in full, gives the collation both by pagination and signatures, and describes in detail the plates. The size of leaf of the Church copy is 7 11/16 x 5 1/16 inches, and of the Brinley copy 7 x 4 3/8 inches.

The engraved plates appear as follows: frontispiece, engraved dedication, "Avena aquatica Sylvestris" at page 31, "Characteristick Chicasaw head" at page 59, "Characteristick Chactaw Busts" at page 82, untitled plate of Choctaw funeral platform at page 89, "Characteristick head of a Creek War Chief" at page 93, untitled plate of Indian hieroglyphics at page 102. In the Appendix are the maps of "Entrances of Tampa Bay" at page lxxviii, "Pensacola Bar" at page lxxxiv, and "Mobile Bar" at page lxxxv. At page 104 is a printed Table of Exports of Produce from the Province of Georgia.

The printer of the book was undoubtedly James Rivington. He had printed in 1774 Hawkesworth's edition of Captain James Cook's *New Voyage*, for which Romans had drawn plates. He owned a large shop, with sixteen workmen, and had a sufficient supply of presses and type. A comparison of the Romans book with at least thirty other Rivington publications of 1774 and 1775 shows that the type, the set-up, and the format were much the same.

Nearly every description of the Romans book comments upon the author's use of the lower case "i" for the personal pronoun, some assuming that the printer had run out of type for the capital letter. But there are hundreds of examples of the general use of the capital "I" throughout the book. In the Errata at the end Romans corrects "I felt" on page 3 to "i felt." Evidently it was an idiosyncrasy, but one which he did not employ in his other publications.

The second edition of Romans's *Concise Natural History* was issued in 1776, identical in text for the narrative, but omitting the Appendix which contained the Directions to Navigators. It did not give the name of the printer but stated that it was sold by R. Aitken, bookseller, "Price, Bound, One Dollar." The type and plates are identical with the 1775 edition, even to defects in the type, showing that the later edition was a re-issue of oversheets of the 1775 volume, or reprint from the original type.

The announcements made by Romans regarding his book and his map cover the years 1773 to 1775. Chronologically arranged they are as follows:

On August 5, 1773, he issued a broadside prospectus dated at Philadelphia, of which there is a copy in the John Carter Brown Library. It is headed "Proposals for printing by Subscription, Three Very Elegant and Large Maps of the Navigation, to, and in, the New Ceded Countries." A description of the three maps is then given — the first from the Mississippi to the Atlantic Ocean and including West Florida and the northern part of East Florida, from 81° to 93° of longitude and 30° to 31° of latitude; the second covering the middle part of East Florida and the Grand Bahama Bank, from 76° to 85° of longitude and 26° to 29° of latitude; the third, the South part of Florida, the Keys and the north side of Cuba, from 76° to 84° of longitude and 23° to 26° of latitude. Accompanying the Maps was to be a book containing "a concise natural History of the said Countries" and directions to navigators, also to include "sundry necessary plates." The maps were to be "engraven by a masterly hand, under the Author's own inspection." The engraver is now employed on the work at New York, at a cost of £3, 14 shillings for every forty-eight hours of work. The price was to be twelve dollars for the complete work, including the book and the maps on fine paper, but nine dollars for "the Direction alone" and the Maps on a more common paper. The work was to be engraved and printed as soon as one hundred and fifty subscribers were secured.

Early in 1774 Romans journeyed to Boston, ostensibly to obtain subscribers for his book. In the *Boston Gazette* of January 10, 1774, he inserted a long advertisement regarding his projected publication. He states that he has "compleated a very large and extensive Survey of the New Ceded Countries," and that "The elegance of the Map added to its large Size, of twelve feet by seven, will likewise render it an ornamental Piece of Furniture." He says that added to the maps is a book of five hundred pages, in octavo, and that a "great Part of the Work is already printed." He adds that his stay in Boston will be short, and thinks that the work will be completed about July, 1774. He obtained in Boston the names of thirty-seven subscribers, who took seventy-two copies, including Cox & Berry who took twenty-five copies. The entire number of subscribers, including those who subscribed during the progress of printing, totalled two hundred and thirty names.

In the *Massachusetts Gazette and Boston Weekly News-Letter* of January 27, 1774, Romans advertised Proposals for his book. The advertisement was dated January 18. The title-page of the *Concise Natural History* is given exactly as it appeared in the printed book, except that the words "Volume I" are omitted, and no mention of an imprint or a printer is included. The conditions are advertised as follows:

> I. The Book will be in two Volumes, each 300 Pages Crown Octavo, printed with a new Type, on a very good Paper.
>
> II. To be delivered about June next.
>
> III. Price sewed Six Shillings Sterling.
>
> N.B. About 150 Pages are already printed.
>
> ☞ Subscriptions taken in for the above Book by Messrs. Cox and Berry and Henry Knox, Boston.

When in Boston, Romans contributed three articles to Isaiah Thomas's *Royal American Magazine*. The first was signed from Boston, January 15, 1774, the second had no place or date line, and the third was dated from New York, March 31, 1774. He also undoubtedly had interviews with Paul Revere, as will be shown later in discussing the engraving of the maps. He was back in New York by February 10, judging by an article in *Rivington's New-York Gazetteer* of that date, when Romans contributed a long communication, defending himself against the charge of piracy.

Work on printing the book and the maps evidently progressed slowly during the summer of 1774. In *Rivington's New-York Gazetteer* of October 20, 1774, Romans inserted the following advertisement:

> Mr. Bernard Romans begs leave to inform the public, that his maps are now ready for publication, the copper-plates being all done, and the paper which he was obliged to get manufactured on purpose, is likewise finished, but not yet received from Philadelphia, or else at least a great part would have been delivered before now: The subscribers may rest assured of receiving the copies within the time prescribed, which is the first day of January next. As his edition is small, it is requested that such Gentlemen who incline to have copies may subscribe, as after publication none will be to be had for less than 16 Dollars.

Hopes for early publication, however, were delayed, as was shown by Romans's advertisement in Rivington's paper of April 27, 1775, as follows:

> Mr. B. Romans has now finished his publication; and though every thing was ready according to promise before the 1st of January last, yet a struggle of above 4 months with the art and mystery of Copper-plate printing has occasioned delays until now; but he succeeds now in that last operation. . . . He returns thanks to his subscribers, whose favours have much exceeded his hopes, they are so numerous, for the whole work, that the book cannot be spared separately. A few complete copies are left to non-subscribers, at 16 dollars each.

A final summary of his publication troubles is found in the "Advertisement" on the last page of his *Concise Natural History*, 1775, as follows:

> The map of the country of the savage nations, intended to be put, facing page 72, was engraved by a Gentleman who resides in the country 60 or 70 miles from New-York, to whom the plate was sent; but when it was sent back, it miscarried, through the carelessness of the waggoner; and though the publication has been delayed some

time on that account, it is not yet come to hand; the reader will therefore please to expect said map with the second volume.

At the first planning of this publication, it was intended only to be a single volume, not exceeding 300 pages, appendix and all; but at the request of some Gentlemen, my friends, i have subjoined so many articles, that it swelled imperceptibly to about 800 pages, which made it necessary to print it in two volumes; and as some unexpected accidents, especially the want of a copper-plate printer, have occasioned delays; i will therefore, to atone in some measure (for said delays) to those kind Gentlemen who favoured me with their subscriptions for the maps, deliver them the second volume gratis, as soon as it is published: It is now in the press.

In commenting on this succession of advertisements, it is evident that, according to his Prospectus of August 5, 1773, Romans employed, or attempted to employ, an engraver working in New York. There is no evidence to show that this unknown engraver succeeded in producing anything. Romans was in Boston early in 1774 and had the opportunity to meet Paul Revere, the engraver. Romans contributed three articles early in 1774 to the *Royal American Magazine* conducted by Isaiah Thomas, the friend and patron of Revere. In April, 1774, Revere was employed by James Rivington, the New York printer, to engrave the frontispiece of Rivington's publication of Captain James Cook's *New Voyage*. Revere's own Day Book, as will later be shown, charged Romans with engraving the Maps of Florida. In his advertisement of October 20, 1774, Romans stated that the copper-plates of his maps were finished, although the necessary paper had not been received. In his advertisement of April 27, 1775, Romans referred to his four months' struggle with "the art and mystery" of printing from copper-plates. Finally, in the advertisement at the end of his published *Concise History*, announced as published in April, 1775, he stated that publication had been delayed for some time because of the loss of a plate of "a map of the country of the savage nations," which he had intended to place facing page 72, and which had been engraved by a gentleman who resided sixty or seventy miles from New York. When the finished plate was sent back to Romans, it was lost in transit and the book had to go to press without it. There is reason to believe that the engraver of the lost plate of "the savage nations" was Abel Buell of New Haven. Buell had had business associations with James Rivington, the printer, was a capable engraver, and

New Haven was about seventy miles from New York. Lawrence C. Wroth, in his interesting book, *Abel Buell of Connecticut*, 1926, page 59, favors the possibility that Buell was the engraver of this plate. Romans promised that the map would appear in his second volume, which unfortunately was never published. He must soon have decided against such publication, as the reprint of his *Concise Natural History*, printed in 1776, does not refer to it, and omits "Vol. I" from the title-page.

Revere's connection with the Romans map is first revealed through his Day Book, where there are three charges against Romans in 1774, as follows:

May 3, 1774

"Capt Bernard Romans Dr	
To Cash paid for letter	1–1
To Engraving a Plate for a Map of East Florida	10–0–0
To the Copper for plate	2–2–8
To prepairing plate for Engraving	1–0–0
To a Wooden Case 1/6 Cartage to Providence 1/6	0–3–0
Capt Bernard Romans Cr	
By Cash Receiv'd to buy Copper plate	1–17–4

July 9, 1774

Capt Bernard Romans Dr	
To Engraving a Copper Plate for part of a map of Florida	7–0–0
To smoothing plate	1–0–0
To Cash paid for two letters	2–3
To Cash paid for bring plate from Providence	
To Dito for carrying it to Salem	1–4

October 21, 1774

Capt Bernard Romans Cr	
To prepairing a Copper plate for Engraving & Engraving	2–8–0
To Cash paid for 4 letters	6–0

The first two entries specifically mention the map of Florida, and the third presumably covers the same subject. The charges for engraving the plates vary considerably. The upper section of the Romans map was divided into three plates of 21 high by 28 inches wide, 21 high by 29.5 inches wide, and 21 high by 33.5

inches wide. The lower portion has an upper half 65 inches wide, divided into three plates each 29 inches high. The lower half is 65 inches wide, divided into 3 plates each 26 inches high. These figures are approximate, as there is a slight variation in measurement between the original and the reproduction due to the stretching of the paper during the process of mounting on cloth, and the measurements are sometimes given for the actual map size and sometimes to include the margin to the plate mark. The 1924 reproduction, furthermore, is confusing since it divides the upper section into four plates instead of three, and the lower section into nine plates instead of six.

The plates therefore average about 21 by 28 inches. Revere's first entry charges £2–2–8 for the copper-plate, before smoothing or engraving. This nearly agrees with Abel Buell's charge in 1774 of £6–5–0 for two coppers each 20 by 27 inches (see L. C. Wroth's *Abel Buell*, page 52). The charges of £10 for engraving one plate, £7 for another, but only £2–8–0 for both preparing and engraving a third plate were probably due to the amount of work required on the various plates.

Judging by the Day Book, Revere engraved only three of the plates of the Florida map. Yet he may have been paid cash for other plates, which would not have required a charge account. From a careful study of the maps, I believe that Revere engraved all nine sections. The lettering is characteristically Revere's, especially the capital letters, and the formation of the symbol "&," the ampersand, is practically his trade-mark. Romans signs the two cartouches as if he both designed and engraved them. He certainly designed them — perhaps he engraved them, whereas Revere engraved the map outlines and the lettering.

There is no question in my mind but that the "Two whole sheet Maps" mentioned on the title-page of Romans's *Concise Natural History*, 1775, refer to the large printed map in two sections, the only complete copy of which is in the Library of Congress. In his Prospectus, Romans describes the maps in detail, as well as the book which accompanied the maps, and promises a price of twelve dollars for the book and the maps on fine paper. In his advertisement of January 10, 1774, he says "There is added to the Maps a Book of 500 pages," and again describes the area covered by the maps. He prints a long "List of Subscribers to this Work," one hundred and seventy-eight in number, and a short list of nineteen "Subscribers for the Book only," plus an additional list of thirty-three late subscribers.

There are three copies, complete or partial, of the large Romans map located. The only complete copy is in the Library of Congress. Its measurements have been described in detail on a previous page — the upper portion 21 inches high by 91 inches wide and the lower portion 55 inches high by 65 inches wide. Mr. Phillips's 1924 reproduction divides the plates differently from the original printing, but the measurements are practically the same. The Florida Historical Society, at Gainesville, has the entire lower portion, 59 by 66 inches including margins. It is in six sections, joined together and mounted. It is believed that the map came to that Society from Francis P. Fleming, president of the Society in 1905. The Clements Library at Ann Arbor has two sections, the west and the east, of the upper portion.

The Clements Library has a Romans manuscript map of areas covering parts of both portions of the printed map, including the drawing from the north line of Florida down to the southern tip of the State. This map is 34 by 21 inches and is described as Number 331 in R. G. Adams's *British Headquarters Maps*, 1928, page 111. That Library also has a manuscript "Map of part of West Florida done under the direction of John Stuart," 1772–1773, 21¼ by 29¾ inches, which includes most of the area shown in the western section of the upper portion of the printed Romans map. Its third manuscript is "A map of West Florida, part of East Florida, Georgia, part of South Carolina," 1773, size 12 by 9 feet, covering the area shown in the entire upper portion of the printed Romans map, and much territory further north. In the Public Record Office in London is a manuscript "General Map of West Florida by Bernard Romans, with an attempt towards a Short Description of West Florida," which scales about four miles to one inch.

I have located at least sixteen copies of the Romans, 1775, *Concise History*, in varying degrees of completeness as to plates. Those copies which are complete are in the American Antiquarian Society, Huntington Library, Newberry Library, New York Historical Society, New York Public Library, Library of Congress, Philadelphia Library Company, and Williams College. The copies owned by the Clements Library, Thomas W. Streeter, and the University of Virginia lack only the plate at page 102. The following lack two or more plates: Boston Athenæum, University of Florida, John Carter Brown Library, John Crerar Library, and the Rosenbach Company. I have a record of all these defects. I have found twenty-one sales of copies at auction, although these are often sales of the same copies.

The Romans Map is not reproduced in this book, because of its large size and since it was carefully reproduced by P. Lee Phillips in the volume accompanying his *Life of Bernard Romans*, 1924.

Anatomical Lectures, 1780

REVERE'S engraving of Dr. John Warren's Anatomical Lectures is known by only two copies, one in the Warren Papers in the Massachusetts Historical Society, and the other in the Library of the American Antiquarian Society. The Historical Society copy is the earlier of the two, and was made out March 28, 1782, for Israel Keith, when the "dissecting Theatre" was in the American Hospital in Boston. As is shown in Plate number 47, this consists of the certificate of attendance, enclosed in a Chippendale border, with the bust of Galen at the top of the engraving, two skeletons at the sides, and an anatomical operation at the bottom. It is signed "P R." Its exact size is 7 9/16 by 5 7/8 inches. As early as 1823, Dr. Ephraim Eliot wrote in manuscript an "Account of the Physicians of Boston," which was printed in the *Proceedings* of the Massachusetts Historical Society of November, 1863, Volume 7, page 177. Dr. Eliot describes Dr. Warren's efforts in 1780 to launch "an incipient medical school institution" for the benefit of the younger medical pupils in Boston. He proposed that Dr. Danforth should conduct courses in materia medica and chemistry, Dr. Rand on the theory and practice of physic, and was willing himself to lecture on anatomy and surgery. The first two doctors declined to accept the proposition, but Warren "agreed to commence a course." Dr. Rand told Dr. Eliot: "Now, Warren will be able to obtain fees from the pupils who will attend his lectures on anatomy and surgery, and turn it to pecuniary advantage." Eliot continues: "At the proper season, Dr. Warren read a very excellent course of anatomical lectures with demonstrations, and exhibited the various operations of surgery. It was renewed the next year."

The most complete early record of the establishment of the Anatomical Lectures is in Dr. James Thacher's *American Medical Biography*, Boston, 1828, Volume 2, page 257. Thacher was a friend and associate of Dr. John Warren during the Revolution and well knew his subject. In referring to Dr. Warren, he says:

"His anatomical pursuits becoming known to his friends in the medical profession, he was solicited by them to extend the benefit of his dissections, and to give a private course of demonstrations or lectures. . . . In the year 1780 he gave a course of dissections to his colleagues with great success. To them the opportunity was so novel and so desirable, that they attended his lectures with zeal; and none of them forgot the impressions they received. These lectures were given in the Military Hospital, which was situated in a pasture in the rear of the present Massachusetts General Hospital, at the corner of Milton and Spring streets. They were conducted with the greatest secrecy, on account of the popular prejudice against dissections. In the following year the lectures, given at the same place, were quite public, and many literary and scientific gentlemen of the town, and the students of Harvard College, were permitted to attend. In this season and at this place, Dr. Warren performed the amputation at the shoulder joint, with complete success. The third course of lectures was given in the year 1782 in the 'Molineaux house,' situated on Beacon street, between Sumner and Bowdoin streets. The attendance of the senior class of Cambridge College upon these lectures led to the design of forming a medical school in connexion with the university."

Edward Warren, in *The Life of John Warren*, Boston, 1874, page 226, adds little to Thacher's account. In referring to his father's lectures, he says: "This was the first attempt at anatomical instruction by actual demonstrations, in Boston. They were conducted with great privacy, on account of the popular prejudice against dissection. They were attended by a small number of medical students and young practitioners, chiefly mates or persons otherwise attached to the army. A few scientific gentlemen were invited to attend."

No records remain of the early history of Dr. Warren's Anatomical Lectures. It is not known what students attended, or how many. Only this certificate reproduced shows that Israel Keith attended and received his diploma, signed by John Warren, "F.M.S." The initials undoubtedly mean Fellow Medical Society, referring to the Boston Medical Society which had been established in May, 1780.

In the volume of Warren Papers, in the Massachusetts Historical Society, page 43, is a document with a list of names, as follows:

Doct. Cheney	Mr. Eliot
Col. Keith, paid	Mr. Bartlett, paid
Doct. Blanchard 2	Mr. Haskins

Doct. Homans
Mr. Templeman
Mr. Cheever, paid 2
Mr. Jackson 2
Mr. Swan
Mr. Peck, paid
Mr. Draper, paid 2

On the reverse of the document is the endorsement: "Subscribers for Copper Plate, 1780." Underneath is the notation: "Dr. Draper paid Col. Revere 9 Crowns & ½ and a Dollar." Revere's Day Book does not include the charge for the engraving, although it does show several accounts with Dr. John Warren, between 1783 and 1796, for the making and engraving of silver.

In the *Quarterly* of the Harvard Medical Alumni Association for July, 1902, pages 201–229, is a sketch of the life of Dr. John Warren, written by John Warren of the Harvard Class of 1900. It refers to the Anatomical Lectures, and reproduces in reduced size the Israel Keith certificate. It is also reproduced in Thomas F. Harrington's *Harvard Medical School*, 1905, Volume 1, page 84.

Israel Keith was a graduate of Harvard in the Class of 1771, the same Class as John Warren's. He entered the service in the Revolution, serving as aid-de-camp to General Heath and rising to the rank of Lieutenant-Colonel. In 1778 he expressed his desire to resign from the army and to pursue the study and practice of law. He was admitted as an attorney by the Superior Court of Judicature on February 15, 1780 (see typed copies of Israel Keith Papers presented to the Massachusetts Historical Society by James B. Wilbur in 1923). With other learned and scientific non-medical men, he attended Dr. Warren's Anatomical Lectures in 1780–1782. He was a close friend of Dr. Warren and a fellow Mason. He delivered an oration before the Grand Lodge on December 27, 1780, which was printed. He married at Boston, September 7, 1783, Caroline Jenkins. He acquired considerable property and removed to Pittsford, Vermont, where he died June 5, 1819, aged about seventy (see *Rutland Herald*, June 8, 1819).

The second known copy of the Revere diploma, owned by the American Antiquarian Society, is made out for Levi Bartlett, dated June 8, 1785, and signed "John Warren, Prof. of Anaty and Surgery, University Cambridge." The engraved words "dissecting Theatre in the American Hospital" are changed by scratching out the words "American Hospital" and substituting in ink "Univer-

Theſe may certify, that Israel Keith Esqr has diligently attended an entire course of my Anatomical Lectures & Demonſtrations; to-gether with Phyſiological & Surgical obser-vations, at the diſsecting Theatre in the American Hoſpital, BOSTON: whereby he has had an opportunity of acquiring an accurate knowledge in the structure of the human body. John Warren F.M.S.

BOSTON March 28 1782.

PLATE 47. ANATOMICAL LECTURES, 1780.

These may certify, that
Mr. Levi Bartlett has diligently
attended an entire course of my
Anatomical Lectures & Demonstrations; to-
-gether with Physiological & Surgical obser-
-vations, at the dissecting Theatre in the
University at Cambridge whereby
he has had an opportunity of acquiring
an accurate knowledge in the structure
of the human body and the surgical Branch
of his Profession

John Warren
Prof. of Anat.
and Surgery
University
Cambridge

BOSTON
June 8th
1785

Plate 48. Anatomical Lectures, 1785.

sity at Cambridge." Also in pen at the end of the diploma are the words "and the surgical Branch of his Profession." (See Plate no. 48.)

The Harvard Medical School was established in 1783, with John Warren as professor of anatomy and surgery. Any reputable candidate could take his course of anatomical lectures, although it was not until 1788 that the first medical class was graduated.

The diploma reproduced was made out for Levi Bartlett and dated June 8, 1785. Levi Bartlett was born at Kingston, New Hampshire, September 15, 1763, and studied medicine with his father, Dr. Josiah Bartlett of Kingston, and Dr. Thomas Kittredge of Andover. He became well known in the medical profession, occupied many civil offices, and died January 30, 1828. He was not the "Bartlett" who was among the subscribers for the copper-plate in 1780, as the student of 1780 was Josiah Bartlett of Charlestown, born in 1759, and later a physician of high standing (see James Thacher's *American Medical Biography*, 1828, Volume 1, page 150).

Buried with Him by Baptism

BURIED with Him by Baptism" is one of the scarcest of the plates signed by Revere. As is shown in Plate number 49, this engraving gives the title at the bottom of the print, with the signature "P Revere Sculp." It shows Jesus being baptized by John in the river Jordan, with two shafts of light coming down from Heaven, one with a flying dove, and the other with the inscription "This is my beloved Son, — hear ye him." The size of the print is 6½ by 4¼ inches.

The title of this allegorical print is derived from the Epistle of Paul to the Romans, Chapter 6, verses 3 and 4: "Know ye not, that so many of us as were baptized into Jesus Christ were baptized into his death? Therefore we are buried with him by baptism into death." The scene of the baptism is from Saint Mark, Chapter 1, verses 9, 10, and 11: "And it came to pass in those days, that Jesus came from Nazareth of Galilee, and was baptized of John in Jordan. And straightway coming up out of the water, he saw the heavens opened, and the spirit like a dove descending upon him. And there came a voice from heaven, saying, Thou art my beloved Son, in whom I am well pleased." In Saint Matthew, Chapter 17, verse 5, the voice is described as saying: "This is my beloved Son, in whom I am well pleased; hear ye him."

The print may have accompanied some book or pamphlet on baptism, but an examination of all the American tracts on baptism from 1760 to 1780, in fact several copies of each tract, shows no evidence that such an engraving or frontispiece was included. Apparently Revere made the engraving as a separately issued item, either for a friend or because of his desire to engrave such a subject. The crudeness of the engraving leads to the belief that Revere designed the print rather than copied it from an English original. At least no copy of such an engraving has been found in an English book or periodical.

Only four copies of the print have been located, two in the American Anti-

PLATE 49. BURIED WITH HIM BY BAPTISM.

quarian Society's collection, one in the Worcester Art Museum, and another which was included in the Dr. Charles E. Clark Sale at Libbie's, January 15, 1901, number 567, where it brought $31. It was bought by E. B. Holden, and next appeared in the sale of his library at the American Art Association, April 21, 1910, number 3698, where it brought $11. It was purchased by the Museum of Fine Arts in Boston, where it is now preserved. William Loring Andrews reproduced the print in his *Paul Revere and his Engraving*, 1901, page 15.

Portrait of Washington, 1780

THE chief reason for including this anonymous woodcut, or line-cut, portrait of Washington is because it has frequently been ascribed to Revere. The story of the ascription is as follows. On October 26, 1781, Paul Revere wrote a letter to his cousin Mathias Rivoire in France, in which he says: "Before this reaches you, you will have heard of the victory gained over the British Army by the Allied Armies commanded by the brave General Washington. (A small engraving of him, I send enclosed, it is said to be a good likeness and it is my engraving)." Rivoire replied, thanking his cousin for the "engraving of General Washington representing a gallant warrior." (E. H. Goss's *Life of Paul Revere*, Volume 2, page 502).

As it happened, late in 1780 or early in 1781, John D. M'Dougall and Company printed *Weatherwise's Town and Country Almanack for the Year of our Lord 1781*. On the fourth leaf, or unnumbered page 7, was a cut of "His Excellency George Washington, Esq: Commander in Chief of the Armies of the United States of America," followed by a long extract from Murray's *Impartial History of the present War in America*, narrating the entry of Washington into Boston and the defense of the town.

The cut, presumably on type-metal, measured 2 15/16 inches high by 2 1/2 wide. As is seen in Plate number 50, it showed the head and shoulders of Washington, surrounded by a mantling of flags, wreaths, and cannon. It was apparently copied from the John Norman copper-plate in the *Philadelphia Almanack* for 1780, engraved and printed in broadside form by Norman and Bedwell in Philadelphia, measuring 10 1/4 by 7 3/4 inches (reproduced in C. H. Hart's *Catalogue of Engraved Portraits of Washington*, 1904, number 42, opposite page 22).

The cut in the Weatherwise Almanac was unsigned, which might account for Revere emphasizing in the letter to his cousin that he engraved it, if he did engrave

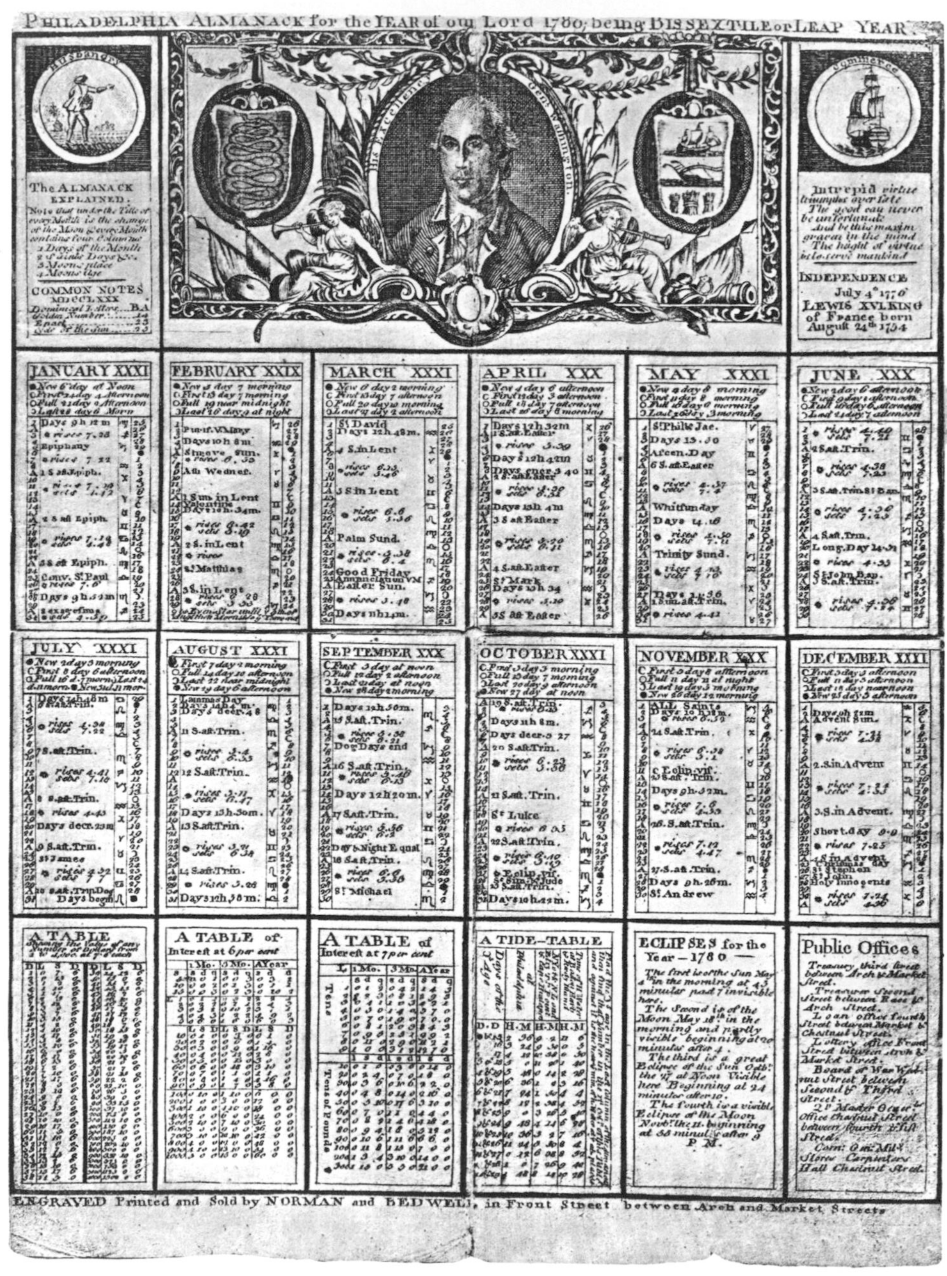

PLATE 50. PORTRAIT OF WASHINGTON, 1780.

it. The portrait certainly did not portray "a gallant warrior," although that might have been Mathias Rivoire's opinion of the General.

The same cut from the same plate was again used in *The New-England Primer Enlarged*, printed at Boston by E. Draper, undated, but probably about 1781. There are two varieties of this Primer, differing in the border around the title-page. The same plate again did duty in a later New England Primer (about 1798, but title-page missing in the American Antiquarian Society copy, the only one located), but in this cut of Washington, the title underneath was "John Adams, President."

In 1904 Charles Henry Hart published his monumental *Catalogue of the Engraved Portraits of Washington*. On page xv of the Introduction, he reproduces the cut of Washington, details the evidence of Revere's letter to his cousin, and of the Weatherwise Almanac, and concludes: "I think therefore, this type-metal portrait of Washington may be accepted as the Revere 'small engraving,' until the ascription is disproved by the production of a copper-plate print bearing his name as engraver."

Mr. Hart's opinion may be correct. The style of engraving in a way is like Revere's work, and the evidence of the letter to his cousin is interesting, if not conclusive. Perhaps some day the problem will be solved.

The American Antiquarian Society has all of the titles mentioned in the above text, except the John Norman sheet Almanac for 1780.

Revere's Bookplates

REVERE'S engraving of bookplates is represented by eleven plates, four signed by him, four which were unquestionably his work, two which were probably his work, and one plate probably by his father, Apollos Rivoire. In general the plates are divided into two groups according to the style of the mantling. In the first group there are seven plates, three signed and four unsigned. They are almost identical, in the elaborate Chippendale style of mantling, scroll work, flowers, and motto ribbon. Revere used the same mantling many times, changing the coat-of-arms, the crest, and the name. It is probable that he used some English bookplate as his model, copying it faithfully, yet I have never located this English plate, although I have examined many thousands by English engravers. It is possible that he used his father's Paul Rivoire plate for a model. The seven plates in the first group are as follows:

Gardiner Chandler. Signed "P Revere sculp." The coat-of-arms and the crest follow the design of the bookplate of his brother, John Chandler, Jr. (1721–1800), earlier engraved by Nathaniel Hurd; but the mantling is more elaborate and is distinctly Revere's. Also the plate bears in the upper left corner the abbreviation "No," with a superior "o" directly above two parallel lines, a characteristic of Revere's bookplates and also of his colonial paper currency. Gardiner Chandler's dates were 1723–1782 and the plate was probably engraved in the 1760's. The original copper was long owned by Mrs. Nathaniel Thayer of Lancaster, who occasionally made restrikes from it on modern paper. Since her death in 1934 the copper has not been found. On the reverse of the copper, in the upper left corner, is a small trial engraving of a coat-of-arms, of which restrikes were made about forty years ago by Mr. Charles E. Goodspeed, to whom the copper had been loaned.

John Gardiner. Almost identical, in mantling and motto ribbon, with the

Plate 51. Bookplates of Chandler, Greene, and Sargent.

PLATE 52. BOOKPLATES OF OLIVER, RIVOIRE, THOMAS, AND GARDINER.

David Greene and Gardiner Chandler plates. Although unsigned this was undoubtedly Revere's work. In addition to the American Antiquarian Society copy, there are copies in the Baillie collection in the Metropolitan Museum and in the Libbie collection at Dartmouth College. John Gardiner (1714–1764) was the fifth proprietor of Gardiner's Island, and his career is well described in Curtiss C. Gardiner's *Lion Gardiner and his Descendants*, 1890, pages xix, 116. Long after his death his grand-nephew, Robert S. Gardiner (1786–1824), used the copper by covering John's name with paper and inserting his own name in handwriting. Robert was the grandson of Colonel Abraham Gardiner, who was John's executor. He died unmarried and the original copper is now unlocated. Another Gardiner bookplate, with "By the name of Gardiner" on the motto ribbon, was used by John-Lyon Gardiner (1770–1816), seventh proprietor of Gardiner's Island. It was engraved about 1800 and copied closely the John Gardiner plate, but was not engraved by Revere. David Gardiner (1772–1815), brother of John-Lyon Gardiner, also used this plate by writing in his own name.

David Greene. Signed "Revere scp." The mantling is almost identical with the Chandler plate. The abbreviation for "No" in the upper left corner is not on the Greene plate. The motto ribbon is filled in with "Nec timeo nec sperno." There is also an identical impression of this plate, but without the Revere signature. David Greene (1749–1812) was a Boston merchant who frequently bought silver from Revere. His son, David I. Greene (1782–1826), later used the plate by having his middle initial engraved on the copper, crowded in between the first and last names. David Greene's grandson, the Reverend David Greene Haskins (1818–1896), also used the plate by covering the engraved name with paper and inserting his own name in handwriting. One example in the American Antiquarian Society carries the name of Mary C. D. Haskins, the Reverend David's wife, and another has the inscription "David Greene Haskins, Jr., from Father, March 5, 1857."

Andrew Oliver. Unsigned, but unquestionably by Revere, and almost identical in design and mantling with the David Greene plate. Bears the motto "Pax quaeritus bello." Andrew Oliver (1706–1774) was Lieutenant-Governor of

Massachusetts and became unpopular in 1765 for his attempt to enforce the Stamp Act. His name is occasionally entered in Revere's Day Book as a purchaser of silver.

Paul Rivoire. Unsigned, but the same design, almost identical, as the Gardiner Chandler plate. This plate was presumably engraved by Paul's father, Apollos Rivoire. Apollos, born in 1702, arrived in Boston from France in 1716, and was indentured to John Coney, silversmith. Coney died in 1722 and Apollos, with the aid of his French relatives, paid off his indenture indebtedness, and succeeded to the business. Coney in his will calls the boy Paul Rivoire. He soon changed his last name to Revere, but apparently used the name interchangeably in the 1720's. In his marriage record in 1729 it is called Revere, but in the same year Samuel Mather's *Life of Cotton Mather* carries the name in the list of subscribers as Paul Rivoire, and in the birth records of his children the name is spelled Rivoire. In the Boston *News-Letter* of May 21, 1730, he advertises over the name of Paul Revere the removal of his shop. Hence this bookplate was undoubtedly made by the father, either from his own design or by copying the mantling from an English plate. If so, it could well have served as the model for the design which the son Paul Revere used in the Chandler, Gardiner, Greene, Oliver, Sargent, and Thomas plates. The father obtained his heraldry from the arms of the Rivoire family of Dauphiny, from which, however, he was in no way descended. Apollos Revere was born at Riaucaud, near Bordeaux, in 1702. The subject of the Revere ancestry in France is interestingly told by Paul F. Cadman in the 1935 publication of the State Street Trust Company, entitled *Boston and Some Noted Émigrés*. The copy of the plate in the American Antiquarian Society is torn at the bottom, but that in the Massachusetts Historical Society, deposited by William B. Revere in 1921, is perfect. If made in the 1720's, young Paul could not have engraved it, as he was born in 1735. There is no reason to believe that it was engraved in England, and it is not in the Franks collection in the British Museum.

Epes Sargent. Signed "P. Revere Sculp," and almost a replica in design of the Gardiner Chandler plate. In Revere's Day Book, under date of September 27, 1764, there is a charge against Epes Sargent, Jun., "To Engraving your Arms on a Copper Plate 0–12–0" and "To 150 Prints at 4s pr Hund. 0–6–0." The American Antiquarian Society copy of the bookplate came from a volume of Lady

Montague's *Letters*, and on the title-page the signature of "Epes Sargent, jun'r, Aug. 3, 1764." Epes Sargent (1721–1779) was a frequent customer of Revere for silver. He seldom used the "Junior" after his father's death in 1762. The original copper of this plate is still owned by members of the Sargent family.

Isaiah Thomas. His first engraved plate, practically a replica of the Gardiner Chandler plate except for the arms. His first bookplate was an oblong printer's type label, dated Charlestown, South Carolina, July 8, 1769. This second plate, unsigned, but unquestionably engraved by Revere, with the characteristic Revere "No" at the top, does not seem to have been used to any extent. Only the copy in the American Antiquarian Society collection is known. It is the supposition, in fact the tradition, that Thomas did not relish that his plate was an evident facsimile of the plate of Gardiner Chandler, and engaged Revere to make a new one, which is described later.

The second group of bookplates designed by Revere is represented by two examples, one signed, one unsigned. The first is that of William Wetmore, signed "Revere sc." It shows a coat-of-arms, surrounded by a mantling of palm branches and flowers, with a crest above and a motto ribbon below. It presumably copied the design of some English plate. The American Antiquarian Society has two copies of the plate in varying shades of blue. The Reverend Robert G. Wetmore (1774–1803) copied the plate, although his was evidently made by another engraver. He was only a distant cousin of William Wetmore (1749–1830), although he had frequent correspondence with William's branch of the family. Also identical with the Robert G. Wetmore plate is that of Thomas Wetmore (1767–1828), brother of Robert and a Loyalist who removed to Nova Scotia, where he became a prominent lawyer and Attorney-General of the Province of New Brunswick.

Perez Morton. Exactly the same mantling and design as the William Wetmore. In addition, it has the characteristic Revere "No" at the top. In Revere's Day Book, under date of July 12, 1784, is entered "Perez Morton Esqr Dr. To Engraving your Arms on Copper 18[sh]. To Printing 100 Impressions 4–6. [Total] £1–2–6." Perez Morton (1750–1837) was a frequent buyer of silver from Revere from 1781 to 1797, invariably with his crest engraved thereon. He was an ardent patriot, speaker of the House of Representatives, and Attorney-General.

There are two plates not signed by Revere but probably his work. One is his own plate, showing a lion holding the Revere coat-of-arms copied from the Paul Rivoire plate. The motto "Pugna pro Patria" might indicate that the plate was engraved after the beginning of the Revolution. The lettering and the engraving look like Revere's work, but the chief argument in favor of his having made it is that he would be unlikely to call upon another engraver to make his own bookplate. The American Antiquarian Society copy of the plate was removed from Volume I of Hugh Latimer's *Sermons*, London, 1758. The original copper is owned by Edward H. R. Revere, of Canton, although in its present state only the last name "Revere" is on the copper. Restrikes in prints were made about fifty years ago, and twenty-five years later restrikes of fifty prints and proofs were made for Mr. Revere by the John A. Lowell Company of Boston.

The second engraved plate made for Isaiah Thomas was probably engraved by Revere. Why Thomas disliked his earlier Revere plate, almost a replica of the Gardiner Chandler plate, we do not know; but when he acquired a new plate there was no one to whom he would have turned more quickly than his friend, Paul Revere. The plate is distinctly in Revere's style, with the characteristic "No" at the top, the drawing of the mantling, and the lettering, both on the motto ribbon and for the script letter of the name underneath. In the American Antiquarian Society copy of the *Royal Magazine* for 1766, Thomas pasted this plate which he numbered "no. 4" and the year "1798," showing that its use was almost at the end of the century.

Revere has only three bookplates noted in his Day Books, which would mean little as this journal was far from complete and contained only charge accounts. In addition to the Sargent and Morton plates noted above, he has an entry under date of January 15, 1765, charging Captain William Ellery, Jr., 12 shillings for "Engraving a Copper Plate with your Arms," and 4 shillings for one hundred prints. Inquiry among members of the Ellery family has so far not resulted in finding the plate.

The only William Ellery, Jr., who bore the title of "Captain" was born in

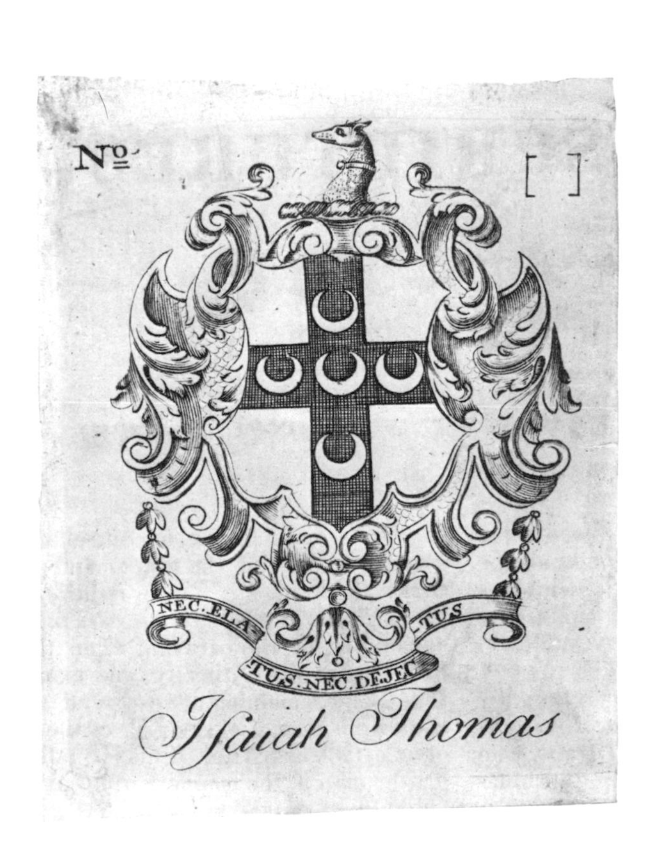

Plate 53. Bookplates of Morton, Revere, Thomas, and Wetmore.

Gloucester in 1694 and died there in 1771. William Ellery (1701–1764) of Newport was the son of Benjamin, and the father of William Ellery of Newport, signer of the Declaration, who apparently had been a naval officer and might have been called "Captain." Benjamin Ellery (1699–1746), of Gloucester and later of Newport, owned a bookplate, or it might have been his grandson Benjamin Ellery (1725–1797) of Newport, who was known, according to his obituary, as "a gentleman of culture." The Benjamin Ellery bookplate was engraved probably by Hurd, but surely not by Revere.

Other eighteenth-century bookplates have been occasionally ascribed to Revere, such as the Minot, William Cabot, and William Bell plates, but they are not characteristic of Revere's style and there is no outside proof, documentary or presumptive, to connect them with his work. Of the plates credited above to Revere, the American Antiquarian Society has all the originals and re-impressions.

Trade Cards

TRADE CARDS, also called advertising cards, business cards, and shopkeepers' cards, were popular in England in the eighteenth century. America followed suit and previous to the Revolution, Henry Dawkins, James Smither and James Turner in Philadelphia, and Nathaniel Hurd in Boston, engraved many cards. Dawkins made some especially beautiful ones, notable for their elaborate Chippendale borders. George F. Dow reproduced many of these in two articles in *Old-Time New England* for April and July, 1936. The cards frequently displayed hanging signs or showed a symbol associated with the trade. Sometimes space was left on the card for description and prices of goods sold, and invariably the reverse was used for a bill of goods made out by hand.

Revere was especially adept in engraving advertising cards and bill-heads, and charges for them were often entered in his Day Books. He was especially fond of elaborate Chippendale borders and mantling, and evidently copied the designs of English cards. But few of Revere's cards have survived to the present day. Of a dozen or more which he is known to have engraved, only five are now to be found, four of them unique examples. All five are in the American Antiquarian Society collection. The five cards located are as follows.

Joshua Brackett. This is rather a bill-head than an advertising card, as it has, on the face, engraved lines for charges. At the top is an ornamental mantled frame with the bust of Cromwell. On ribbons above is the name "Joshua Brackett," and below "O. Cromwell's Head. School-Street," and underneath is the word "Boston." It is signed "P Revere sc." It measures 6¼ inches high by 3⅞, to the edge of the plate mark. (See Plate no. 54.)

Joshua Brackett for nearly twenty-five years was the proprietor of the well known Cromwell's Head Inn on School Street. His father, Anthony Brackett, had

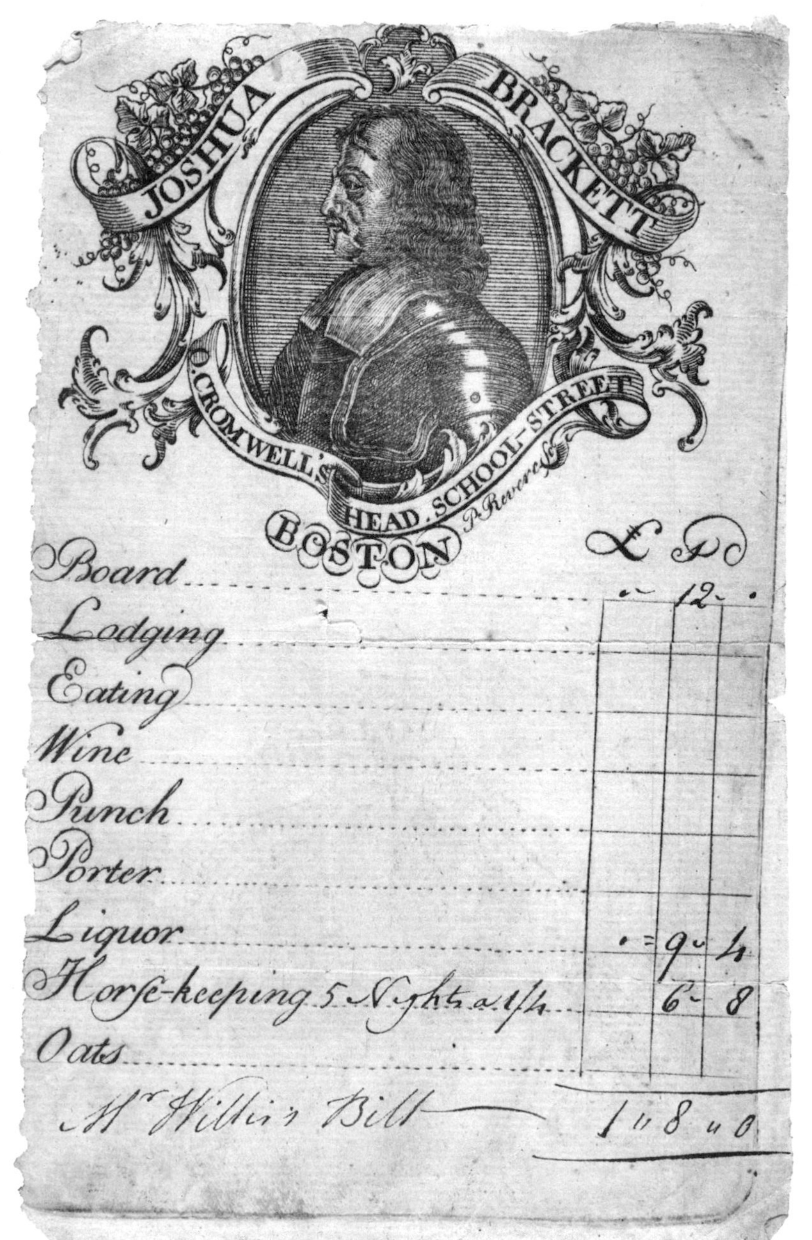

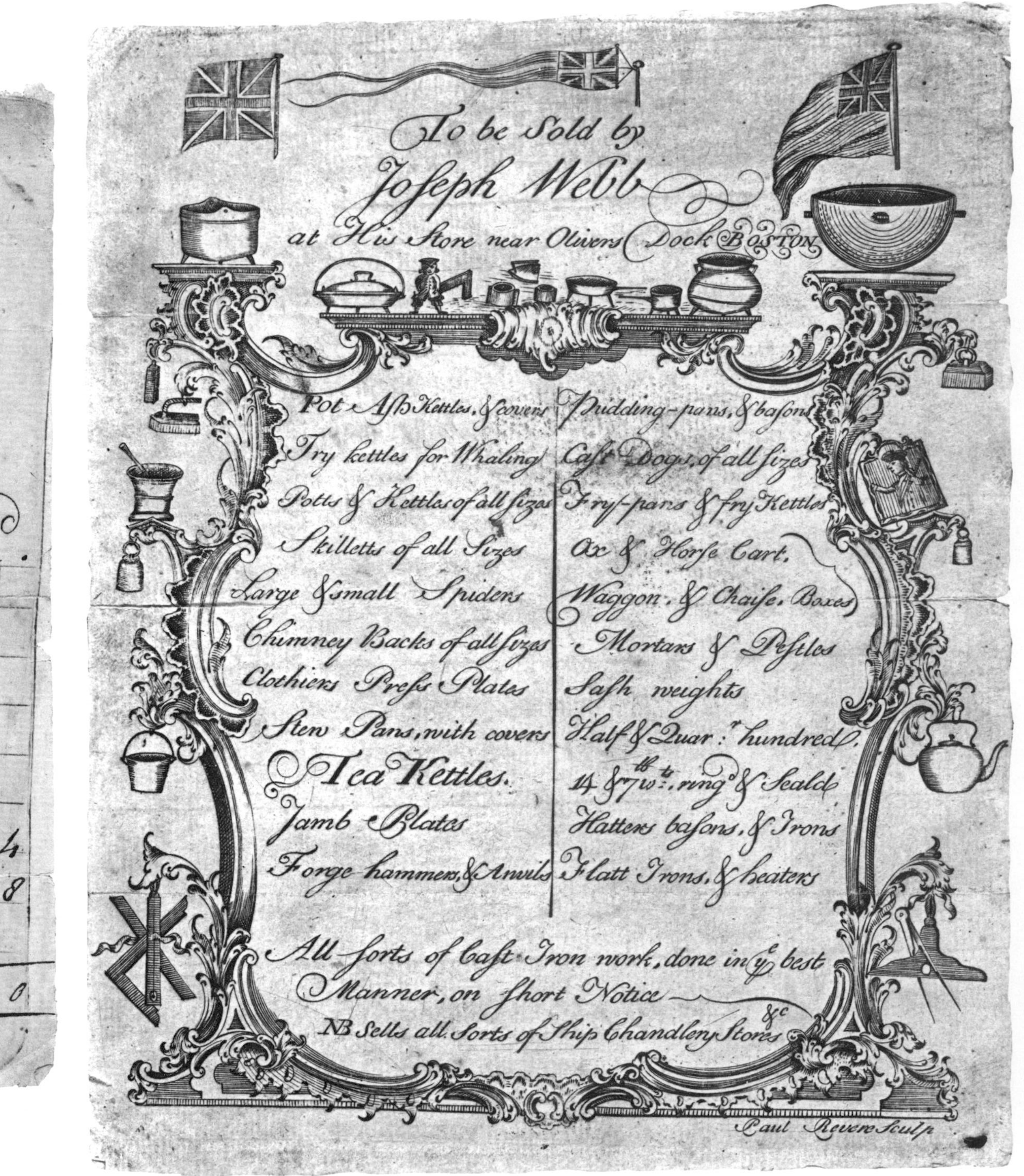

Plate 54. Joshua Brackett and Joseph Webb Trade Cards.

established the Inn, and when he died in 1764 was succeeded by his widow. Upon her death in 1768, Joshua followed as inn-keeper. He was born in 1738, married Abigail Pond in 1763, and died in 1794 (see *Brackett Genealogy*, 1907, page 106). Revere in his Day Book charged Joshua Brackett for shoe and knee buckles in 1761, and made similar charges in 1762, 1763, 1781, and 1785. But there was no charge for engraving the bill-head. The plate was engraved before 1771, as that date appears in manuscript on a copy owned by Samuel A. Drake, seen by Goss, and mentioned in his *Paul Revere*, Volume 1, page 95. Joseph Callender, the Boston engraver, later engraved another version of the Cromwell's Head plate with the head of Cromwell facing to the front. It is reproduced in Alice Morse Earle's *Stage Coach and Tavern Days*, 1900, page 86, and there is another copy in the Bostonian Society which has a manuscript date of 1785.

William Breck. This Boston importer and merchant had a shop "at the Golden Key near the draw-Bridge." His business card, which is 7 inches high by 5⅜ wide to the edge of the plate mark, is set in a Chippendale frame with an elaborate mantling of flowers and leaves, and a large design of a key at the top. It is signed "P Revere sculp." Revere copied an English original for the frame and presumably his model was the trade card of Joseph Welch of London, hardware merchant. The Welch card is in the large collection of English trade cards owned by the Metropolitan Museum of Art in New York. (See both cards Plate no. 55.) This frame served Revere as the model for the Breck card and also the William Jackson trade card.

Breck was a well known Boston merchant, who was born in 1745, married Margaret Thomas of Plymouth in 1771, settled at Claremont, New Hampshire, in 1794, and died in 1819 (see *Breck Genealogy*, 1889, page 39). He advertised his wares in the *Boston Gazette* of June 1, 1767, giving his location at the North End, near Hancock's Wharf. On the back of the American Antiquarian Society's copy of the print, William Breck signed a receipted bill, dated October 7, 1770. Revere did not enter in his Day Book the charge for engraving this print, but he did charge Breck eighteen shillings for three hundred prints under date of September 29, 1772. He also charged him two shillings, on March 25, 1774, for "a Print of Adams & Handcock," evidently the prints in the *Royal American Maga-*

zine of February and March, 1774, and for making a silver porringer in April, 1781.

Isaac Greenwood. The trade card of "Isaac Greenwood Ivory Turner Next door To Doctr John Clark's, at the North End Boston" is in plain script lettering, without ornamentation, and is signed "P Revere sculp." The measurements, to the outside of the border lines, are 5¾ by 4½ inches. The card lists Greenwood's numerous items of turned work in ivory, wood, and metal, ending with "Makes Umberilloes." (See Plate no. 56.) In Revere's Day Book there are five charges against Isaac Greenwood, from 1762 to 1774, for minor kinds of engraving, such as "Engraving two Cane Heads," and payments on account. There is no charge entered for engraving a trade card.

Isaac Greenwood, Jr., born at Cambridge in 1730, married Mary I'ams in 1757, and died in 1803, carried on the business of mathematical instrument maker, ivory turner, and importer of hardware. After the Revolution he conducted the business of a dentist, making artificial teeth, and specialized in the making of umbrellas. There is a long account of him in Isaac J. Greenwood's *Greenwood Family*, 1934, pages 68–78, where the trade card is reproduced at page 74, and in Bernard W. Weinberger's *Introduction to History of Dentistry*, 1948, Volume 2, pages 119–134, where the card is reproduced at page 127. In the *Boston Gazette* of May 20, 1771, he advertised his manufacture of "umbrilloes," which was continued for several weeks. He also advertised in the *Boston Gazette* for May 29, 1769, August 10, 1772, and May 10, 1773. It was presumably in 1771 that his trade card was engraved by Revere. The card was at one time owned by the late Hollis French and was presented by him to the American Antiquarian Society in November, 1937.

William Jackson. The trade card of William Jackson, importer and merchant, is an artistic design set in a Chippendale frame. The lettering begins "William Jackson at the Brazen Head, next ye Town House Boston." At the top is an imaginary bust, on a pedestal, assumedly portraying a brazen, or brass, head. Although unsigned it is surely Revere's engraving. In fact, the card is identical in design with that of William Breck, except for the top ornament and the lettering. The measurements, to the plate lines, are 6⅞ by 5¾ inches. The advertising

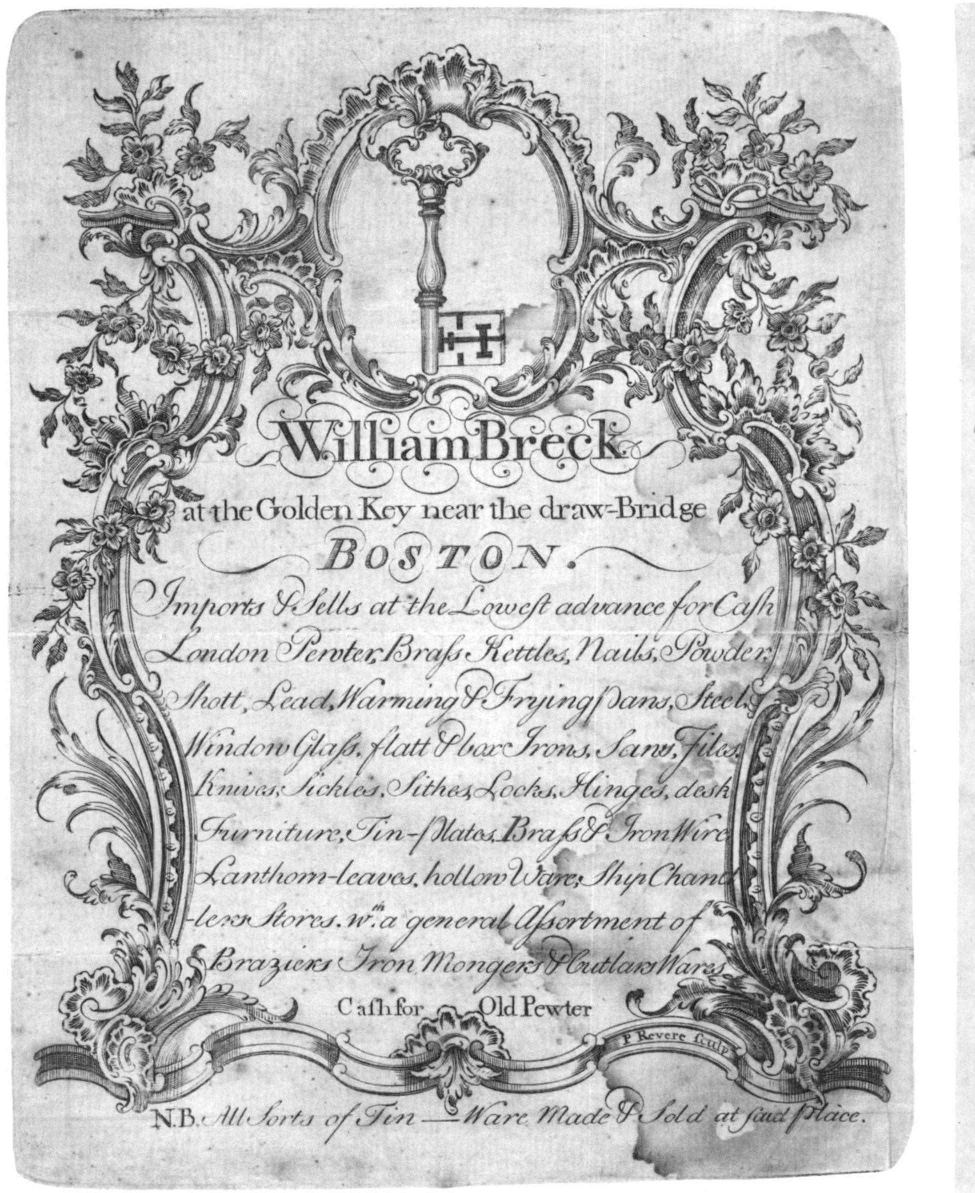

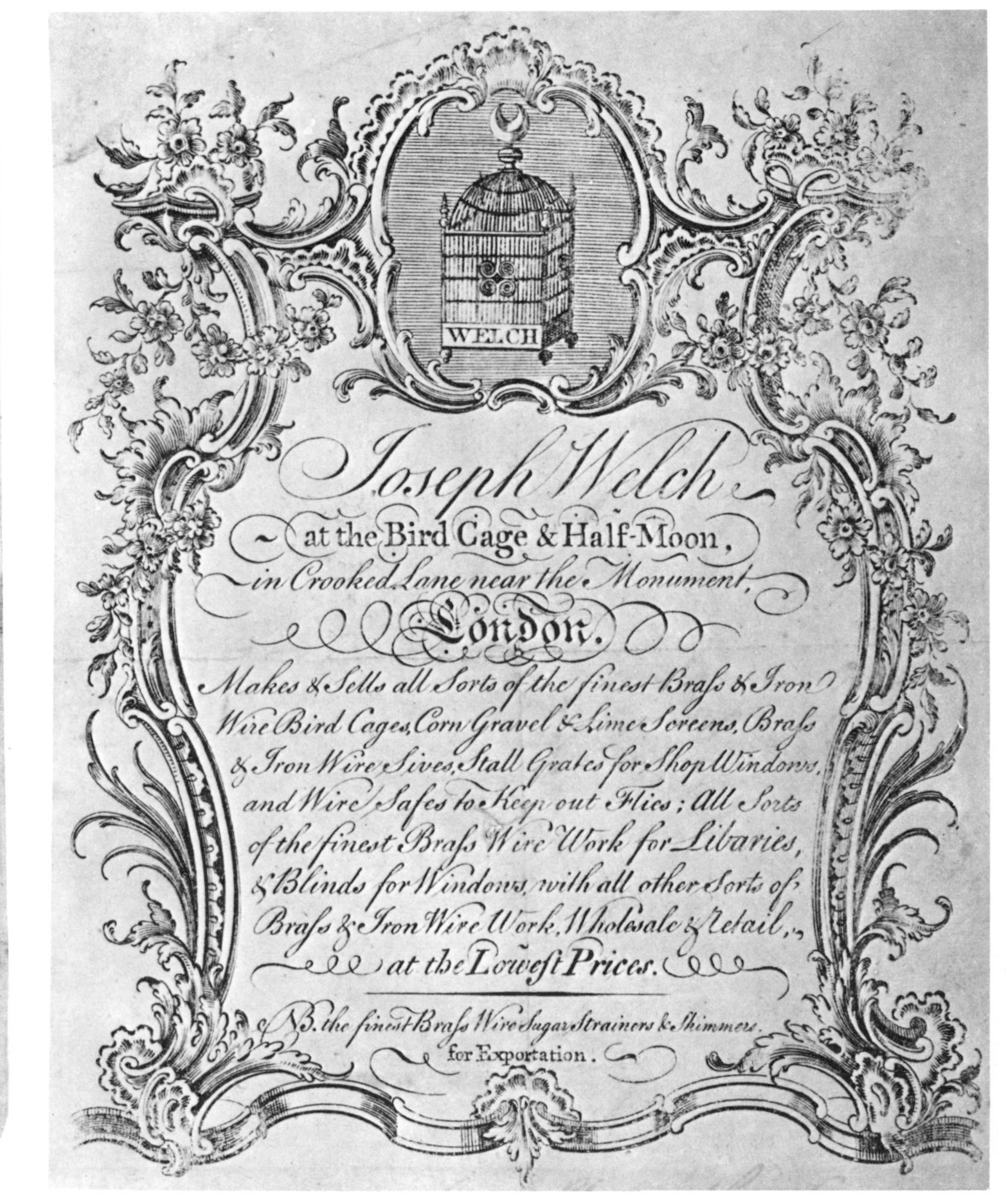

Plate 55. William Breck, and Joseph Welch, English Trade Card.

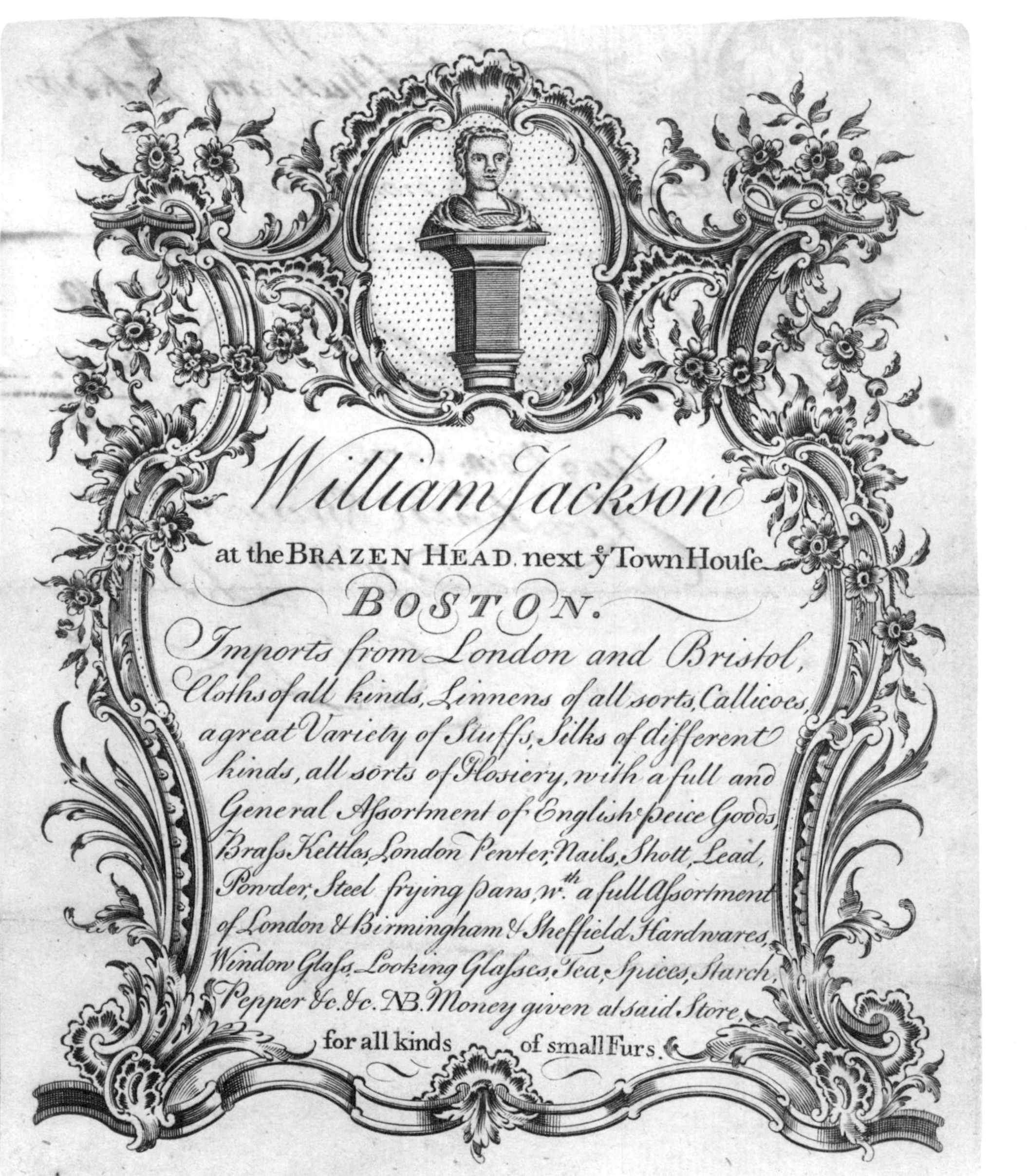

William Jackson
at the BRAZEN HEAD, next y^e Town House
BOSTON.
Imports from London and Bristol,
Cloths of all kinds, Linnens of all sorts, Callicoes,
a great Variety of Stuffs, Silks of different
kinds, all sorts of Hosiery, with a full and
General Assortment of English peice Goods,
Brass Kettles, London Pewter, Nails, Shott, Lead,
Powder, Steel frying pans, wth a full Assortment
of London & Birmingham & Sheffield Hardwares,
Window Glass, Looking Glasses, Tea, Spices, Starch,
Pepper &c. &c. NB. Money given at said Store
for all kinds of small Furs.

Isaac Greenwood IVORY·TURNER
Next door To Doct[r]. John Clark's, at the North End
Boston. Turns all Sorts of Work in Ivory, Silver, Brass,
Iron, Horn, Wood &c, Such as Billiard Balls, Tea Boards,
Scollopd & Plain Salvers, Decanter Stands, Pestles & Mortars,
Chocolate Mills, Lemon Squeesers, Walking Sticks, Ivory
& Nut heads & Ferrells for ditto, Ends for Prospective Glasses,
Joints for German Flutes, Large Wooden Cocks for distillers
Butts, Small ditto for Spirits. Turns Work for Gold=
=smiths, Such as, Tankards; Canns, Casters, Salts, Iron
Hand Irons for Smiths. Plain & Twisted Bannisters, &
Posts for Stair Cases, & Turretts, Pillars for Frontispieces &
Makes Handles for Coffee Potts, Tea Potts, Chafing dishes
& Warming Pans, Patterns for Goldsmiths & Founders,
Wooden Leggs, and many other Articles, too many
to be here enumerated with Fidelity & Dispatch at
a very reasonable Rate — Makes Umber=
=elloes

P. Revere sculp

PLATE 56. WILLIAM JACKSON AND ISAAC GREENWOOD TRADE CARDS.

describes imports from England of cloths, linens, calicoes, and silks, as well as hardware of various kinds. On the back of the American Antiquarian Society copy is a receipt for £44, signed William Jackson and dated August 28, 1773. He advertised in the *Boston Evening Post* of October 17, 1768, that he "is just arrived . . . from London," and in the same paper of January 16, 1769, he printed a long description of his importations. Presumably the card was engraved in 1769. J. Tracy Wiggin of Attleborough found in 1957 a copy of this card with a receipt, dated October 16, 1769, on the back. It went to the Pocumtuck Valley Memorial Association of Deerfield in 1959. (See Plate no. 56.)

William Jackson was a prominent and consistent Tory. As early as 1770 he continued to import British goods contrary to the sentiments of the majority of Boston merchants. The Sons of Liberty issued a broadside asking patriots not to buy from William Jackson (see Justin Winsor's *Narrative and Critical History of America*, Volume 6, page 80). He was one of the Addressers of Hutchinson in 1774 and of Gage in 1774 and 1775. With other Loyalists he purchased a large brig, filled it with imported goods, and set sail for Halifax in April, 1776. But the vessel was captured by a privateer and sent into Beverly. Jackson made his way finally to Boston where he was cast into jail, and there remained for one hundred and twenty-six days (see Albert Matthews, *Publications of the Colonial Society of Massachusetts*, 1906, Volume 8, page 99, and E. A. Jones's *Loyalists of Massachusetts*, 1930, page 178). He remained for a time in Boston, where he suffered several indignities, but after he was named in the banishment act of October 16, 1778, he left for England on a British ship. He is last recorded in the *Columbian Centinel* of March 28, 1810, as having died in England, aged seventy-nine.

Joseph Webb. The most elaborate of Revere's trade cards, in a Chippendale frame, with all kinds of utensils hung on the mantling—skillets, pots, kettles, pans, fire-backs, andirons, mortars, dividers, sash weights, and flat-irons. The card is headed "To be Sold by Joseph Webb at His Store near Olivers Dock Boston" and is signed "Paul Revere Sculp." The interior of the frame is filled with the names of the wares to be sold. The measurements, to the edge of the plate mark, are 7⅛ by 5⅞ inches. The mantled frame is almost identical with that used for the Saint Peter's Lodge notification. (See Plate no. 54.)

Revere in his Day Book enters the charge for this trade card, under date of September 28, 1765, as follows: "Mr Joseph Webb Dr settled/ To Engraving a Copper Plate for Advertisements 3–0–0/ To 150 Advertisements Printing at 4–1 pr Hdd 0–7–0."

Joseph Webb, Jr., merchant and ship-chandler, was born in Boston, October 28, 1734, son of Joseph and Abigail Webb, and married in November, 1759, Penelope Phillips of Marshfield. In 1760 his shop, which was at the lower end of Water Street, suffered in the fire which destroyed much of the Boston business section. He began business again in Long Lane, later Federal Street, where he also had his residence, erected in 1767. In 1765 his place of business was at the head of Oliver's Dock. He was one of the leaders in colonial resistance, with Warren, Revere, and Otis. He was prominent as a Mason, being Master of Saint Andrew's Lodge in 1765–66, and Grand Marshal in 1769; and he was Grand Master of Massachusetts Grand Lodge from 1777 until his death, on April 26, 1787 (see sketch in Oliver A. Roberts's *History of Ancient and Honorable Artillery Company*, 1897, Volume 2, page 109).

The American Antiquarian Society has a receipted bill, signed by Joseph Webb, Jr., March 10, 1759, charging for kettles, pots, skillets, and other wares.

In Revere's Day Book there are many charges for engraving advertising cards and bill-heads for merchants, or for the sale of prints. But since no specimens of such cards have survived, there is no way of describing them, or proving that they were engraved. A list of such charges follows:

> 1762 August 18. "Mr. William Hichborn Dr/ To Cutting a Copper for hatt Prints 0–10–4/ To 100 Prints 0–2–8." Subsequent charges on October 28, 1763, for 200 "Hatt Prints," and on September 2, 1773, for 100 "Hatt Bills."
>
> 1764 June 14. "Mr Nathl Fosdike Dr/ to 100 Hatt Bills 0–2–8."
>
> 1764 June 14. "Mr Increas Blake Dr/ To Cutting a Copper Plate 1–16–0/to 100 Prints."
>
> 1764 August 28. "Mr Nathaniel Baker Dr/ To Engraving a Copper plate for hatt bills 0–10–8/ To 100 Prints 0–2–8."

1765 May 7. "Mr Matthew Lindsey Dr/ To a Engraving a Copper Plate 0–6–0/ To two Hudd Prints at 2/8 0–5–4."

1771 January 3. "Mr Samuel Hewes Dr/ To Engraving a Copper plate for sper'ceti Cans 3–10–0/ To two Hund. prints 0–9–4." On April 15, 1772, there was a charge for 350 Prints at 5 sh., 6d.

1773 January 1. "Mr William Boardman Dr/ To 200 Hatt Bills 0–6–0." Subsequent charges on September 2, 1773, for 100 "hatt bills," and on February 6, 1774, for 200 "Hatt Bills."

1773 May 10. "Mr Ezra Collins Dr/ To 100 Hatt Bills 0–2–4." Subsequent charges on October 25, 1773, for 100 "Hatt-Bills," on June 7, 1774, for 100 "Hatt Bills," and on March 20, 1775, for 100 "Hatt Bills."

1774 June 7. "Mr John Piemont Dr/ To two Hundred prints 0–8–0." It is not known whether this charge was for bill-heads, or for blank Masonic notifications. Piemont was a prominent Mason, and became an inn-keeper at Danvers in 1773. The charge of four shillings per hundred prints, however, is lower than Revere's usual charge for stock Masonic notifications.

1783 October 10. "William Boardman & Son Dr/ To Engraving a plate for Hatt Bills 0–15–0/ To printing 300 @ 4s. 0–12–0/ To printing 500 @ 4s 1–0–0." During the years 1787 to 1797 Revere entered twenty-one charges against William Boardman & Sons for a total of 7897 hat bills.

1784 August 10. "Mr Abraham Adams Dr/ To Engraving two plates for hatt Bills 0–18–0/ To printing to hund Bills 0–6–8."

1786 March 13. "Benjm Warren Plimouth Dr/ To printing one hundred Compass Cards 0–18–0." He advertised in the *Plymouth Journal* of March 19, 1785, to sell seamen's and surveyor's instruments. There may be a copy at Yale. The E. C. Streeter Collection of Weights and Measures contains a compass card with Warren's name thereon.

1792 April 16. "Mr William Williams Dr/ To Engravg plate for hatt bills 0–18–0/ To 2 hund prints 0–6–0." From June 24, 1792, to January 28, 1797, Revere entered twelve charges, amounting to £14–15–0, against William Williams for 8500 hat bills.

1792 April 16. "Mr Sarson Belcher Dr/ To Engravg a plate for hatt bill 0–15–0/ To 150 prints 0–4–6."

1792 November 15. "Mr Charles Smith Dr/ To printing 200 hatt bills 0–6–0." Also charge of 6 sh. for 200 "hatt bills" on December 9, 1792, and 17 sh. 6d. for 500 on January 24, 1793.

1794 December 9. "Mr Samuel Barry Dr/ To 310 hatt bills 0–12–0."

Clock Advertisements

REVERE'S Day Book shows three charges against Simon Willard for prints to be placed in clocks, as follows:

> April 11, 1781, "Mr Simon Willard Dr/ To printing a number of sheets of / Prints to go into time pieces 1–12–0."
>
> June 14, 1781, "Mr Simon Willard Dr / To printing 18 Sett of prints to / go into time pieces 0–18–0."
>
> July 3, 1781, "Mr Simon Willard Dr / To Printing 18 Sett of prints / for your time pieces 0–18–0/ To Cash paid for Vermillion 0–3–0/ To 100 prints for your Br Aron for Watches 0–6–0."

All of these charges were made against Simon Willard. Simon was the second oldest of the Willard brothers who were clock-makers. Benjamin was born in 1743, Simon in 1753, Ephraim in 1755, and Aaron in 1757. Benjamin had a shop in Grafton and sold tall clocks in Roxbury as early as 1771. Simon spent most of his business life in Roxbury, and made tall clocks and wall clocks, mostly the latter. Ephraim lived at Medford during the eighteenth century and made comparatively few clocks. Aaron established his clock business in Boston, later moved to Roxbury, and in 1792 returned to Boston. He made clocks on a large scale, employing many workmen.

Although all of the above entries for clock prints were charged against Simon Willard, no print with Revere's characteristic engraving has ever, to my knowledge, been found in a Simon Willard clock. In the 1790's he used a printed label, printed by Isaiah Thomas, Jr., advertising his various kinds of clocks, and giving directions as to operation.

All of the clock labels, surely engraved by Revere, carry the name of Aaron Willard and are found in Aaron Willard clocks. I have located more than twenty. The label is 5⅞ inches high by 3⅞ wide, to the edge of the engraving. It shows a Chippendale type of border of scroll work and flowers, with a shelf clock at the top, and with the engraved advertisement "Common House Clocks, Table Spring

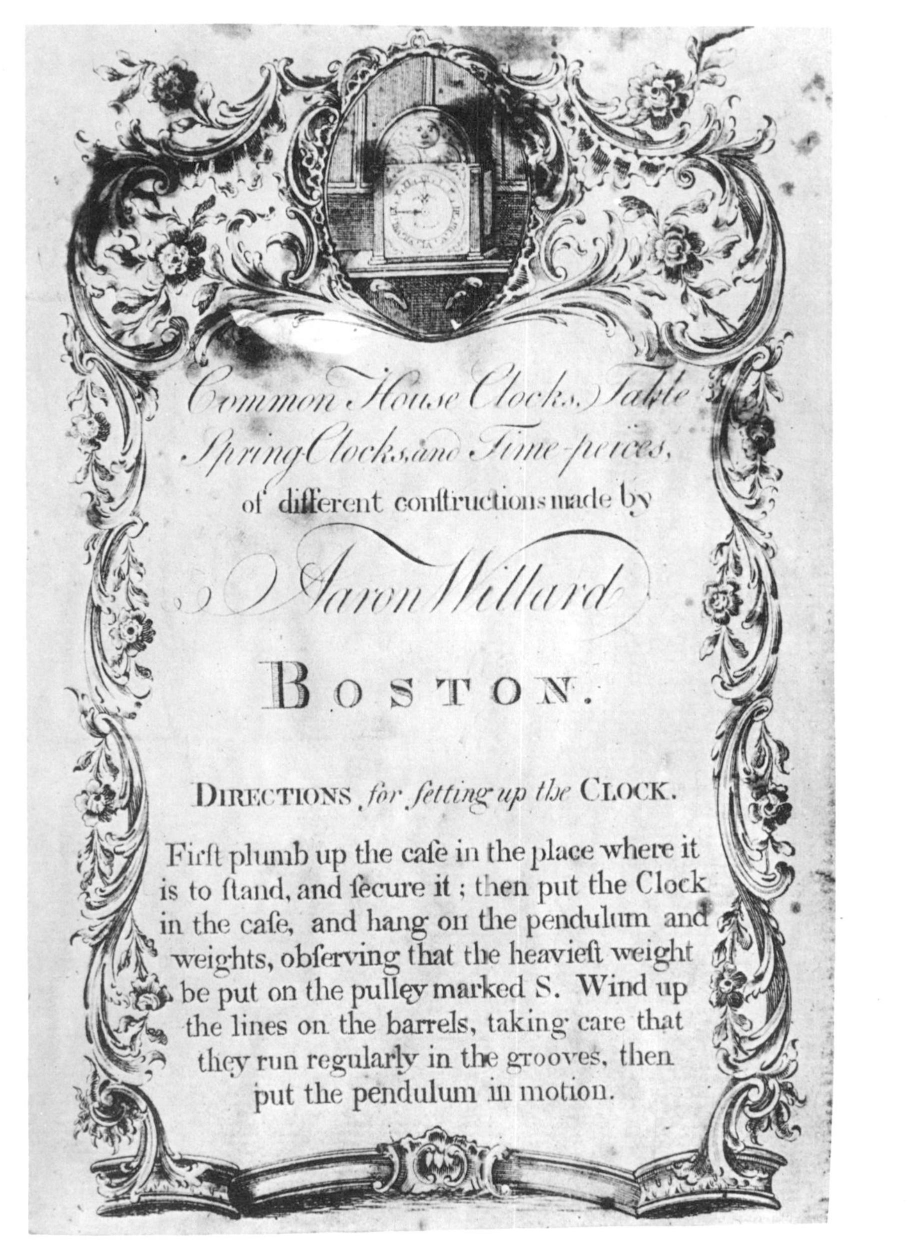

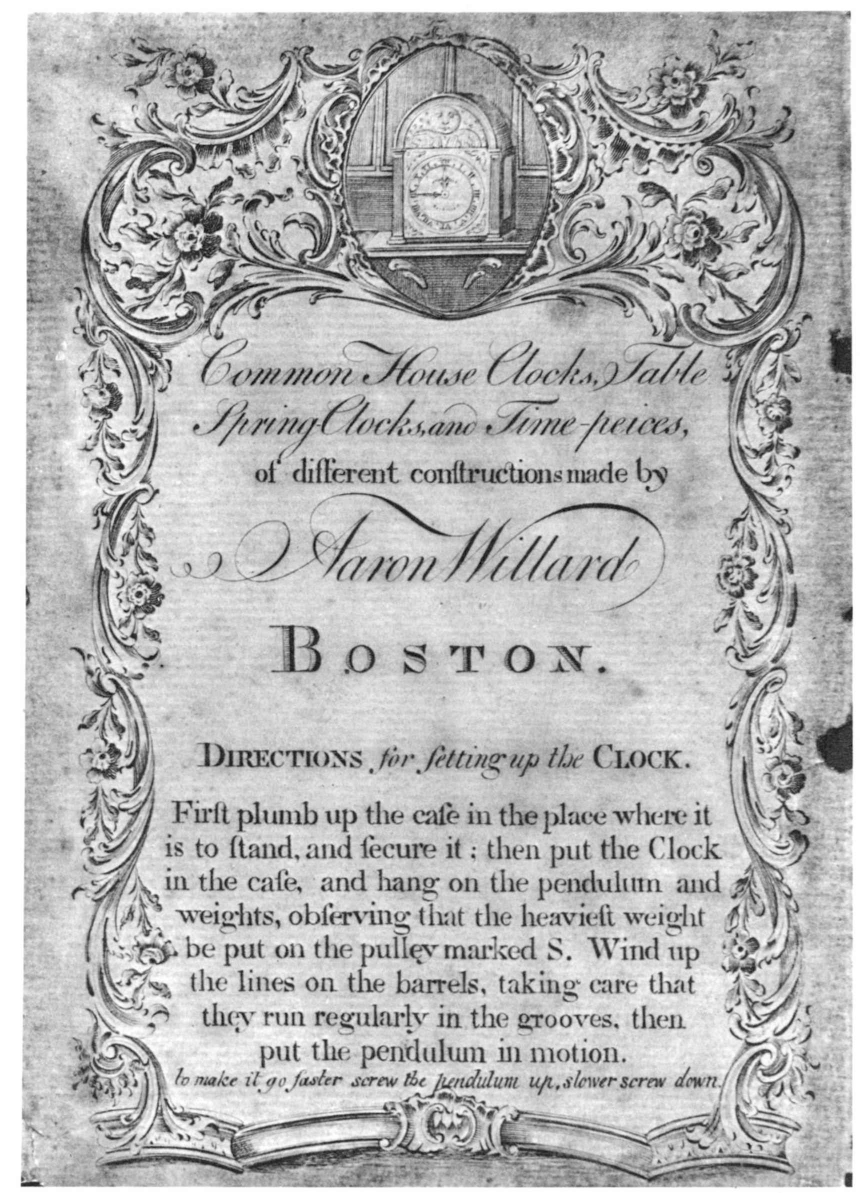

PLATE 57. WILLARD CLOCK ADVERTISEMENTS, BOSTON VARIETIES.

PLATE 58. WILLARD ROXBURY CLOCK ADVERTISEMENT AND WILLARD WATCH PAPER.

Clocks, and Time-peices, of different constructions made by Aaron Willard Boston," followed by "Directions for setting up the Clock." There are three varieties — the first with "Roxbury," a second with "Boston," and a third with "Boston" and a line inserted at the bottom "to make it go faster screw the pendulum up, slower screw down." The chronological order of the three labels is not certain. All of the three labels are herewith reproduced, Plates 57 and 58. The American Antiquarian Society has only the last of the three prints.

The engraving is in Revere's characteristic style, both in the border and in the lettering. The fact that no such labels are found in Simon Willard clocks, and all located are in Aaron Willard clocks, would lead to the belief that Simon was assuming the charge in the Day Book in behalf of his brother Aaron. This belief is heightened by the fact that the last Revere charge is for one hundred prints for "Your Brother Aron for Watches."

I have not attempted to list the owners of tall clocks which still retain the engraved label. I have found over twenty and have a dozen photographs. The print is reproduced, in slightly reduced form, in Wallace Nutting's *Clock Book*, 1924, plate 112, and in his *Furniture Treasury*, 1928, Volume 2, number 3452.

As for the watch paper engraved for Aaron Willard, the Revere Day Book in July, 1781, specifically charges Simon Willard with six shillings for 100 prints for "Your Br Aron for Watches." The search for such a watch paper has gone on for many years. In 1935, John M. Phillips of Yale University acquired such a paper from Francis H. Bigelow of Cambridge. He gave it in 1947 to Mark Bortman of Boston, and Mr. Bortman in turn presented it to the American Antiquarian Society in 1948. The paper is circular in shape, to fit the back of a watch, and shows an angel blowing a horn at the top, a branch of a tree, a watch, Father Time, a rooster, and in the center the advertisement of "A. Willard Watch & Clock Maker Boston." It is typically engraved in Revere's style and is unquestionably his work. It is reproduced, Plate no. 58. The Bortman copy shows only the outside ornamental border line, but another copy recently acquired by the American Antiquarian Society shows also an outside plain border line. The diameter of the label is 1⅞ inches, to the plain border line. The two copies owned by the American Antiquarian Society are the only ones located.

Masonic Engravings

REVERE'S engravings of Masonic notifications and certificates, or diplomas as they were frequently called, constituted an important feature of his work. They are rare, perhaps because they were destroyed by the families of their owners, or because local Lodges were not careful in preserving their records. Of the seven Masonic engraved designs known, the American Antiquarian Society has six. Occasional copies are in Masonic libraries, especially the Massachusetts Grand Lodge Library in Boston.

Revere was the most prominent Mason in New England during his period. The chapter on Masonic History in E. H. Goss's *Life of Paul Revere*, 1891, Volume 2, pages 465–495, gives the best account of the subject. Revere became a member of Saint Andrew's Lodge of Boston in 1760, its Secretary in 1769, and Master from 1770 to 1771, and 1777 to 1782. When the Massachusetts Grand Lodge was formed in 1769, Revere was made Senior Grand Deacon. In 1783 when the question of allegiance arose as to whether Saint Andrew's Lodge should be under the jurisdiction of the Massachusetts Grand Lodge or of the Grand Lodge of Scotland, Revere, losing his preference for adhering to the Massachusetts Grand Lodge, withdrew from Saint Andrew's and organized a separate Saint Andrew's Lodge in February 1784 which in September 1784 changed its name to Rising States Lodge, of which Revere became the first treasurer. In 1792 all differences of opinion were settled, Saint John's Grand Lodge, which had been formed in 1733, and the Massachusetts Grand Lodge, were united, taking the title of the Grand Lodge of Massachusetts. Revere was Grand Master of the united body from 1794 to 1797.

Revere, as a goldsmith and engraver, was constantly employed in making Masonic jewels and engravings on parchment and paper, and in 1800 he made the gold urn designed to preserve a lock of Washington's hair. Undoubtedly Revere copied the general designs and ornamental frames of his Masonic engravings from English sources. The earlier English Lodges used engraved notifications and certificates, and many of them are shown in J. Ramsden Riley's monograph on "Masonic Certificates" in the *Quatuor Coronatorum Antigrapha*, Masonic Reprints, Volume 8, 1895. Although in this volume most of the reproductions are of

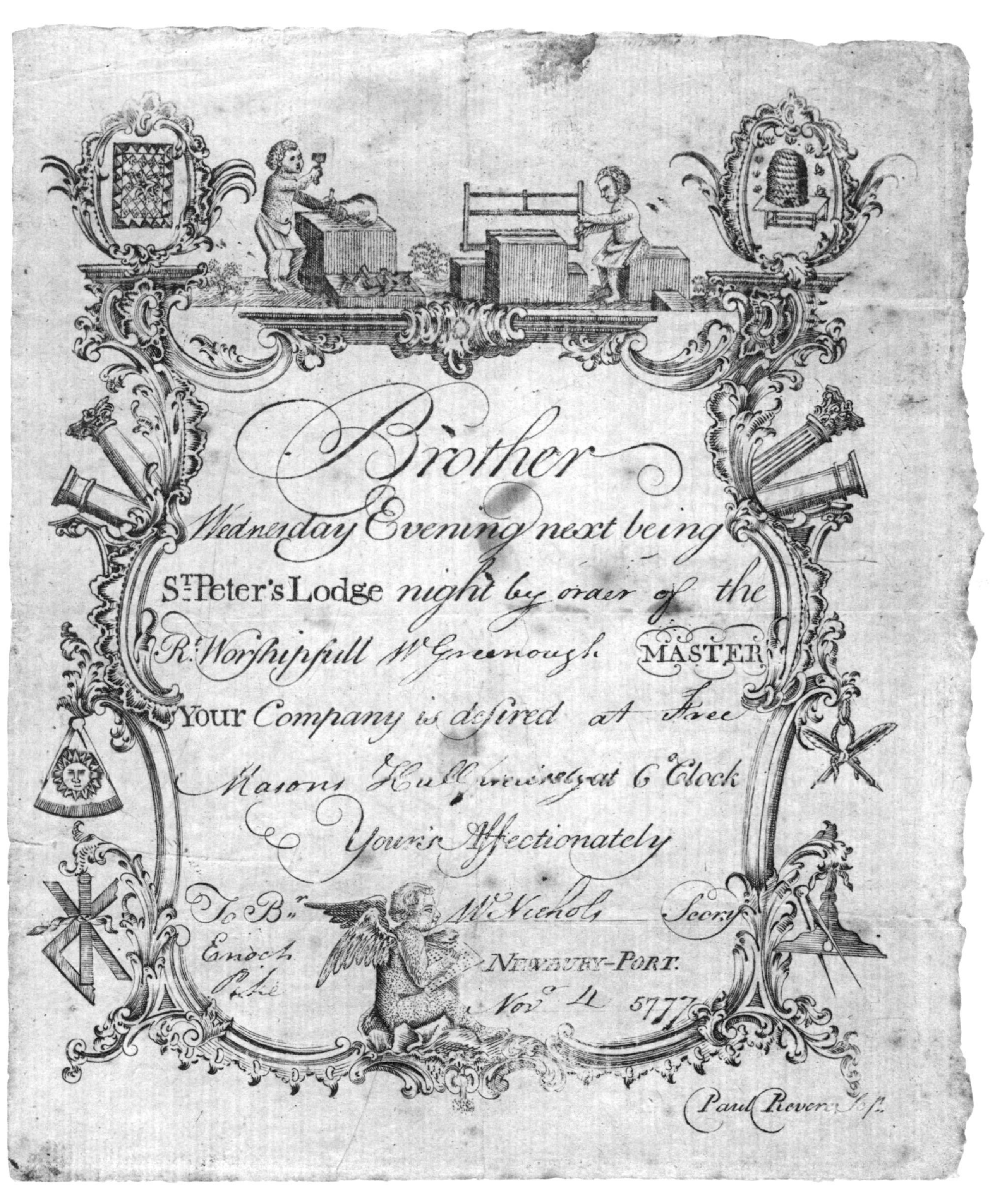

Brother

Wednesday Evening next being

St. Peter's Lodge night by order of the

Rt. Worshipfull Wm Greenough MASTER

Your Company is desired at Free Masons Hall precisely at 6 O'Clock

Your's Affectionately

To Br. Wm Nichols Secry

Enoch Pike

Newbury-Port. Nov. 4 5777

Paul Revere Sculp.

Plate 59. St. Peter's Lodge Notification, Engraved in 1772.

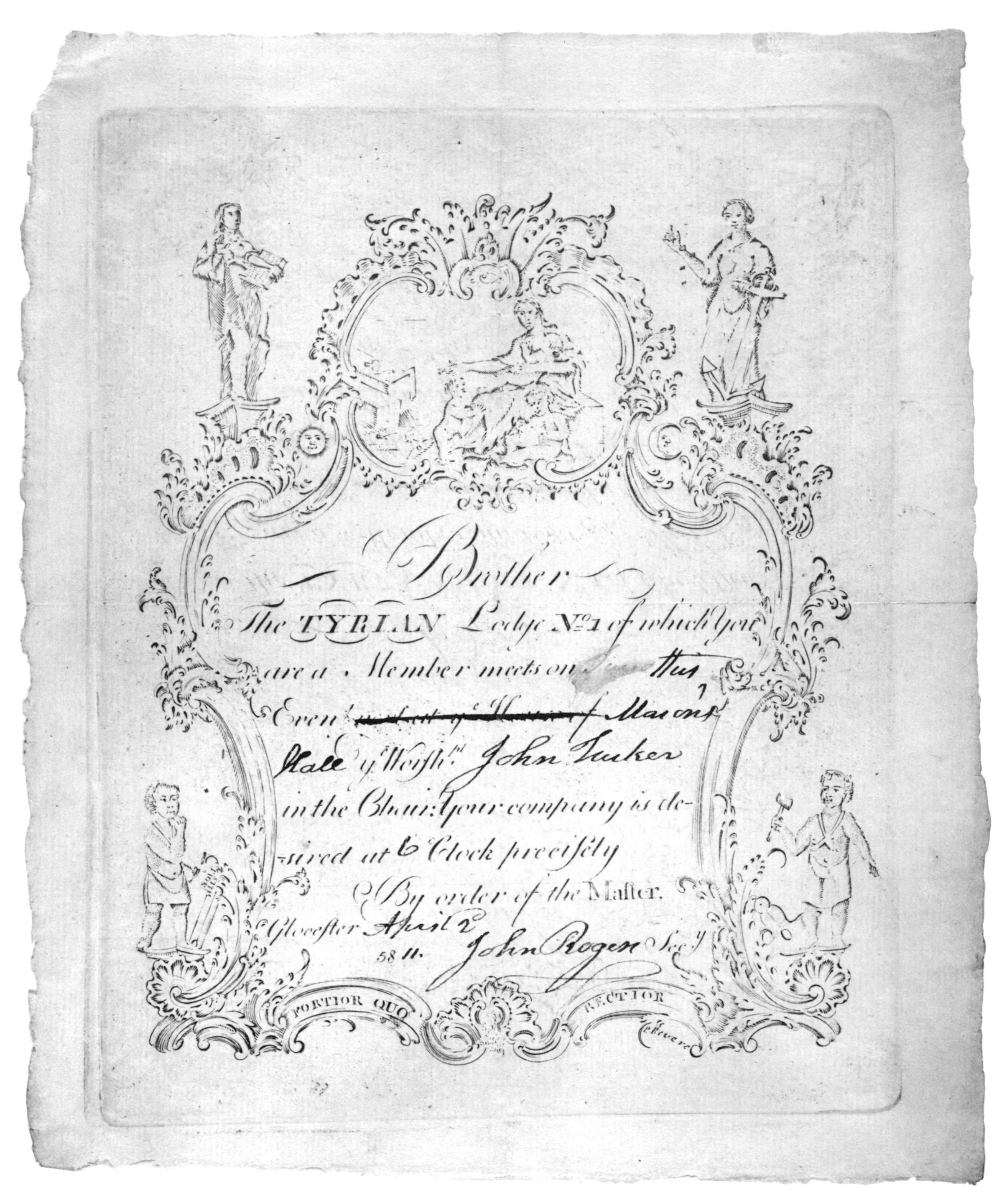

Brother

The TYRIAN Lodge No. 1 of which You are a Member meets on Thurs. Even[g] Masons Hall ye Worshl. John Tucker in the Chair: Your company is de-sired at 6 Clock precisely

By order of the Master.

Glocester April 2
5811. John Rogers Secy

FORTIOR QUO RECTIOR

Revere sc

Plate 60. Tyrian Lodge Notification, Engraved in 1773.

PLATE 60A. LODGE 169 NOTIFICATION, ENGRAVED IN LATE 1760'S.

engravings after 1780, the frontispiece shows an engraved certificate called the "Three Graces" which was apparently the model that Revere used for his small certificate which in the American Antiquarian Society collection is filled in for Samuel Welch of Rising States Lodge of Boston. Before engraved certificates were procurable from Revere in Boston, many Lodges made out such diplomas by hand. The Massachusetts Grand Lodge Library has examples in manuscript made for John Pulling in 1761, Winthrop Sargent in 1776, and John Stacey in 1777.

Revere in his Day Book enters several charges for Masonic engravings, some of which cannot be located. He had for sale a stock of notifications and certificates, to be filled in for various Lodges, and entered the record of the names of the purchasers. He also engraved Masonic prints which were not entered in his Day Book. The following record of his Masonic engravings is in the main chronological.

Under date of March 22, 1762, Revere entered in his Day Book the following charge: "Mr John Pulling Junr Dr/ To Cutting a Copper Plate for Notifications 1–4–0/ To 2 Hundred Notifications at 6s P Hundd 0–12–0." The plate may have been simple in style, as the charge was smaller than usual for similar work. On June 7, 1762, Revere charged "Capt. John Pullings" for making a coffee-pot and a child's porringer with spoon £20–1–0. Revere's friend, John Pulling, Jr., was generally called Captain Pulling. He was born in 1737, married Annis Lee of Marblehead, January 14, 1768, and died in 1787. John Pulling was a member of the Lodge at Marblehead chartered in 1760 and received an elaborate certificate from that Lodge on June 9, 1761. The certificate, written by hand, was long owned by Alfred Pratt of Weston (see reproduction in *Proceedings* of Massachusetts Grand Lodge for 1909, page 26), and after his death was presented to the Grand Lodge Library by Mrs. Pratt. Although Pulling was made a Mason in Marblehead Lodge, he was soon a member of the Lodge of Saint Andrew in Boston, as is shown by the record of his presence at the meetings of that Lodge in 1761 and 1762. If the copper-plate for the notification cut for him by Paul Revere was a Masonic notification, it could have been for the use of either Marblehead or Saint Andrew. It might have been made for some other form of notification, such as the call for the meetings of a social organization. It should be noted, moreover, that the Lodge of Saint Andrew engaged Paul Revere to cut a plate for a "summons" in March, 1784.

On November 14, 1766, Revere in his Day Book entered the following charge: "Capt Caleb Hopkins Dr/ To Engraving a Copper Plate for Notifications for a Masons Lodge in Surinam 3–6–8/ To 500 Prints from it at 6/8 pr Hudd 1–13–4." Although this entry is specific, no such print has been discovered. Revere worked often for Captain Caleb Hopkins from 1763 to 1767 and entered charges for shoe buckles, gold buttons, and spectacles. Caleb Hopkins was a leading patriot, a Son of Liberty in 1769, and had his name inscribed on the famous Liberty Bowl of 1768. In a Loyalist list of Boston "rebels" of 1775 he is described as "Caleb Hopkins. Mariner, a Northern politician, talks on both sides the question occasionally" (Massachusetts Historical Society *Proceedings*, Series 2, Volume 12, page 141). The Lodge at Surinam was listed as one of the Lodges in the jurisdiction of Saint John's Grand Lodge from 1761 to 1767, although at no time was it represented at the meetings. The *Freemason's Calendar* for 1776 lists the following Dutch Lodges in Surinam—La Vertieuse 1769, La Fidèle Sincérité 1771, Concordia 1762, La Zelée 1767, and La Croissant des Trois Clefs 1768 (article by C. M. Stow in *Transactions* of American Lodge of Research for 1947–49, Volume 5, page 18). Surinam, or Dutch Guiana, had considerable trade with New England, exporting sugar and cocoa to the colonies. One of the most interesting of eighteenth-century colonial paintings, presumably by John Greenwood in the late 1750's, was a scene in Surinam, showing a score of New England masters of ships, mostly from Rhode Island, carousing in a tavern. This large painting, long owned by the Cushing family in North Providence, is now in the St. Louis Art Museum. It is reproduced in Edward Field's *Esek Hopkins*, 1898, page 28, and in M. B. Davidson's *Life in America*, 1951, Volume 1, page 116. The Surinam Masonic notification, engraved by Revere, will some day be discovered, but unfortunately not in time for the present volume.

A summons for the meeting of Lodge No. 169 Antient York Masons of Boston was engraved and signed by Revere. This was probably done in the late 1760's, but no charge for it appears in his Day Books. Lodge No. 169 was chartered prior to 1772 by the Atholl Grand Lodge of England. It had but a brief existence.

In his Day Book, under date of September 15, 1772, Revere enters the following charge: "Mr. Simon Greenleaf Newbury-port Dr/ To Engraving a plate

These do Certify that
the Bearrer hereof William Peirce
Has been regularly initiated into the first degree of
Masonry As such He has been received by Us.
And being a true & faithfull **BROTHER** is hereby Recommended
to the Favour of all Free and Accepted Masons
wheresoever dispersed.
Given under our Hands and Seal at Boston
New England in St. Andrews Lodge Jany 14th AD 1779 &
of Masonry 5779.

Paul Revere M
Wm. Hoskins SW
Jona. W. Edes JW
Jas. Carter Sec.

William Peirce Jr.

I have caus'd said brother to affix his Name
in the Margin — J. C. Secy

Engraved Printed & sold by Paul Revere BOSTON

PLATE 61. LARGE GENERAL CERTIFICATE, ENGRAVED ABOUT 1773.

for Notifications 2–8–0/ To 300 Prints 0–18–0." Greenleaf was a charter member of Saint Peter's Lodge of Newburyport, March 23, 1772, and served the Lodge as Treasurer and Secretary. He was born in 1752 and died in 1776. The American Antiquarian Society has a fine, clear copy of this notification made out to Enoch Pike, by order of Mr. Greenough, Master, and signed by Mr. Nichols as Secretary, dated Nov. 4, 1777. It is set in a Chippendale frame, 7 inches high by 5¾ inches wide to the edges of the printing, and is signed "Paul Revere Scp." It has the water-mark of the figure of Britannia, surmounted by a crown, and underneath the initials of "I.B," James Boies, who operated the paper-mill in Milton. This copy is reproduced, Plate no. 59. Essex Institute has the same engraving made out to J. Lock, February 24, 1797, by order of Jona. Gage, Master, and signed by A. Perkins as Secretary. The Pennsylvania Grand Lodge Library in Philadelphia has the same made out to N. Long, by order of Jona. Gage, Master, and signed by A. Perkins as Secretary, June 24, 1797. The American Antiquarian Society has a second copy made out to P. Brown, by order of Jona. Gage, Master, and signed by A. Perkins as Secretary, October 28, 1798. In these later copies the plate was much worn. The Saint Peter's Lodge notification, so far as the mantled border was concerned, was almost identical with the Joseph Webb trade card. See reproduction in chapter concerning Trade Cards.

Revere, under date of June 15, 1773, entered the following charge: "The Tyrian Lodge Dr/ To Engraving a Plate for summons 3–0–0/ To 400 Impressions 1–4–0/ To P Cross Keys 0–18–0/ To two Stewards Jewils 0–18–0." Summons in this charge was the equivalent of notifications, used to notify members of a meeting, although the word summons was generally used for a meeting held for some special purpose. The print is 6¼ inches high by 5¼ wide, to the extreme borders of the printing. The notice is set in an elaborate Chippendale border, and is signed "P Revere," or possibly it is "Revere" with only an ornament instead of a first initial. The earliest example of the Tyrian Lodge notification is dated May 18, 1795, with Nathaniel Warner in the Chair and signed by John G. Rogers as Secretary. It is reproduced in E. H. Goss's *Life of Paul Revere*, 1891, Volume 2, page 481, at that time owned by George W. White of Melrose, but now unlocated. Tyrian Lodge has a reproduction of a copy dated March 4, 1811, with John

Tucker in the Chair, signed by John Rogers as Secretary, this copy formerly owned by Edgar S. Taft of Gloucester. The American Antiquarian Society owns an original print dated April 2, 1811, with John Tucker in the Chair, signed by John Rogers as Secretary. This copy is reproduced, Plate no. 60. Essex Institute has an example dated September 2, 1811, addressed to Jacob Smith, and signed by John Tucker as Master and John Rogers as Secretary. The 1811 copies show the plate somewhat worn. The Massachusetts Historical Society has copies dated October 6, 1806, October 8, 1811, and June 22, 1822.

About 1773, or earlier, Revere engraved a large copper-plate as a certificate, or diploma, with blank spaces for the name of the recipient, the nature of his degree, the date, the name of the Lodge and the signatures of the officers granting the degree. The print measures 12¼ inches high by 9⅝ wide, to the extreme borders of the print. It is signed "Engraved Printed & sold by Paul Revere. Boston." The print shows tall columns at the left and right, surmounted by statues, an angel blowing a trumpet above, a mother with three infants in lower left corner, and a large tablet for names of officers in lower right center. Evidently Revere carried this print in stock and sold it over the counter to Masonic buyers. One of the earliest dated copies is owned by the Grand Lodge Library in Boston, dated December 21, 1774, and made out for Joseph Coffin, of Union Lodge in Nantucket, who was granted his third degree. A slightly earlier copy on parchment is owned by the Grand Lodge, dated February 3, 1774, and made out for Shubal Downes of Saint Andrew's Lodge in Boston. The Lodge also has a photograph of a certificate, dated in 1778, made out for Jacob Oliver of Saint Andrew's Lodge. The American Antiquarian Society has another example, dated January 4, 1779, made out for William Peirce of Saint Andrew's Lodge. This copy is herewith reproduced, Plate no. 61. All of these certificates were impressions from what might be called the first state of the plate. Apparently Revere used this same copper in 1796, engraving a few additional symbols, and sold the plate to Elias Perkins of New London. (See description of plate below, under 1796.)

Under date of April 27, 1782, Revere entered in his Day Book the following charge: "Doc John Blanchard Dr/ To engraving a Copper plate for/ Certificates 4–10–0/ To printing 2 hr impressions 0–16–0." Captain John Blanchard was a member of Washington Lodge Number 10, an Army Lodge chartered by the

And the DARKNESS comprehended it not.
In the EAST a place of LIGHT where reigns SILENCE & PEACE.

We the Master, Wardens, and Secretary, of
LODGE held in the TOWN of
Boston and State of Massachusetts
Do Certify that the BEARER hereof our worthy
BROTHER Saml Welch Has been regularly
initiated in to the Second degree of Masonry.
As such He has been receiv'd by Us: And being a true &
faithfull BROTHER is hereby recommended to the Favour
and Protection of ALL Free and Accepted MASONS
wheresoever dispersed. In witness whereof we have
caus'd the Seal of our said Lodge to be hereunto affix'd.
this 25 day of Salvation 1790
and of Masonry 5790

Paul Revere M
Robert Rogers S.W
J.W
Sec.y

Printed & sold opposite Liberty Stump BOSTON

Plate 62. Small General Certificate, Engraved about 1780.

PLATE 63. ST. ANDREW'S LODGE NOTIFICATION, ENGRAVED IN 1784.

Massachusetts Grand Lodge October 6, 1779, and active during the American Revolution. John Blanchard served as a surgeon's mate in the Hospital Department in 1776. Captain John Blanchard was listed among the officers retiring from the Fourth Massachusetts Regiment, December 29, 1783 (Pickering Papers in Massachusetts Historical Society). If this was a certificate engraved especially for Washington Lodge, no copy of it has been located.

In the small book of charge accounts kept by Paul Revere and owned by the Massachusetts Grand Lodge, under date of March, 1784, Revere enters the following charge against Saint Andrew's Lodge: "To Engraving Copper plate for summons 4–10–0/ To printing 400 Impressions @ 8s 1–12–0." In the records of Saint Andrew's Lodge, December 12, 1783, is found the following vote: "Voted . . . that the Secy' supply the Lodge with blank summonses as many as he shall think necessary for the two following years." The American Antiquarian Society has an original of this print, not filled in, measuring 7¼ inches high by 5⅞ wide, to the edges of the printing. It is a graceful design, almost identical with his engraving of the notification for Saint Peter's Lodge in 1772. It is signed "Engrav'd, Printed, & Sold, by Paul Revere, Boston," and is here reproduced, Plate no. 63.

Revere frequently entered charges in his Day Book for the sale of blank Masonic certificates. Under date of June 26, 1784, he made the following charge: "Mr. James Avery Dr/ To 5 Masons Jewels for Warren Lodge 9–0–0/ To printing 5 Certificates @ 1s 0–5–0." These were presumably blank certificates to be filled in for the recipient. James Avery was a member of Machias Lodge, later Warren Lodge, in 1778.

Another charge for the sale of blank certificates entered by Revere in his Day Book was dated June 1, 1792, as follows: "Mr. Eveleth Dr/ To printing 12 paper & 12 parchment Certificates 1–2–0." These were for James Eveleth, who obtained the charter for Lincoln Lodge of Wiscasset, Maine, June 1, 1792, and was its first Master.

Again, on May 18, 1796, was entered this charge: "Mr David How Dr/ To 12 Certificates 0–12–0." David Howe was Master of Hancock Lodge in Penobscot, Maine (later Castine) in 1796. The small certificates which Revere kept in stock and sold to James Avery were undoubtedly often used. At least four of them, identical in design, have been preserved. Essex Institute has an example, filled in for Hale Hilton, of Amity Lodge of Beverly, dated May 30, 1780; the Massachusetts Grand Lodge Library in Boston has one, on parchment, filled in for Joseph Walles, Jr., of Warren Lodge of Machias, June 25, 1785; the American Antiquarian Society has another, also on parchment, filled in for Samuel Welch of Rising States Lodge of Boston, July 25, 1790; a fourth copy is owned by Lincoln Lodge of Wiscasset, Maine, made out on parchment for John Haupt, September 21, 1792. All have the engraved imprint "Printed & Sold opposite Liberty Stump, Boston." They measure 7 inches high by 6 inches wide, to the border lines which enclose the print, although the wrinkling of parchment in some of the copies seen causes variation in the measurements. The American Antiquarian Society copy, which is signed by Paul Revere as Master, is the one which is reproduced, Plate no. 62.

"Liberty Stump" for many years was a familiar site at the corner of Essex and Washington (then Newbury) Streets in Boston, marking the location of the famous Liberty Tree which the British had cut down late in August, 1775. Although unsigned by Revere, the "Liberty Stump" engraving was unquestionably by him. It is characteristically his work, and is almost identical, although smaller, with the large certificate which he engraved and signed in about 1773, previously described. This smaller engraving, judging from the use of the location of the "Liberty Stump," must have been engraved certainly before 1780, since one copy of the certificate is signed in that year. Revere owned the land at the corner of Newbury (Washington) and Boylston Streets, opposite "Liberty Stump," from early in the Revolution. He sold part of the land to David Moseley, silversmith, in 1784, and again in 1797. Moseley in the early Boston Directories was located on Frog Lane, later Boylston Street. Paul Revere's brother, Thomas Revere, is listed in the first Boston Directory of 1789 as "silversmith" on Newbury Street. Revere's Day Book shows that he resumed engraving and the sale of merchandise in December, 1778. He removed from the "Liberty Stump" shop in 1786, as is shown by an advertisement in the *Independent Chronicle* of January 26, 1786, as follows: "Paul Revere, would respectfully inform his customers, and the public,

And the DARKNESS comprehended it not.
In the EAST a place of LIGHT where reign SILENCE & PEACE.

We the Master, Wardens, and Secretary, of St. Peters LODGE held in the TOWN of Newburyport, and State of Massachusetts Do Certify that the BEARER hereof our worthy BROTHER [illegible] Has been regularly initiated in to the Third degree of Masonry. As such He has been receiv'd by Us: And being a true & faithfull BROTHER is hereby recommended to the Favour and Protection of ALL Free and Accepted MASONS wheresoever dispersed. In witness whereof we have caus'd the Seal of our said Lodge to be hereunto affix'd, this 7th day of [illegible] Salvation 179[illegible] and of Masonry 579[illegible]

Jon^a Gage M.
[illegible] S.W.
Benj Tucker J.W.
Geo. [illegible] Sec-y

We have caused the Bearer to affix his Firm in the opposite Margin.

PLATE 64. SMALL GENERAL CERTIFICATE, ENGRAVED ABOUT 1790.

Gift - Mark Bortman, Oct. 31, 1960

IN ANGUSTIIS AMICI

Sir,

BOSTON March 4. 1782

The RELIEF-SOCIETY of which you are a Member, meets on Thurs-day Evening next, at the Green Dragon precisely at 7 O.Clock at which Time & Place you are desir'd to give your punctual Attendance.

Eben Oliver Clerk.

To Mr Andrew Brimmer

P. Revere sculp

Plate 64a. Relief Fire Society Notification, Engraved Circa 1782.

that he has removed from the south part of the town, opposite Liberty-Pole, to Dock-Square, in the store adjoining Mr. Joseph Bush, near the Market."

Revere used the same copper, described in the preceding paragraph, for his small stock certificate. But he erased the imprint of "Printed & sold opposite Liberty Stump, Boston," and left the lower margin clear. This new version of the same copper he must have produced soon after 1790. The example owned by the American Antiquarian Society is dated September 7, 1794, and is filled in for Theophilus Bradbury, Jr., who received his third degree from Saint Peter's Lodge of Newburyport. The certificate, or diploma, is on parchment, reproduced, Plate no. 64. It measures 7⅛ inches high by 5¾ wide. It bears a ribbon and a seal, which is omitted in the reproduction since it covers a portion of the print. The Library of the Supreme Council in Washington has a parchment certificate made out for John Howland of Rising States Lodge, December 6, 1794, signed on the tablet by Paul Revere as Junior Warden, with other officers. This also omits the engraver's line on the lower right margin. The Massachusetts Grand Lodge Library has a photostat of another copy of this certificate, made out for Nathan G. Doak of Rising States Lodge, March 8, 1796.

In 1796 Revere took the large copper-plate which he had cut for certificates, or diplomas, about 1773 (described above), engraved a few additional symbols, and sold it to Elias Perkins of New London. The additions consisted of the inscrtion of a line at the top, under the figure of the angel with the trumpet, reading "And the Darkness comprehended it not; In the East a place of light," the insertion of a circular moon at the upper left and a sun at the upper right, and seven stars at the extreme upper left between the clouds. Otherwise the two plates seem to be identical. They are both signed "Engraved Printed & sold by Paul Revere. Boston." The original bill, formerly owned by Ernest L. Gay, and now in the Harvard College Library, reads: "Elias Perkins Bot of Paul Revere Boston Jany 4, 1796/ One Engravd Copper-plate for Mason Certificates 6–0–0/ Receivd pay Paul Revere." Elias Perkins was Junior Warden and later Master of Union Lodge of New London in 1796 (see E. G. Storer's *Records of Freemasonry in Connecticut*, 1859, pages 73, 76, 404).

There are at least three original impressions from this plate. The American

Antiquarian Society has an example for Daniel Huntington receiving his Master degree, not dated, signed by Joseph Huntington, Master, Jabez R. Packard, Senior Warden, and Benjamin Collier, Secretary. (Plate no. 65.) It is 12¼ by 9⅝ inches. Daniel Huntington belonged to Somerset Lodge, Norwich, Connecticut, and the date of the certificate was probably 1799. The Iowa Masonic Library, Cedar Rapids, has a copy for Walter Burdick of Union Lodge, December 19, 1799. Forest H. Sweet, Battle Creek, Michigan, has a copy for Benjamin Stark of Union Lodge, December 17, 1812.

The original copper-plate still exists; on the obverse Revere had engraved his famous "Obelisk print," later using the reverse for the Masonic diploma. The plate was owned successively by Thomas S. Collier, R. B. Jacobs, A. S. W. Rosenbach, and Lessing J. Rosenwald. When Jacobs owned it in 1921, he had a few restrikes made of the Masonic diploma, of which the American Antiquarian Society has a copy. The Society also has the restrike made by Rosenwald in 1943, before he gave the copper to the National Gallery in Washington.

Paul Revere ceased making Masonic copper-plates in the late 1790's. Others were making Masonic engravings then — Samuel Hill in Boston, Amos Doolittle in Connecticut, Andrew Billings and William Rollinson in New York, and Joseph Bowes in Philadelphia. A monograph on early Masonic engravings would supply a neglected phase of Masonic history and would provide material for the study of American engraving.

RELIEF FIRE SOCIETY

A hitherto unlocated Revere print, discovered in 1957, is the notice for meetings of the Boston Relief Society, dated March 4, 1782, and signed "P. Revere sculp." It was given to the American Antiquarian Society by the late Mark Bortman. The Relief Fire Society was founded in 1773. The Boston Public Library has the minutes of the Society from 1773 to 1807. From these it appears that Revere cut a plate for membership tickets, a plate for the head of the printed articles of the Society, and a plate for notices — all after June 2, 1773. The Public Library also has *Rules and Orders for the Relief Society*, with a list of members in manuscript, and a cut, presumably by Revere, in type metal, of an ornamental design at the head of the broadside.

And the DARKNESS comprehended it not; In the EAST a place of light

These do Certify that

the Bearer hereof Daniel Huntington

Has been regularly initiated into the Master degree of

Masonry. As such He has been received by Us.

And being a true & faithfull BROTHER is hereby Recommended

to the Favour of all Free and Accepted Masons

wheresoever dispersed. Throughout the Globe

Given under our Hands and Seal

in Lodge

Joseph Huntington M

Jabez R. Packard SW

JW

Benj. Collins Sec.

Engraved Printed & sold by Paul Revere. BOSTON.

PLATE 65. LARGE GENERAL CERTIFICATE, ENGRAVED IN 1796.

Revere's Metal Cuts, 1762-1781

THESE cuts were all made in lead except for one of 1781 made in brass. Although frequently termed woodcuts, the cuts for eighteenth-century newspapers, almanacs, pamphlets, and broadsides were almost invariably engraved on type-metal, which was an alloy of lead, antimony, and tin. Revere undoubtedly made his own metal cuts by combining the proper proportions of lead, antimony, and other compounds, so that the result would take cutting and not be too brittle. In the earliest sketch of Revere in the *New England Magazine* for October, 1832, page 307, the anonymous author stated that Dr. Benjamin Waterhouse "found Mr. Revere the only man, in 1794, who appeared to know any thing of the discrimination between the ores of the seven metals."

None of Revere's "leaden," or metal, cuts were signed except for the 1770 "Prospective View of the Town of Boston." The only way of identifying them is through the charges entered in Revere's Day Books, the originals of which are in the Massachusetts Historical Society. There are twenty-two cuts representing seventeen charges, which can be thus reasonably identified, and they all bear the characteristic marks of Revere's style. Six of the cuts mentioned in the charges defy identification. The twenty-two which can be ascribed to Revere are herewith reproduced from the originals in the American Antiquarian Society. Revere undoubtedly made other metal cuts, which for one reason or another were not entered in his charge accounts, but it would be unwise to include them, even if they seemed to be possibly cut by Revere.

1765. Cut of Eclipse of Sun in Nathaniel Ames's *Astronomical Diary; or, Almanack for 1766*, Boston: W. M'Alpine and J. Fleeming [1765]. The cut is on the first page in signature C, size 1½ by 3 inches. (See Plate no. 66.) In Revere's Day Book, under date of September 28, 1765, is the following charge: "Messr McAlpine & Fleming Dr/ to Cutting 12 half figures at 2d/ 0–2–0/ to Cutting a Leding Plate for the Eclipse of the Sun/ 1–0–0." What the twelve half figures are is not known. In the second edition of the Ames Almanac for 1766, there is a cut of the eclipse, but it differs from the cut supposedly made by Revere.

The pirated edition of the Ames Almanac for 1766 does not include the special cut of the eclipse.

1770. Masthead of *Boston Gazette* first used January 1, 1770, showing a seated figure at right, with liberty cap, bird cage in center, and view of a town at left (see Plate no. 67). The size is 2¼ by 8½ inches. In Revere's Day Book, under date of January 10, 1770, is the following charge: "Messrs Edes & Gill Dr/ To Engraving a Leading plate for newspaper/ 0–12–0." Isaiah Thomas describes the symbolism of the cut in his *History of Printing*, 1874 edition, Volume 2, page 55.

1770. Prospective View of the Town of Boston in *Edes & Gill's North-American Almanack for 1770*, Boston, Edes & Gill; and T. & J. Fleet. The plate is signed "P. Revere" and is 3⅜ by 6 inches (see Plate no. 68). In Revere's Day Book, under date of January 10, 1770, is the following charge: "Messrs Edes & Gill Dr/ To Engraving plate for Almanack/ 2–8–0/." This cut was reproduced in S. G. Drake's *History of Boston*, 1856, page 747; in S. G. Drake's *Old Landmarks of Boston*, 1873, page 119; and in Winsor's *Narrative and Critical History*, 1888, Volume 6, page 81. The imprint of the Almanac states that it was printed on paper made in America.

1770. Cut of five coffins for Boston Massacre. In Revere's Day Book, under date of [April] 9, 1770, is the following charge: "Messrs Edes & Gill Dr/ To Engraving 5 coffings for Massacre/ 0–6–0/." In the *Boston Gazette* of March 12, 1770, is a long account of the Massacre, illustrated by a cut of four coffins, marked with the initials of the four men who were killed, and in the issue of March 19 is an additional cut with the initials of another victim who died after March 12. (See Plate no. 69.) A broadside of two pages, entitled *An Account of a late Military Massacre at Boston, or the Consequences of Quartering Troops in a populous Town* (original in Boston Public Library and photostat in American Antiquarian Society) reprints the identical text of the *Boston Gazette* of March 12, 1770, but the four cuts of the coffins are slightly different in design. There is a large broadside entitled *A particular Account of the most barbarous and Horrid Massacre! Committed in King-Street, Boston, on Monday, March 5, 1770, by the Soldiery quartered in Said Town* (originals in American Antiquarian Society and John Carter Brown Library). There are cuts of five coffins at the top, but the coffins are

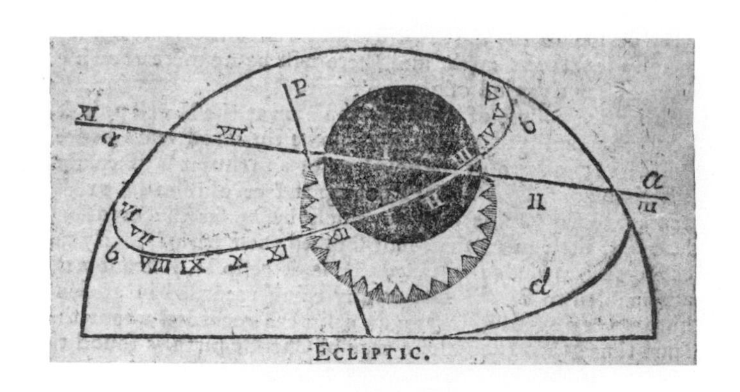

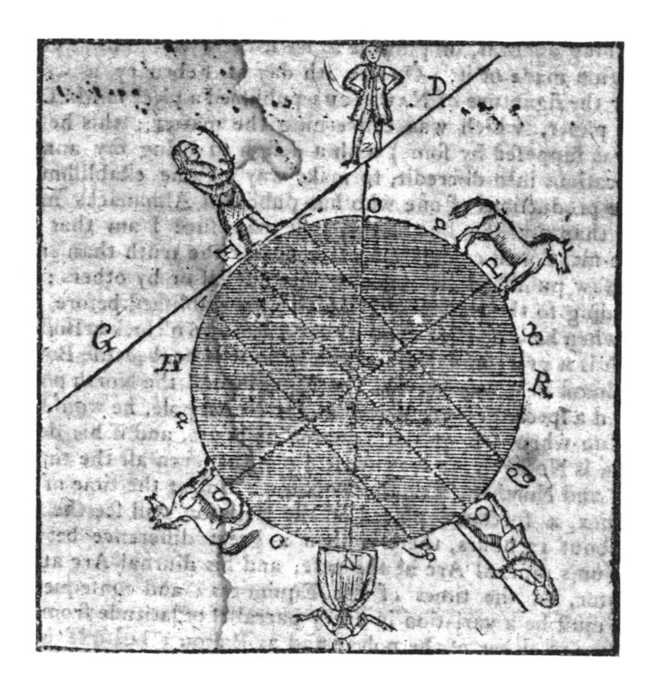

PLATE 66. CUT OF ECLIPSE, 1765. CUT OF COMPASS, 1771.
CUT OF GLOBE, 1773.

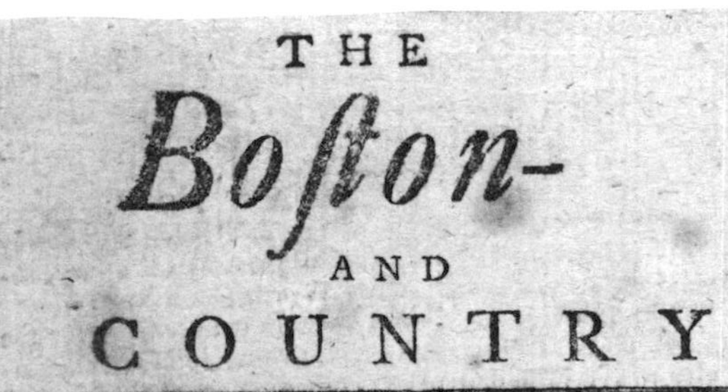

THE
Boston-
AND
COUNTRY

Gazette,
JOURNAL.

No. 769.

Containing the freshest Advices, Foreign and Domestic.

MONDAY, January 1, 1770.

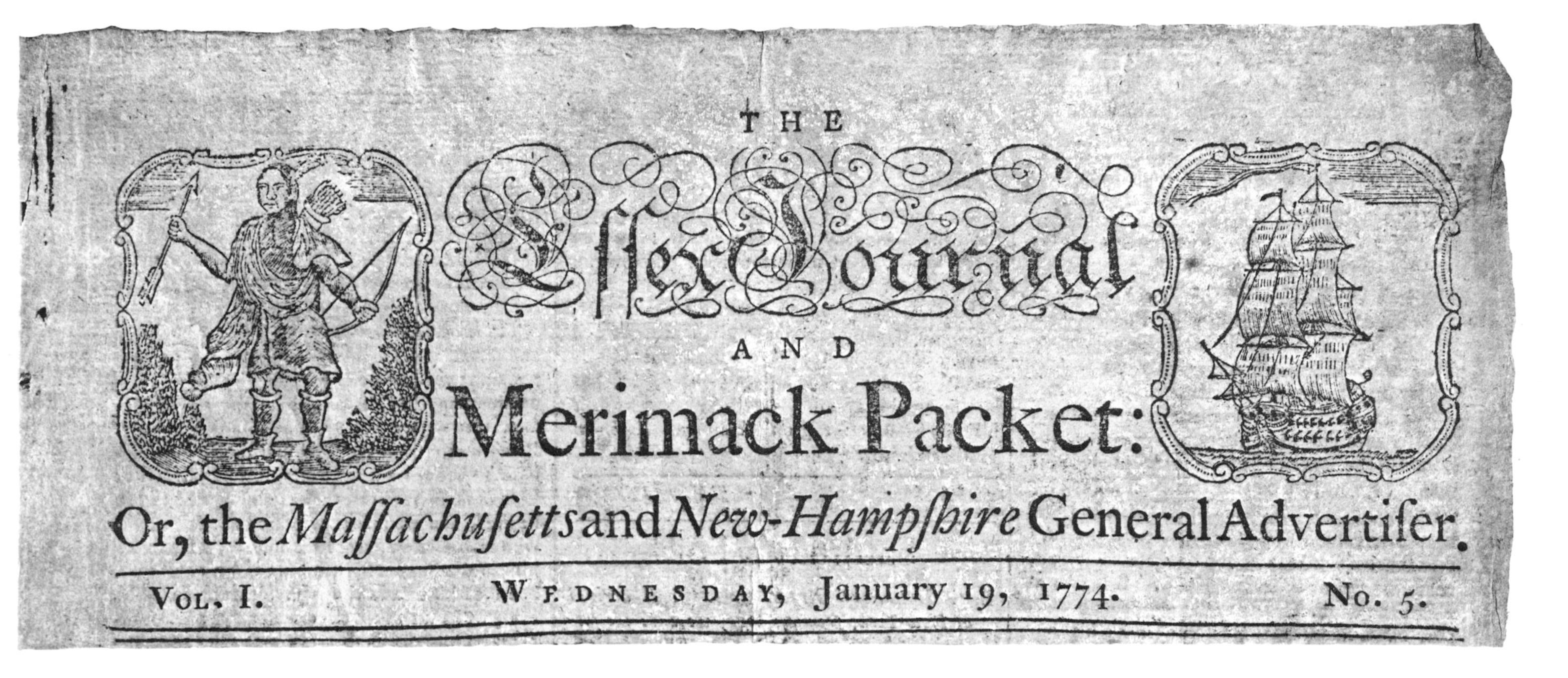

THE
Essex Journal
AND
Merimack Packet:
Or, the *Massachusetts* and *New-Hampshire* General Advertiser.

VOL. I. WEDNESDAY, January 19, 1774. No. 5.

PLATE 67. MASTHEAD BOSTON GAZETTE, 1770. MASTHEAD ESSEX JOURNAL, 1774.

much larger than those in Edes's *Boston Gazette*. There is also a smaller broadside entitled *A Poem, In Memory of the* (*never to be forgotten*) *Fifth of March, 1770,* with narrow cuts of five coffins at the top. An original is in the Massachusetts Historical Society, with photostat in the American Antiquarian Society. But the only cuts of the coffins positively printed by Edes are in the *Boston Gazette*.

1771. Masthead of Isaiah Thomas's *Massachusetts Spy* of March 14, 1771. In Revere's Day Book, under date of March 12, 1771, is the following charge: "Mr Isaiah Thomas Dr/ To engraving a plate for Newspapers/ 2–8–0." It was an elaborate scroll title, with figures at either side. It was first used in the issue of March 14, 1771, and was continued until Thomas removed to Worcester in April, 1775, with an additional design of the well known snake device, with a dragon added, under the title engraved by Revere, for the issue of July 7, 1774. It was ten inches wide. (See Plate no. 70.) Thomas used part of the cut, omitting the figure at the right, in his paper published at Worcester through May 17, 1781.

1771. Cut of compass in Stearns's *North-American's Almanack, for 1772.* In Revere's Day Book, under date of September 20, 1771, is the following charge: "Messr Edes & Gill Dr/ To Engraving a Compass for Almanack/ 0–18–0." Edes & Gill, in company with R. Draper and T. & J. Fleet, published *The North-American's Almanack for 1772* in the fall of 1771, and on the title-page is an elaborately drawn compass in Revere's characteristic style of lettering. (See Plate no. 66.) The size was 2 5/16 by 2 5/16 inches. Edes & Gill advertised the publication of the almanac in the *Boston Gazette* of September 23, 1771.

1771. Cuts in Ames Almanac for 1772, printed for and sold by Ezekiel Russell. In Revere's Day Book, under date of December 16, 1771, is the following charge: "Mr Ezekiel Russel Dr/ To Engravin two plates for Ames's Almanack/ 2–0–0." Yet there are three cuts in the Ames *Astronomical Diary; or Almanack for 1772,* printed for Ezekiel Russell — one of a dwarf on the title-page, one of John Dickinson on the fourth page, and a third of Mrs. Catharine M'Caulay on the seventh page. The sizes of the three items were 3 5/8 by 2 3/4, 3 5/8 by 2 3/4, and 3 5/8 by 2 3/4 inches. If Revere's charge is correct, which were the two cuts made by him? The cuts of Dickinson and Mrs. M'Caulay seem to be in Revere's style. All three are reproduced, and the reader can take his choice. The Dickinson portrait was apparently copied from a frontispiece in Dickinson's *Letters of a Farmer*, Philadelphia, 1769. (See Plate no. 71.)

An additional complication is caused by another charge in Revere's Day Book, under date of December 21, 1771, as follows: "Messrs Edes & Gill Dr/ To Engraving 3 plates for Ames Almanack/ 2–14–0." But there is no Ames Almanac for 1772 with an Edes & Gill imprint. There is an almanac with only this imprint: "Price 2s. 8d [per?] Dozen, and Six Coppers single." This may well have been the Edes & Gill edition. The three cuts are the same subjects as those in the E. Russell edition of Ames, but they are different in the cutting. Did Revere re-cut them for Edes & Gill from the Russell originals? The three varying cuts are not reproduced herewith. Any reader can consult the original almanacs in the American Antiquarian Society and other libraries.

1771. Cut of Boston Massacre in Isaiah Thomas's *Massachusetts Calendar, or an Almanac for 1772*. The cut was on the reverse of the first leaf, and measured 4¾ inches high by 3⅞ wide, to the border lines. It was not signed but was unquestionably Revere's work. Revere did not charge Thomas for the cut in his Day Book, although there was a charge, under date of December 21, 1771, as follows: "Mr. Isaiah Thomas Dr/ To Engraving Copper Rules/ 0–10–0." The same woodcut was again used on a large broadside entitled *A Monumental Inscription on the Fifth of March*, printed in 1772. These cuts are discussed in more detail in the chapter on the Boston Massacre, where both are reproduced.

1772. Cuts in *North-American's Calendar for 1773*, by Samuel Stearns, printed by Edes & Gill. In Revere's Day Book, under date of September 15, 1772, is the following charge: "Messr Edes & Gill Dr/ To Engraving 3 plates for Almanack/ 1–16–0." The three plates in the above almanac are "A Projection of the Twelve Signs of the Zodiack" on the title-page, a cut of the Anatomy of Man's Body on the second page, and a cut of the Eclipses on the third page — all reproduced. (See Plate no. 72.)

1773. Two cuts in *A Vision of Hell*, Boston: John Boyle, 1773. In Revere's Day Book, under date of August 7, 1773, is this charge: "Mr John Boyles Dr/ To Engraving two leading plates/ 0–12–0." The two plates are found in *A Vision of Hell*, by Theodorus Van Shemain [Jacob Green], Boston: Printed and Sold at

Plate 68. View of Boston, 1770. Cut of Skeleton, 1773.
Cut of Devils, 1773.

The Maſſachuſetts CALENDAR;
OR AN
ALMANACK
FOR THE
Year of our Lord Chriſt 1774;
Being the ſecond after Biſſextile or Leap Year;
By EZRA GLEASON

The wicked Stateſman, or the Traitor to his Country, at the Hour of DEAT[illegible]

B[illegible]: Printed by ISAIAH THOMAS: S[illegible]d at his P[illegible]ntin[illegible]
Office near the Market, and at his ſhop [illegible]ear the Mill B[illegible]id[illegible]
[illegible]

THE
Royal *American* Magazine,

OR UNIVERSAL
Repoſitory of *Inſtruction* and *Amuſement*.

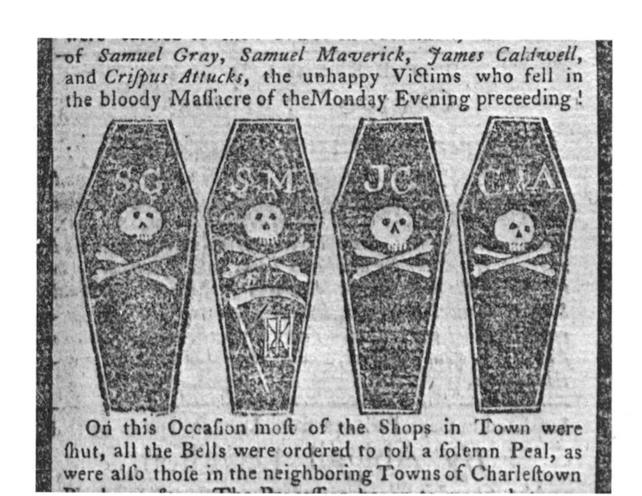

of *Samuel Gray*, *Samuel Maverick*, *James Caldwell*, and *Criſpus Attucks*, the unhappy Victims who fell in the bloody Maſſacre of the Monday Evening preceeding!

On this Occaſion moſt of the Shops in Town were ſhut, all the Bells were ordered to toll a ſolemn Peal, as were alſo thoſe in the neighboring Towns of Charleſtown

PLATE 69. CUT OF WICKED STATESMAN, 1773. TITLE-PAGE VIGNETTE, 1774.
CUT OF FOUR COFFINS, 1770.

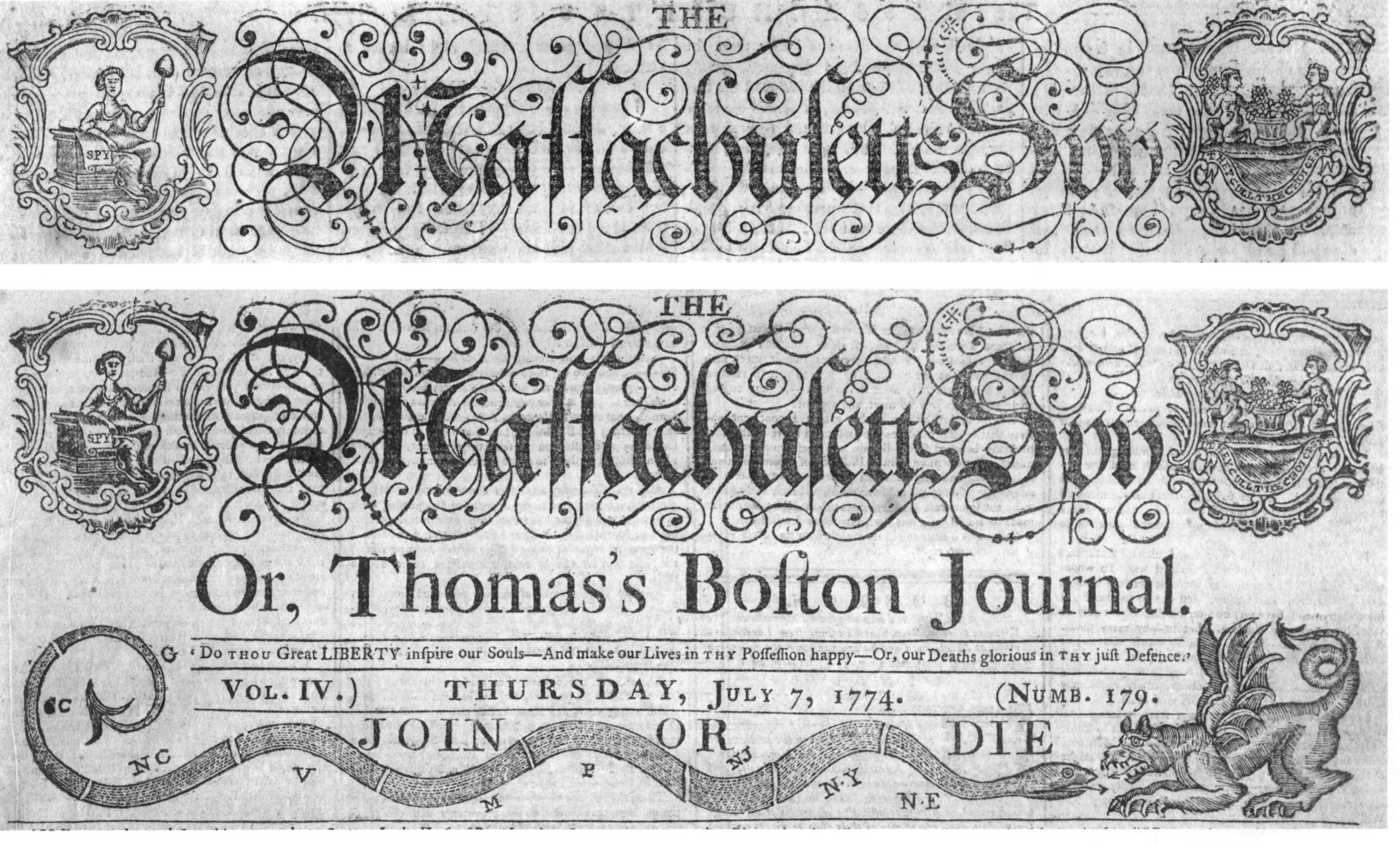
THE
Massachusetts Spy
SPY
THEY CULL THE CHOICEST
THE
Massachusetts Spy
Or, Thomas's Boston Journal.
'Do THOU Great LIBERTY inspire our Souls—And make our Lives in THY Possession happy—Or, our Deaths glorious in THY just Defence.'
VOL. IV.) THURSDAY, JULY 7, 1774. (NUMB. 179.
JOIN OR DIE
G
SC
NC
V
M
P
NJ
N·Y
N·E

THOMAS'S
Massachusetts Spy
LIBERTY DEFENDED FROM TYRANNY
UNION

THE PATRIOTIC AMERICAN FARMER.

Mrs. CATHARINE M'CAUL AY.

PLATE 71. CUT OF DWARF, 1771.
CUT OF JOHN DICKINSON, 1771. CUT OF MRS. M'CAULAY, 1771.

John Boyle's Printing-Office, 1773, an octavo pamphlet of twenty pages. The first is a view of four devils, one with a pitchfork, grouped at right, and the monstrous open jaws of a fish-like animal, with flames pouring out from its mouth — this on the title-page. This latter design is almost the same as Revere's drawing for his plate "A Warm Place – Hell," issued in 1768. The second cut is of a man conversing with a skeleton. Both cuts are reproduced. The latter cut was also used by Boyle on the title-page of a sixteen-page pamphlet entitled *A Dialogue between a Blind-Man and Death*, by Richard Standfast, which he printed in 1773. The two cuts measure 1¾ inches high by 3½ wide, and 3⅜ by 2⅝ inches to the borders of the cut. (See Plate no. 68.)

1773. Cut of Globe in Samuel Stearns's *North-American's Almanack for 1774*. In Revere's Day Book, under date of September 9, 1773, is this charge: "Messr Edes & Gill Dr/ To Engraving a leading Plate for Sterns's Almanack/ 0–18–0." The plate, which is on the title-page and measures 3⅛ by 3 inches (see Plate no. 66), attempts to illustrate the Globe, indicating by letters the North and South Poles, the axis, the equator, the sun's declination, etc. The description of the illustration is given on the second page. The almanac is advertised in the *Boston Gazette* of September 27, 1773, as "now in the Press," and on October 11, 1773, as "To be sold by Edes & Gill."

1773. Cut of "The wicked Statesman, or the Traitor to his Country" in *The Massachusetts Calendar for 1774*, by Ezra Gleason, Boston, Printed by Isaiah Thomas. In Revere's Day Book, under date of October 15, 1773, is this charge: "Mr Isaiah Thomas Dr/ To Engraving a plate for Almanack/ 0–18–0." The plate has the inscription underneath, "The wicked Statesman, or the Traitor to his Country, at the Hour of Death." On the second page is a fifteen-line statement regarding the virtues of patriotism and the wretchedness of disloyalty. The size of the cut is 3¾ by 3 inches. (See Plate no. 69.)

1773. Masthead of *Essex Journal* of December 4, 1773. In Revere's Day Book, under date of December 15, 1773, is this charge: "Mr Isaiah Thomas Dr/ To Engraving head for Essex Gazette/ 1–16–0." Revere confused the *Essex Gazette* with the *Essex Journal*. Samuel Hall was publishing the *Essex Gazette* at Salem in 1773 and it carried a title which it had long used. Isaiah Thomas established the *Essex Journal* at Newburyport on December 4, 1773, and he obtained his masthead design from Revere, showing the figure of an Indian at the left, and a ship at the right. The size of the cut is 2¼ by 8½ inches. (See Plate no. 67.) The issue reproduced is that of January 19, 1774.

1774. Vignette on title-page of *Royal American Magazine*, January, 1774, showing an Indian seated, offering a calumet of peace to a woman portraying the Genius of Knowledge (I. Thomas's *History of Printing*, 1874 edition, Volume 2, page 72). In Revere's Day Book, under date of February 6, 1774, is this charge: "Mr Isaiah Thomas Dr/ To Engraving a Leading Cutt for Magazine/ 0–16–0." The cut was used on the title-page through the issue of December, 1774, and on the front cover for the issues of January to March, 1775. The size of the cut is 2 by 3¼ inches. (See Plate no. 69.)

1774. Masthead of *Massachusetts Spy* of July 7, 1774. In Revere's Day Book, under date of July 6, 1774, is this charge: "Mr Isaiah Thomas Dr/ To Engraving leding plate for News/ 0–12–0." The cut in question was the famous "Join or Die" inscription under the title of the newspaper. The cut was higher at the left and right, leaving room for type lettering in between. Revere had already engraved the scroll-work title for the issue of March 14, 1771. (See Plate no. 70.) Thomas used the "Join or Die" wording until his last issue in Boston, April 6, 1775. The cut was 3⅞ by 10 inches.

1781. Masthead of *Massachusetts Spy* of May 24, 1781. In Revere's Day Book, under date of May 2, 1781, is this charge: "Mr Isaiah Thomas Dr/ To Engraving a head for a Newspaper on Brass/ 9–0–0/ To the Brass & prepareing/ 1–4–0." This cut, which measured 1⅞ by 8⅜ inches, contained the title, with a figure of Liberty at the left, and crossed hands with sword at the right. (See Plate no. 70.) It was the only metal cut made by Revere for newspapers and almanacs after 1774, so far as his Day Book shows, and it was the only one cut on brass. Thomas used the cut until the issue of December 30, 1784.

Unidentified

In Revere's Day Book, under date of March 25, 1762, is this charge: "Messr Fowle & Draper Dr/ To Cutting a Leaden Plate/ 0–12–0." The only illustrated

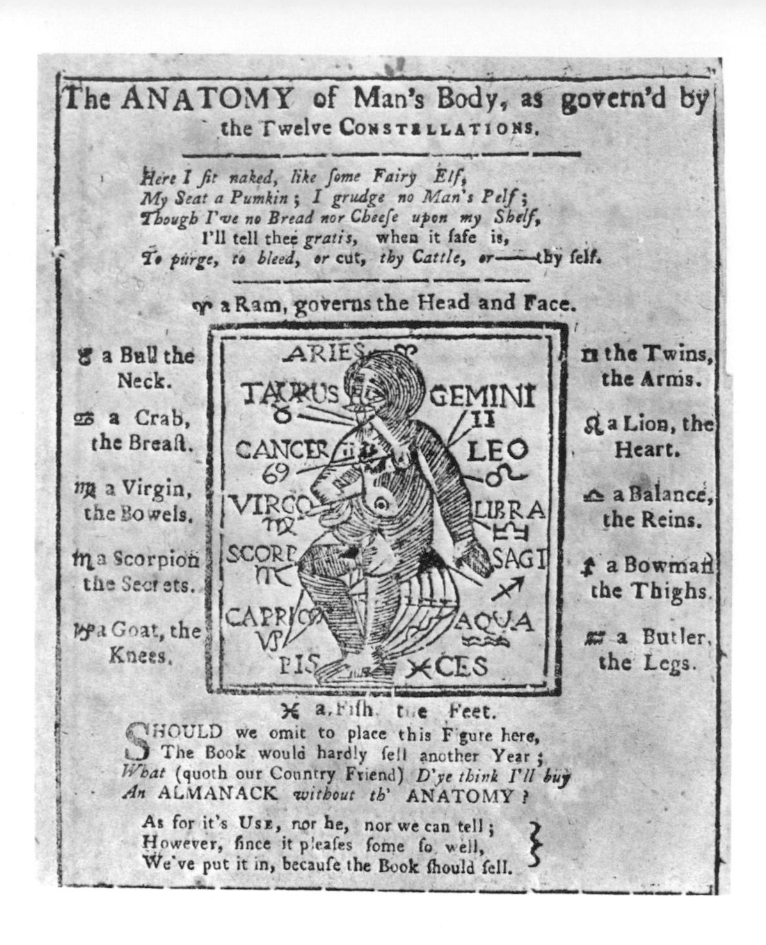
The ANATOMY of Man's Body, as govern'd by the Twelve CONSTELLATIONS.

Here I sit naked, like some Fairy Elf,
My Seat a Pumkin; I grudge no Man's Pelf;
Though I've no Bread nor Cheese upon my Shelf,
I'll tell thee *gratis*, when it safe is,
To purge, to bleed, or cut, thy Cattle, or——thy self.

♈ a Ram, governs the Head and Face.

♉ a Bull the Neck.
♊ the Twins, the Arms.
♋ a Crab, the Breast.
♌ a Lion, the Heart.
♍ a Virgin, the Bowels.
♎ a Balance, the Reins.
♏ a Scorpion the Secrets.
♐ a Bowman the Thighs.
♑ a Goat, the Knees.
♒ a Butler, the Legs.

♓ a Fish the Feet.

SHOULD we omit to place this Figure here,
The Book would hardly sell another Year;
What (quoth our Country Friend) *D'ye think I'll buy*
An ALMANACK *without th'* ANATOMY?

As for it's USE, nor he, nor we can tell;
However, since it pleases some so well,
We've put it in, because the Book should sell.

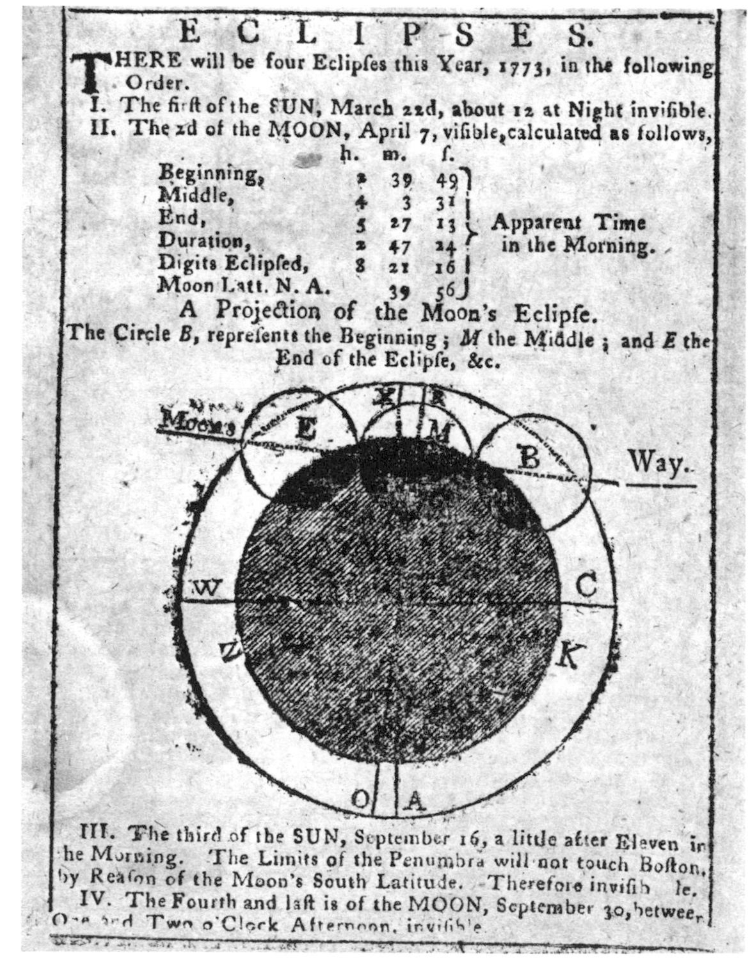
E C L I P S E S.

THERE will be four Eclipses this Year, 1773, in the following Order.

I. The first of the SUN, March 22d, about 12 at Night invisible.
II. The 2d of the MOON, April 7, visible, calculated as follows,

	h.	m.	s.	
Beginning,	2	39	49	Apparent Time in the Morning.
Middle,	4	3	31	
End,	5	27	13	
Duration,	2	47	24	
Digits Eclipsed,	8	21	16	
Moon Latt. N. A.		39	56	

A Projection of the Moon's Eclipse.
The Circle *B*, represents the Beginning; *M* the Middle; and *E* the End of the Eclipse, &c.

III. The third of the SUN, September 16, a little after Eleven in the Morning. The Limits of the Penumbra will not touch Boston, by Reason of the Moon's South Latitude. Therefore invisible.
IV. The Fourth and last is of the MOON, September 30, between One and Two o'Clock Afternoon, invisible.

PLATE 72. CUTS OF ZODIAC, ANATOMY OF MAN'S BODY, AND ECLIPSES, 1772.

pamphlet published by Fowle & Draper in 1762, that I can find, is James Hervey's *Treatise on the Religious Education of Daughters*, which contains a title-page cut showing two young people, kneeling and reading books. It looks like Revere's work, but the plate was used earlier by Fowle & Draper in D. Jones's *Discourse upon the Great Fire of London* in 1760.

1765. In Revere's Day Book, under date of January 20, 1765, is the following charge: "Mr Shubal Hews Dr/ To Engraving a Leding Plate/ 0–16–0." Shubal Hewes was a tallow chandler in Boston in 1765. What the cut was for is not known, possibly for some form of advertisement. Later, during the early days of the Revolution, Shubal Hewes was well known as butcher for the British army quartered in Boston (see Eben Putnam's *Lieut. Joshua Hewes*, 1913, page 331).

1768. In Revere's Day Book, under date of February 1, 1768, is the following charge: "Messrs Eades & Gill Dr/ To engraving 16 leading plates at 5s/ 4–0–0/ To engraving 9 Dito at 5s/ 2–5–0/ To engraving 4 small Dito at 2s/ 0–8–0." These twenty-nine cuts are not identified. Edes & Gill published the *Boston Gazette* in 1768, but none of the issues from January to June have cuts, and none of their books or pamphlets of 1768 examined have cuts. Perhaps the cuts could have been used in some broadside or pamphlet not carrying the Edes & Gill imprint.

1768. In Revere's Day Book, under date of February 1, 1768, is the following charge: "Mess. Mein & Fleming Dr/ To engraving 3 leading plates at 8s/ 1–4–0." The identity of these cuts has not been discovered. Mein & Fleeming early in 1768 were publishing the *Boston Chronicle*, but the only cut in all the issues from January to June, 1768, was a single cut of a coffin in the issue of January 25. They also published *Bickerstaff's Boston Almanack* for 1768, presumably printed in October, 1767, and this included two full-page cuts. But Revere, if he made either of these cuts, would have charged over £2 for a single plate. *Mein & Fleeming's Register* for 1768 contains a crude cut of an eclipse. They used several crude cuts for *Bickerstaff's Boston Almanack* from 1768 to 1773, and these were continued by Mills & Hicks in 1774 and 1775. Both firms were Loyalist and opposed in their publications the revolutionary cause. Revere, as an intense patriot, would presumably not have engraved for either firm during this period. Callender signed one plate in the Almanac for 1774. All of the four Loyalists removed to Great Britain during the early days of the Revolution.

1771. In Revere's Day Book, under date of April 3, 1771, is the following charge: "Messrs Edes & Gill Dr/ To 6 Types for Newspaper at 2s/ 0–12–0." An examination of the *Boston Gazette* for the first six months of 1771 reveals no especially cut type. There is a display article in the issue of March 11, 1771, but it seems to be made up of ordinary printer's type.

1773. In Revere's Day Book, under date of February 11, 1773, is the charge: "Messr Edes & Gill Dr/ To Cutting Plate for Indenture/ 1–10–0." This may well have been a copper-plate. It is not identified.

Paper Money

THE problem of identifying the notes and bills of credit engraved by Revere during the Revolution is difficult. Revere did not enter the charges in his Day Book and in no case are the engravings signed. Only through the various records of the Provincial Congress and of the General Court, and the records of payment made to Revere, can his part in the engraving of the bills be determined. It should always be kept in mind that the large-sized notes were for loans to the Colony filled in for the amounts loaned and redeemable at certain fixed dates, whereas the small-sized bills were printed for stated amounts and were to supply currency for public use.

The first Revere engraving was for the notes authorized by the Provincial Congress on May 3, 1775 (Lincoln, *Journals of Provincial Congress*, page 185), confirmed by the General Court August 23, 1775. The issue was for £100,000, to be dated when borrowed and to be paid with six per cent annual interest on June 1, 1777. The form of the note was given in exact wording. A committee was appointed, consisting of Samuel Dexter, Joseph Warren, and Moses Gill, to procure a copper-plate for the Province notes and to countersign them. It was also resolved that Henry Gardner, the Receiver-General, should not issue any notes for a sum less than four pounds. Moses Gunn replaced Dr. Warren on June 17, 1775, after the latter's death at Bunker Hill, and Stephen Hall replaced Gunn on July 10. Later Lemuel Kollock, Daniel Hopkins, Samuel Phillips, and Edward Rawson countersigned, although no record of their appointment is found.

The entire note is engraved except for the number of the note, the month, date, the name of the lender and the amount lent, and the signatures of the Receiver-General and of the countersigners. At the left border of the plate is an elaborate rectangular design, with a codfish at the top, and the rather crude figure of a patriot holding in his right hand a staff surmounted by a liberty cap. Underneath are the words "American Paper." There are at least three different water-marks in the specimens examined. One of the water-marks is the large design of Britannia, surmounted by a crown, and underneath "J.B.," the initials of James Boies who operated the paper-mill at Milton. The engraving is unquestionably Revere's. The lettering is characteristic, especially the engraving of the abbreviation "No" in brackets, which Revere almost alone used in his bookplates and many other designs. In the American Antiquarian Society collection are ten examples of this note dated in July and August, 1775. The payment for engraving this note was included in the payment of £50 to Revere, July 1, 1775, for engraving four plates, the details of which will be given later. (See Plate no. 73.)

After ordering the £100,000 issue of notes upon which money could be borrowed for the Colony, the Provincial Congress took up the matter of providing advance pay for the soldiers through one-year notes. On May 15, 1775, the Congress appointed a committee to draw up a form for such notes and to employ an engraver to prepare a plate for printing them (Lincoln, *Journals of Provincial Congress*, page 228). It was originally intended to pay the soldiers in two twenty-shilling bills as advance pay. On May 20, 1775, the Congress ordered that Colonel Jedediah Foster, Dr. Samuel Holton, and Major Eleazer Brooks "be a committee to confer with Mr. Revere, respecting his proposal for an alteration in the value of the colony notes, which have been ordered to be struck off" (Lincoln, page 244). On the same day the committee brought in lengthy resolves, which were accepted, providing that soldiers would be paid twenty shillings, lawful money, as advance pay, or if they would accept, they would be paid forty shillings in three notes on 6 per cent interest to be paid one year from the date of the notes. The resolve provided for an issue of £26,000, made up in notes of 20, 18, 16, 15, 14, 12, 10, 9 and 6 shillings, with 4333 of each denomination (Lincoln, page 246, and original resolve in Massachusetts Archives, Volume 157, page 464). The wording of the note, dated May 25, 1775, was given, and followed exactly by the engraver.

The Journal of the Provincial Congress from May 21 to May 31, 1775, was not kept or at least is not preserved, although a few fragmentary records have been gleaned from original documents in the Massachusetts Archives. Therefore some

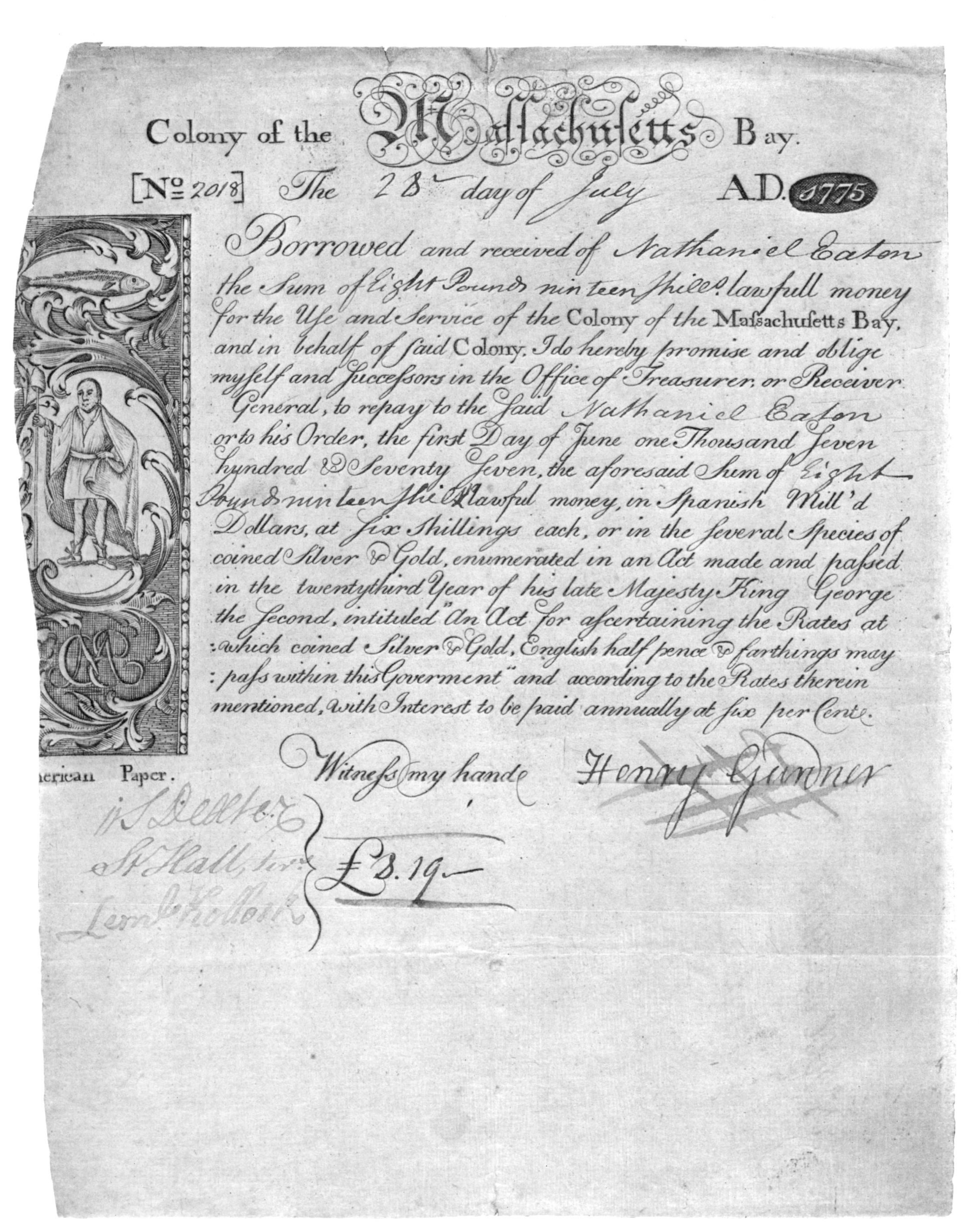

Colony of the Massachusetts Bay.

[No. 2018] The 28 day of July A.D. 1775

Borrowed and received of Nathaniel Eaton the Sum of Eight Pounds ninteen Shills. lawfull money for the Use and Service of the Colony of the Massachusetts Bay, and in behalf of said Colony, I do hereby promise and oblige myself and Successors in the Office of Treasurer, or Receiver General, to repay to the said Nathaniel Eaton or to his Order, the first Day of June one Thousand Seven hundred & Seventy Seven, the aforesaid Sum of Eight Pounds ninteen Shils lawful money, in Spanish Mill'd Dollars, at Six Shillings each, or in the several Species of coined Silver & Gold, enumerated in an Act made and passed in the twentythird Year of his late Majesty King George the Second, intituled "An Act for ascertaining the Rates at which coined Silver & Gold, English half pence & farthings may pass within this Goverment" and according to the Rates therein mentioned, with Interest to be paid annually at six per Cent.

Witness my hand Henry Gardner

erican Paper.

£8.19

PLATE 73. NOTE OF JULY 28, 1775.

possible references to the engraving or signing of the notes may be lost for these ten days. On June 1, 1775, the Receiver-General stated that he had several hundred of the advance-pay notes ready to deliver and that he should be able to pay off at least one regiment a day (Lincoln, page 282). On June 2, Colonel Ezra Richmond was deputed to countersign the advance-pay notes in place of Major Abraham Fuller (Lincoln, page 291). On June 3, Mr. Revere was requested "to attend the business of stamping the notes for the soldiers, all the ensuing night, if he can, and to finish them with the greatest despatch possible" (Lincoln, page 296). On June 4, it was ordered that two members "be appointed to attend Mr. Revere whilst he is striking off the notes for advance pay to the soldiers, night and day, till they are all struck off."

The detail of numbering and countersigning the notes was constantly before the Congress. On June 5, it was ordered that John Pickering, Jr., Samuel Phillips, and Ichabod Goodwin, Jr., be appointed to number the notes for advance pay — Mr. Pickering to number the sheets struck off on the first plate, Mr. Phillips those of the second, and Mr. Goodwin those of the third; also that Colonel Jedediah Foster be appointed to countersign the 20, 14, and 6 shilling notes (Lincoln, page 297). On June 14, Samuel Thatcher was appointed to number the notes in place of Samuel Phillips, and Colonel James Prescott was chosen to countersign the notes in place of Colonel Foster (Lincoln, page 333). On June 16, Deacon Thomas Plympton was appointed to countersign the "small notes," in place of Colonel Richmond (Lincoln, page 347). On June 21, a committee was ordered "to apply to Mr. Paul Revere, desiring him to take care, that he does not leave his engraving press exposed, when he is absent from it; and said committee are directed to take the plates into their hands, and deliver them to this Congress, when the notes are all struck off" (Lincoln, page 369). On June 22, Major Abraham Fuller was appointed to take care of the plates until further order of the Congress (Lincoln, page 375). On June 23, 1775, William Holmes was appointed to number the notes signed by Deacon Plympton (Lincoln, page 381).

Revere submitted to the Congress his bill for engraving and printing the notes, on June 22, 1775. The original bill is in the Massachusetts Archives, Volume 157, number 477. It shows a charge for engraving four copper-plates of the Province notes, at £6 each, or £24; and for printing 14,500 impressions, at £3–6–8 per thousand, or £48–6–8. This made a total of £72–6–8. The account was assigned to a committee on June 22, was re-committed on June 27, was deferred on June 29, was considered and the committee report not accepted on July 1, until finally, on the afternoon of July 1, 1775, it was resolved that "there be paid, out of the public treasury of this colony, to Mr. Paul Revere, or order, the sum of fifty pounds, in full, for procuring and engraving four plates, and printing 14,500 impressions of colony notes" (Lincoln, pages 375, 404, 421, 437, 441). The four plates comprised the large plate for the £100,000 loan, and the three small plates for the soldiers' pay notes.

The nine engraved notes for soldiers' pay were engraved on three plates — the 20, 14, and 6 shilling bills on one plate, the 10, 18, and 12 shilling bills on another plate, and the 16, 15, and 9 shilling bills on a third plate.

In the American Antiquarian Society collection are examples of seven of the nine notes. Other examples are scattered in collections throughout the country. All of the notes are indented through the engraving at the left margin to match the cutting on the stub. One whole bill is preserved by the American Antiquarian Society with the contemporaneous inscription, written in the handwriting of Paul Revere, "This was the Patern Bill Struck for the 26,000 £ Emission and can be of no use but to keep in being the form and Tenour thereof that those who Come after may see the same." It is this specimen which is reproduced. (See Plate no. 74.)

On July 7, 1775, the Provincial Congress provided for more paper currency to pay small bills. It was resolved that, since the plates engraved for the payment of the soldiers "are still sufficient for the striking off a number of impressions on each plate," that there be struck off 667 sheets on the 10, 18, and 12 shilling plate, 667 sheets on the 16, 15, and 9 shilling plate, and 540 sheets on the 20, 14, and 6 shilling plate. From the last plate 127 sheets had already been struck off, but unsigned, which made 667 sheets for this plate also. This made a total of 2001 sheets which, since each sheet impressed currency to the amount of 40 shillings, made a total of £4002. This, added to the sum of £25,998, already perfected of the notes, made a total emission of £30,000. A committee was appointed to agree with Mr. Revere, or some other suitable person, for the striking off the above number of sheets. Captain William Holmes was "directed to inquire of Mr. Revere, how many sheets of notes or bills of credit can be struck off, from the plates he now has by him, more than six hundred and sixty-seven, which were directed to be struck off, by a resolve of this Congress, this day passed" (Lincoln, pages 464–467).

In furthering the details of this additional printing, the Congress on July 8 voted that Abraham Fuller should countersign and number the 18, 12, and 10 shilling notes, Stephen Hall the 16, 15, and 9 shilling notes, and Lemuel Robinson the 20, 14, and 6 shilling notes. They resolved that Mr. Paul Revere should be employed to strike off the 1874 sheets, at the rate of six shillings for each hundred sheets, provided said Revere find ink, and house room, and procure suitable paper, the Colony to pay only the prime cost of said paper. The committee was "instructed to direct Mr. Revere to alter the date of the notes to July 8th, if it can be done" (Lincoln, pages 472–473). On the same date the Congress resolved that the sum of twelve shillings be paid to John Cook, for the use that Mr. Paul Revere had made of his house, while he was striking off the Colony notes.

The Provincial Congress was dissolved July 19, 1775. On the same day the new House of Representatives was formed at Watertown, and thenceforth the record of currency legislation is to be found in the original printed *Journals* of that body, and in the manuscript records of the Council. On August 5, 1775, the House received from Paul Revere his account "for Printing two Thousand Sheets of Soldiers Notes, &c." (*Journal*, page 46), although the actual bill, dated August 2, was for printing one thousand impressions. On August 12 the Treasurer was directed to enquire of Mr. Revere how long before he can "strike off any Number of the Bills he was ordered by the House to print." He replied that he would not be able to strike off any bills until Thursday or Friday next. It was ordered that he "strike off 500 more Blanks for Province Notes" (*Journal*, page 69). On August 17 it was voted that one thousand more blanks for Province notes be struck off and that Daniel Hopkins, Samuel Phillips, and Edward Rawson should countersign the same (*Journal*, page 76), amended two days later to substitute Thomas Rice and Dummer Jewet in place of Mr. Phillips and Deacon Rawson.

In the Massachusetts Archives, Volume 164, number 3, is a manuscript account in the handwriting of Paul Revere, as follows:

1775	The Colony of Massachusetts Bay to Paul Revere Dr	
	To riding for the Committee of Safety	
	from April 21 1775 to May 7th, 17 Days at 5s	4–5–0
	To my expences for self & Horse during that time	2–16–0
May 6th,	To keeping two Colony Horses 10 Day at 1s per horse	1–0–0
Augt 2d	To Printing 1000 impressions at 6s per Hund	3–0–0
	Errors Excepted	£11–1–0

PAUL REVERE

At the bottom of the document is written, in the hand of a member of the committee the words "Soldiers Notes" under the charge for printing, and "N.B. ye Government does not charge ye Charges of Impression for ye Money emitting for other Uses than ye Army," and further "reduced his Labour to 4s per Day." This lower charge for "riding" made the bill amount to £10–4–0. On the back of the document is entered the vote of the House of Representatives dated August 22, 1775, authorizing the payment of £10–4–0 to Revere, and signed by James Warren, Samuel Adams, James Otis, John Adams, and other members of the Council.

In the Massachusetts Archives, Volume 206, number 294a, is a bill in the handwriting of Paul Revere, dated July 17, 1775, as follows:

1775	The Colony of the Massachusetts Bay to Paul Revere Dr	
July 17	To printing 2000 Sheets of Soldiers Notes at 6/pr Hudd	£6–0–0
	To two Reams of Paper at 18/	1–16–0
	To Printing 1000 Colony Notes at 6/	3–0–0
		£10–16–0

Errors Excepd.
PAUL REVERE

On the reverse of the document are entered the votes of the House and of the Council, dated August 24, 1775, approving the account. In the printed *Journal* of the House, page 105, under date of August 24, 1775, is the resolve for paying £10–16–0 to Paul Revere.

Colony of the Massachusetts Bay. [No] May 25 1775

No

The Possessor of this Note shall be Intitled to receive out of the Publick Treasury of this Colony the sum of Ten shillings lawfull Money on the twenty fifth day of May A.D. 1776 with Interest at the Rate of six p. Ct. p. Annum; And this Note shall be received in all payments at the Treasury, at any time after the date hereof for the principal sum without Interest, if so paid before the said 25th day of May A.D. 1776.

American Paper.

Receiv.r Gener.l

This was the Patern Bill Struck for the 26,000 £ Emission and can be of no use but to keep in being the form and Tenour thereof that those who Come after may See the Same

Handwriting of Paul Revere

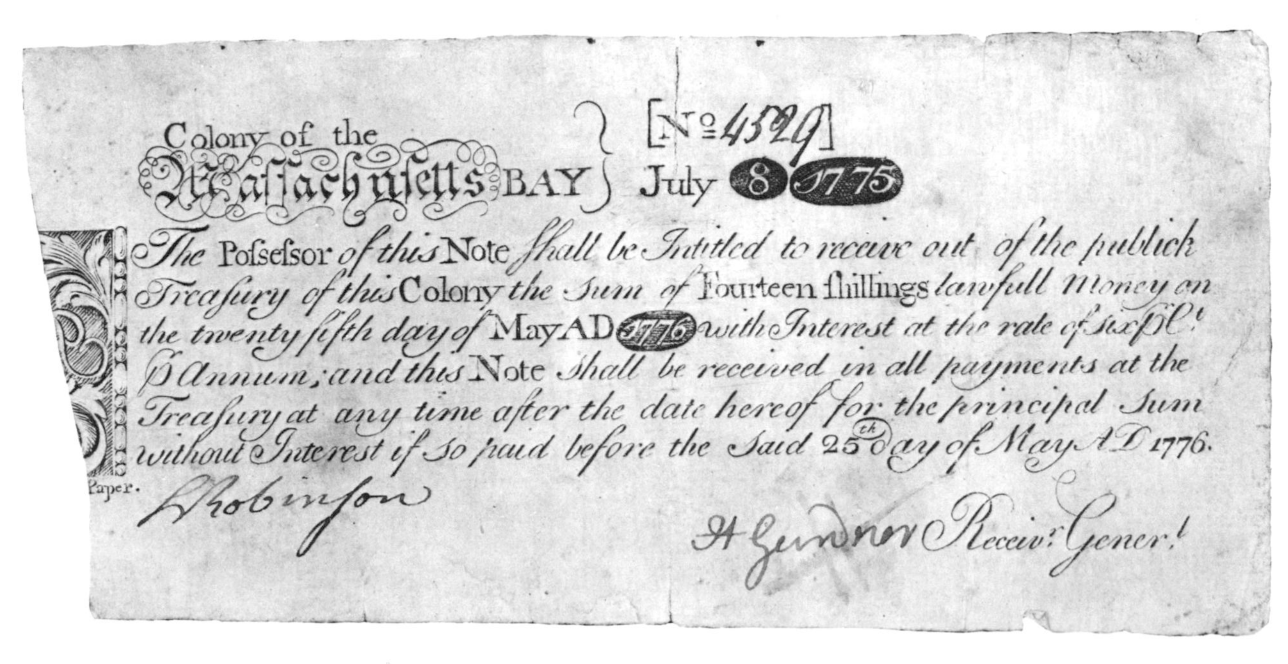
Colony of the Massachusetts BAY } [No 4529] July 8 1775

The Possessor of this Note shall be Intitled to receive out of the publick Treasury of this Colony the Sum of Fourteen shillings lawfull Money on the twenty fifth day of May AD 1776 with Interest at the rate of six p. Ct. p. Annum; and this Note shall be received in all payments at the Treasury at any time after the date hereof for the principal Sum without Interest if so paid before the said 25th day of May A.D. 1776.

Paper.

Robinson

H Gardner Receiv.r Gener.l

PLATE 74. NOTE OF MAY 25, 1775. NOTE OF MAY 25, 1775, REVERSE. NOTE OF JULY 8, 1775.

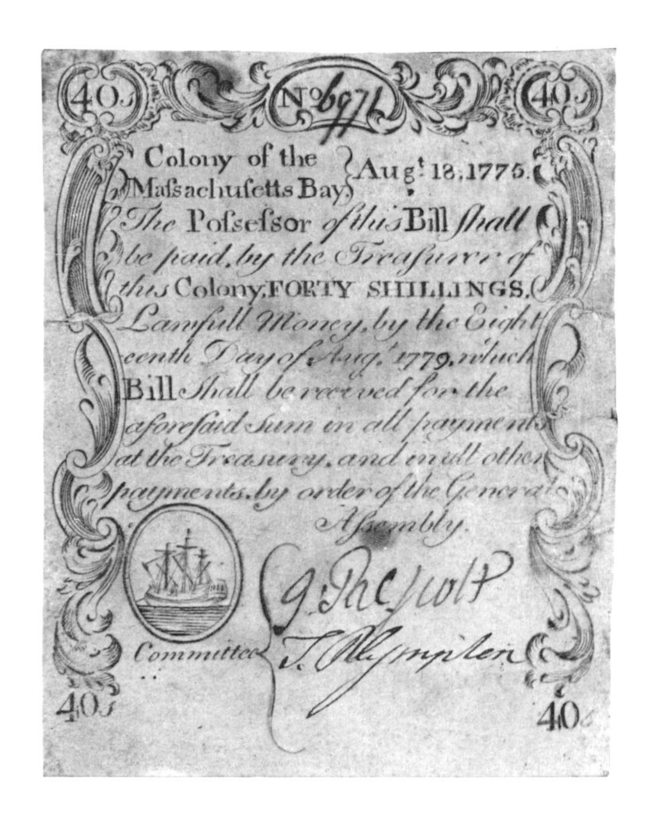

Plate 75. Bill of Aug. 18, 1775, and Reverse. Bill of Dec. 7, 1775, and Reverse.

The nine additional notes for soldiers' pay were identical with the May 25, 1775, issue except that they were dated July 8, 1775. The American Antiquarian Society has only one specimen, that for 14 shillings, although there are examples for 9, 12, 14, and 16 shillings in the F. C. C. Boyd collection. It is true that the issue was very small, with the chance of but few surviving. That they were identical with the May 25 issue, except for the change of date, is shown by the original copper-plates which still survive and are in the office of the Massachusetts Archives. (For reproduction, see Plate no. 74.)

There are six copper-plates in the State Archives office. Three of these are for the issue of July 8, 1775, altered by Revere from the earlier issue of May 25, 1775, and can be described as follows:

The plate for the 10, 12, and 18 shilling notes is defaced, and is 9¼ inches high by 8⅛ inches wide. On the reverse is Revere's original plate of the Boston Massacre, cut off at the top and at the bottom to bring the plate down to proper size.

The plate for the 6, 14, and 20 shilling notes is slightly defaced and is 10¼ inches high by 7⅜ inches wide. On the reverse is Revere's original plate of Harvard College, cut off at the left, constituting half of the original copper.

The plate for the 9, 15, and 16 shilling notes is not defaced in any way, and measures 10⅞ inches high by 7⅜ inches wide. On the reverse is the original engraving of Samuel Willard which was the frontispiece of Samuel Willard's *Compleat Body of Divinity*, Boston, 1726.

There have been restrikes on modern paper of all of these plates, with impressions from both sides. The three other coppers, for the issues of December 7, 1775, and November 17, 1776, and the "Rising Sun" emission of 1779, will be described later.

The two emissions of notes above described established a loan to the Province of £100,000 on May 3, 1775, and an issue to pay the soldiers on May 20, 1775, of £26,000, later increased, by altering the dates on the notes, to £30,000. Then came the problem of defraying the public expenses and providing a paper currency for the people to use in business transactions. After occasional discussion of the subject, the Committee of Safety on July 6, 1775, recommended that the Provincial Congress should provide for an issue of £100,000 of bills of credit, suggesting details as to the size and number of the bills, although many of these suggestions were not followed (Lincoln, page 588). The Congress dissolved July 19, and further action on the subject was brought before the newly created House of Representatives. On July 27 a committee reported in favor of an emission of £100,000, with the amounts extending from one to forty shillings (House *Journal*, page 17). The House, on August 1, appointed a committee to procure suitable paper for the printing of the bills and ordered that the bills should be printed on types (*Journal*, page 31). On August 4 the House voted that the bills should be printed on copper-plates and that an agreement should be made with Mr. Revere for printing the same (*Journal*, page 46).

Finally, the House and the Council agreed upon the details of the emission and the Act authorizing the bills of credit was passed on August 23, 1775. This provided for an issue of £100,000, to be "stamped on copperplates," of the following denominations: 1, 2, 2/6, 4, 5, 6, 7/6, 8, 10, 11, 12, 17, 20, 24, 30, and 40 shillings, with 10,000 of each denomination. Four-tenths of each issue was to be redeemable on August 18, 1778, three-tenths on August 18, 1779, and three-tenths on August 18, 1780. On the back of each bill was to be stamped its value, its date, and the figure of an American, with a sword in his right hand, with the inscription suspended therefrom, "Ense petit placidam sub libertate quietem;" and from his left hand, "Magna Charta," and around the figure these words "Issued in Defence of American Liberty." A tax was levied, as part of the Act, to take up the payment of the bills.

A committee was appointed by the House, on August 23, to attend Mr. Revere while he is striking off the bills, that they take the plates into their own hands when Mr. Revere has done with them, and that Joseph Wheeler, Daniel Hopkins, Ebenezer Sayer, and William Story, with such others as shall be joined with them, be a committee to sign and number the bills; that any three of the committee be sufficient to sign the bills (House *Journal*, page 96). On the same day it was ordered that one of the committee should sign in red ink, one in black, and one in blue. Later in the day Thomas Plimpton was put on the committee in place of Mr. Story (*Journal*, pages 97, 99). On August 24 it was voted that Joseph

Wheeler, Joseph Cushing, Ebenezer Sayer, and Thomas Plimpton number and sign the bills, any three, in red, blue, and black ink. The House then adjourned to September 20, 1775.

On September 22 it was ordered that the first thousand of the bills of lower denominations, from one to eight shillings, should be signed by any two of the committee and the remaining nine thousand by any one of the committee. Since four thousand of the bills from ten to forty shillings had already been signed by three signers, the six thousand remaining bills were to be signed by any two of the committee (*Journal*, page 114). On October 17, an order was passed for the removal of the chest containing the bills of credit and the plates, to the Treasurer's office, since all the bills had been stamped (*Journal*, pages 172, 174).

On October 20, 1775, the House resolved that £133–6–8 be paid to Paul Revere for his printing 133,000 bills for the use of the Colony (*Journal*, page 179). This action was confirmed by the Council, October 21, 1775 (Manuscript Records, Volume 17, page 140). On November 11, 1775, the House adjourned to November 29. On December 22, James Prescott, who had been on the committee for signing the bills, petitioned for a discharge from the trust, since the committee had finished the business, and on January 9, 1776, it was discharged (*Journal*, page 133).

The bills of credit, as made by Paul Revere, were engraved exactly in accordance with the provisions of the Act of August 23, 1775. They were dated August 18, 1775, and were four inches high by three wide. There were sixteen denominations, 1, 2, 2/6, 4, 5, 6, 7/6, 8, 10, 11, 12, 17, 20, 24, 30, and 40 shillings, and each plate had to be separately engraved. On each plate in the lower left corner was an oval frame with a cut of a ship or tree, each different in design. The mantling, the lettering, and the usual abbreviation of "No," were all characteristic of Revere's engraving. On the reverse was drawn a soldier, with a sword in his right hand, and a scroll with the words "Magna Charta" in his left; with two mottoes, "Issued in defence of American Liberty" above, and "Ense petit placidam sub Libertate Quietem" below; also the amount and the date. Each denomination had a different date of payment, August 8, 1778, 1779, and 1780. Of the sixteen denominations those for 1, 2, 2/6, 4, 5, 7/6, 10, 12, 30, and 40 shillings are in the

American Antiquarian Society collection, with one or more variations of each. The F. C. C. Boyd collection has examples of every denomination. The bill reproduced is that for forty shillings, both front and reverse, and is signed by J. Prescott and T. Plympton. (See Plate no. 75.)

Scarcely was the £100,000 emission of August 18, 1775, put in circulation before another issue was required, in order to take care of the public debts. During the month of December, 1775, the details of a new issue of bills of credit for £75,000, were agreed upon, although not until December 22, 1775, was the Act passed by the General Court. It provided that an issue of £75,000 of bills of credit, to be dated December 7, 1775, should be stamped on copper-plates, with denominations of 8d, 1/4, 1/6, 2/8, 3, 3/4, 4/6, 7, 10, 14, 16, 22, 28, 36, 42, and 48 shillings. It should be noticed that every denomination, except for the ten shilling issue, was different from those in the previous emission. There were to be 6250 of each denomination, with four-tenths of each denomination redeemable on December 7, 1781, three-tenths on December 7, 1782, and three-tenths on December 7, 1783. The reverse of the bill was to have the same design as the previous issue of August 18, 1775.

In the meanwhile, since the provisions of the Act were already agreed upon, plans were made to prepare the bills. Paul Revere, writing from Watertown, December 8, 1775, sent to the House the following message:

> "I the Subscriber agree to Engrave the Plates & make the necessary alterations in the same, and Print the number of Bills the Honble House of Represtas. shall order, for the sum of one penny half penny old Tenor, each Bill, and finde the Paper, and all the materials, the paper to be equal to the last Emmission.
>
> As the alteration & engraving will not be quite so much work as the last, I agree to alow thirty Shillings L. Money out of the whole PAUL REVERE
>
> Memorandum
>
> The Paper for the last, cost me Six dollars, a Rheam, when I did not expect to give but four, which made 44 Dollers odds, the Committee of the House ordered the paper to be made, & did not agree for the price, & I was obliged to pay the paper maker his demand."

(Original, in Paul Revere's hand, in Massachusetts Archives, Volume 138, number 271.)

On the document appeared the record ordering "Mr. Cooper to bring a resolve for Engaging the above price to Mr. Revere & to direct ye plates to be dd to him."

On December 8, 1775, the House passed the following resolve:

> "Resolved, That Henry Gardner Esqr; Receiver General of this Colony be, and hereby is directed to deliver unto Mr. Paul Revere, Engraver, the two Pair of Copper-Plates, now in the keeping of said Receiver General, from which the last Emission of Bills was struck off; one Pair of said Plates to be delivered upon the return of the other, and that Mr. Revere be directed to proceed with all expedition, in the cutting or engraving a New Sett of Plates for the striking off Bills of public Credit, to the Amount of Seventy-five thousand Pounds, of the Denominations specified in the Bill, now pending for the Emission of said Sum, provided the same passes into an Act, and that he be allowed for said Service One Penny and a Half Penny O. T. for each Bill he shall strike off, he finding Paper, and every Material that shall be necessary, and allowing a Deduction to be made from the foregoing Allowance of the Sum of Thirty Shillings Lawful-Money for the Advantage he will receive from the old Plates; and that Col. Thompson be a Committee to take into keeping said Revere's Press, until the Plates shall be ready for the striking off said Bills, or any Part of them. Sent up for Concurrence." (House *Journal*, page 28.)

For six weeks after the passage of the Act, both the House and the Council spent much time trying to find members who could afford the time to sign the bills. Members were appointed, and then were excused or replaced. To sum up the votes, Joseph Wheeler, Abner Morgan, Daniel Hopkins, Joseph Batchelder, William Pynchon, Dummer Sewall, Thomas Rice, and Benjamin Ely were chosen at different times, but some of the votes included the names, adding "and others." The only names which I have found on the bills were those of J. Wheeler, Benja. Ely, J. Batchelder, Wm. Pynchon, D. Hopkins, Thos. Rice and A. Morgan.

It was also voted, on December 30, 1775, that the bills from eight pence to seven shillings should be signed by any one of the committee, and the bills from ten to forty-eight shillings by any two, one in black ink and one in red (House *Journal*, page 94). By January 24, 1776, it was stated that all the bills had been struck off.

There were sixteen denominations of the December 7, 1775, issue, with 6250 of each denomination. On January 24, 1776, the House authorized the payment of £81–16–8 to Paul Revere for printing 100,000 bills at sixteen shillings, eight pence, per thousand (House *Journal*, page 197). This was confirmed by the Council, January 29, 1776 (Manuscript Council Records, Volume 17, page 236).

Revere's work in engraving the bills of December 7, 1775, was comparatively small as his chief labor was in altering the dates and lettering of the previous emission. Of the sixteen denominations in the December 7 issue the American Antiquarian Society has fourteen — those for 8d, 1/4, 1/6, 2/8, 3, 3/4, 4/6, 10, 14, 16, 28, 36, 42, and 48 shillings. The F. C. C. Boyd collection has all sixteen denominations. The bill for 36 shillings is in the best condition and is the one reproduced. (See Plate no. 75.)

In the Massachusetts Archives is the original copper-plate, with reverse blank, for eight of the December 7, 1775, bills. The plate measures 7⅞ inches high, by 12½ inches wide. The denominations of the bills are for 8d, 1/4, 1/6, 2/8, 3, 3/4, 4/6, and 7 shillings. In the Montrose Natural History and Antiquarian Society of Montrose, Scotland, is the original copper-plate for the 42 shilling bill of the December 7, 1775, issue, which was picked up in a brass founder's shop at Montrose in 1868. An impression from the plate is in the American Antiquarian Society collection.

In an early ledger of Vose, Lewis & Crane, of Milton, owned by the Crane and Company Museum at Dalton, is entered the charge, dated January 4, 1776, against Major Abraham Fuller and John [Jonathan] Brown of £26 for thirteen reams of "Money Paper," at forty shillings. The debt was discharged by an abatement of £2–8–0 on the paper, and a cash payment, on January 11, 1778, of £23–12–0 from Paul Revere. Major Fuller and Jonathan Brown generally obtained the paper from Milton for the General Court. But why Revere paid up the account as late as 1778 is not shown by any records.

In the spring of 1776 Paul Revere entered into military service. On April 10 the House of Representatives appointed him Major of the regiment to fortify the town and harbor of Boston, for a service of thirty days. On May 10 he was chosen Major in Lieutenant-Colonel Thomas Craft's artillery regiment, and on November 27 Lieutenant-Colonel of the regiment. He continued in service until May 4, 1780, including the command of Castle Island in 1778 and 1779, and his participation in the Penobscot expedition in the summer of 1779.

As a result of his career in the army, Revere did not have too much time for engraving. In the year 1776 the earliest concern of the Province was to borrow money on notes. The last note previously issued was that of July 28, 1775, engraved by Revere. There were four issues of notes in 1776, the Acts being dated May 8, July 2, December 2, and December 6 (*Acts and Resolves*, 1886 edition, pages 504, 551, 604, 608). The total amount to be raised was slightly over £550,000. All of the four notes were printed, with a border of type ornaments. They were identical typographically, except for the insertion of such explanatory words as "Bounty Note" or "Commtte War." The last two issues, those of December, 1776, had the word "State" in place of "Colony," and also were embossed with a stamp with the motto "Dat Vires Unio." The American Antiquarian Society owns examples of the two December issues.

The earliest 1776 issue of bills of credit, or paper currency for the Province, was that of June 18, 1776. There were twenty-four denominations, from three pence to forty-eight shillings, of which the American Antiquarian Society collection has nineteen. They were all printed from type by Benjamin Edes, the smaller denominations, about two by three inches in size, having a single border of type ornaments, and reverse blank. The higher denominations were about 3½ by 2¾ inches, with an ornamental design in type metal and the reverse carrying the value, translated into dollars.

The next issue of bills of credit was that dated September 17, 1776, authorized September 16 (*Acts and Resolves*, 1886 edition, page 559). The issue was for £50,004, in denominations of 10, 14, 16, 22, 28, 36, 42, and 48 shillings, with 4630 bills of each denomination. It was ordered that these bills should be stamped on copper-plate. On September 6, 1776, the House appointed a committee "to wait upon Mr. Revere, to know if he can recut the former plates, to answer in part for the new emission of bills; agreed to be emitted," and also to obtain from the Treasurer the copper-plates in his possession for the emission of December 7, 1775. On September 10, Oliver Wendell was ordered to "wait on Mr. Revere, to desire him to alter the word *Colony*, in the plate on which the bills of credit are to be struck off, and insert *State* in the room thereoff." On September 16 a committee consisting of John Murray, Thomas Cook, Abraham Fuller, Jonas Dix, John

Bliss, Jonathan Brown, John Lewis, and Henry Hill were authorized to sign and number the bills, but the same day Aaron Davis and Ichabod Goodwin were substituted for Fuller and Bliss. Any two of these men could sign. On September 18 Captain Brown of Watertown was ordered to bring paper for the money from Milton to Watertown (House *Journal*, pp. 93, 95, 97, 108, 109, 112).

The eight denominations from ten to forty-eight shillings were chosen because they were the same as the higher denominations on the bills of December 7, 1775. Thus the copper-plates could be easily altered by inserting the date of September 17, 1776, and the word *State* in place of *Colony*. The Boston Public Library (Chamberlain Coll.) has the original bill from Revere to the State of Massachusetts Bay, 1776, as follows:

Sep 27	To printing 37040 Bills @ 2d O. Tr/pr Bill	41-3-1½
Nov'r	To engraving two plates anew	8-0-0
17	To Printing 37040 Bills @ 2d O. Tr/pr Bill	41-3-1½
		£90-6-3

Errors Excepted Paul Revere

On the reverse it was noted that the bill was allowed on December 30, 1776, and receipted by Revere on January 2, 1777. Eight denominations of 4630 bills each would total 37040 bills. The Massachusetts Historical Society has an example of the 36 shilling bill of this issue. (Plate no. 76.) The Boyd collection has the bills for 14, 22, 36, and 48 shillings.

When this issue of September 17, 1776, was planned, it was at first intended to have an additional issue of £100,000, engraved on two plates of twelve bills each — the smaller for bills from two pence to four shillings sixpence, and the larger for bills from one dollar to twelve dollars. A committee recommended this on September 16 but no resolve was passed (House *Journal*, p. 109).

On October 29, 1776, an Act was passed for an issue of £50,004, to be dated November, 1776 (*Acts and Resolves*, 1886 ed., Vol. 5, p. 589). They were to be engraved from the same plates by Revere, and were to be numbered and signed by any two of Jonas Dix, Jonathan Woods, Jonathan Brown, Ichabod Goodwin, Israel Hubbard, William Drew, Ezra Sergeant, and Joseph Noyes. But this Act seems to have been repudiated by that of December 6, 1776.

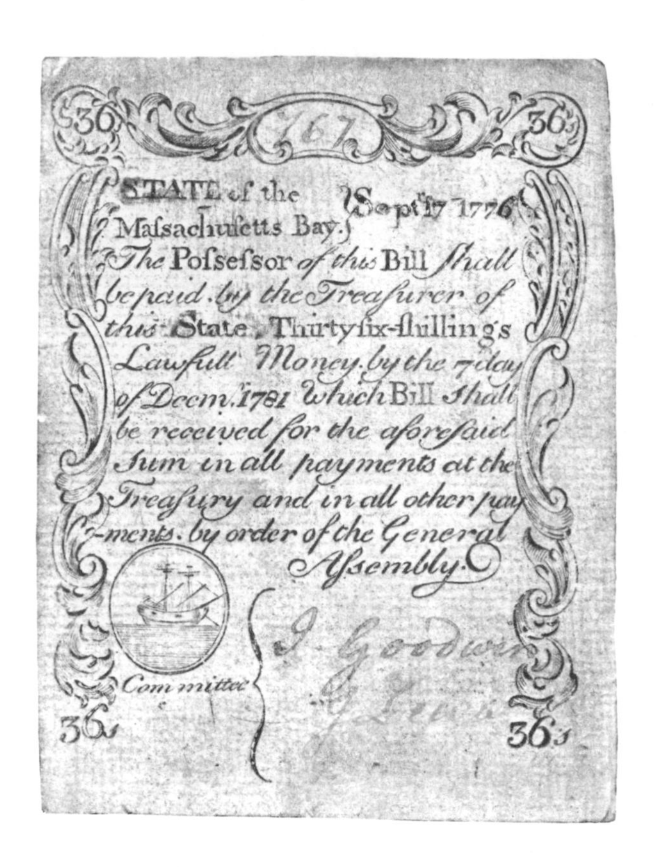

Plate 76. Bill of Sept. 17, 1776, and Reverse. Bill of Nov. 17, 1776, and Reverse.

In December, 1776, two Acts were passed providing for more bills of credit. On December 6 an Act provided for an issue of £20,034 to be dated November 17, 1776. The denominations were 10, 14, 16, 22, 28, 36, 42, and 48 shillings, with 1855 bills of each denomination, and the bills were to be redeemed December 7, 1781 (*Acts and Resolves*, 1886 edition, Volume 5, page 606). On December 5 it was stated that this issue was to be "from the last plates," and on December 7, a committee was appointed "to agree with some persons to strike off the last emission of bills, and to inspect the press." On the same day it was ordered that Joseph Henderson, Dummer Jewett, Thomas Ivers, Nehemiah Abbot, Ezra Sergeant, Henderson Inches, Jonathan Hastings, Jr., and David Cheever, or any two of them, should sign and number the bills (House *Journal*, pages 186, 189). Three days later Nathan Adams was appointed to sign the bills in place of Henderson Inches, and Nathaniel Barber in place of Joseph Henderson. Barber was later replaced by George Partridge.

The selection of the eight denominations on the issue of November 17, 1776, from ten to forty-eight shillings, was because these were the denominations on the previous issue of September 17, 1776. The new issue required only the altering of the date; also on the reverse the words "Magna Charta" on the scroll were changed to "Independence." Undoubtedly this was done by Revere, as he originally engraved the plates and the change would have required little time on his part. On December 2, 1776, he submitted the bill cited above to the House of Representatives, which was read and committed to the Committee on Accounts (House *Journal*, page 180). The House printed record, however, does not state the amount or nature of the account. In the American Antiquarian Society collection are the 10, 16, and 48 shilling issues. The Boyd collection has the 10, 14, 16, 22, 36, 42, and 48 shilling issues. In the Massachusetts Archives is the original copper heavily defaced, showing the reverse of the eight issues of November 17, 1776. Many restrikes have been made from this copper. On the opposite side of the copper is Revere's plate of the View of the Town of Boston and the Landing of the Troops, issued in 1770. The plate was cut at the left and bottom sides, to suit the size of the currency plate. (The bill of November 17, 1776, is shown on Plate no. 76.)

The second issue authorized in December, 1776, was planned nearly two months earlier. On October 10, 1776, the House appointed a committee to prepare a bill for an emission of £75,000. The bill was read on October 19 for the third time, engrossed and sent up to the Council for concurrence (House *Journal*, pages 116, 127). But the Council did not act upon the bill until December 7.

On November 6, 1776, the House voted that "Col. Orne be added to the committee to get the plate for the last emission of bills compleated; and that if the committee shall think proper, they take the plate from Mr. Hurd, and employ some other person to compleat the same." On November 27 it was ordered "That the committee appointed to cut plates for a new emission of money, take from Mr. Hurd the plates he began to engrave, and deliver the same to Mr. Revere, to be compleated" (House *Journal*, pages 145, 175).

The Council finally, on December 6, 1776, concurred with the House in passing the bill and on December 7 it was enacted. The Act provided for an emission of £75,000, dated October 18, 1776, of the following denominations: 2, 3, 4, 6, 8, 9 pence, 1, 1/6, 2, 3, 4, 4/6, 6, 12, 18, 24, 30, 36, 42, 48, 54, 60, 66, and 72 shillings. There were to be 5143 bills each of the lower denominations to 4 shillings 6 pence, and 3000 of each denomination from 6 to 72 shillings. The front of the bill was to be engraved on copper-plate, "with a handsome border" and the back of the bill was to be printed on type metal, with suitable ornaments (*Acts and Resolves*, 1886 edition, Volume 5, pages 610, 693). (See Plate no. 77.)

The bill itself was 2½ inches high, by 3 inches wide. The engraved face included columns at either side, a codfish at the top, a scroll with the words "Massachusetts State," and the amount of the bill in several places. The reverse carried a border of ornaments, the value of the bill, a tree, and the imprint of "Boston: Printed by John Gill. October 1776," all in type metal. The American Antiquarian Society has all of the bills under 6 shillings, and the 30 shilling bill, and the Boyd collection also has the 12, 18, 36, 48, 66, and 72 shilling bills. The reason for the scarcity of the bills of larger denomination was because they were called in, October 13, 1777, to be exchanged for notes. On February 9, 1779, the House voted that such bills turned in should be burned. The same committee which was to number and sign the bills of the issue of November 17, 1776, also signed this

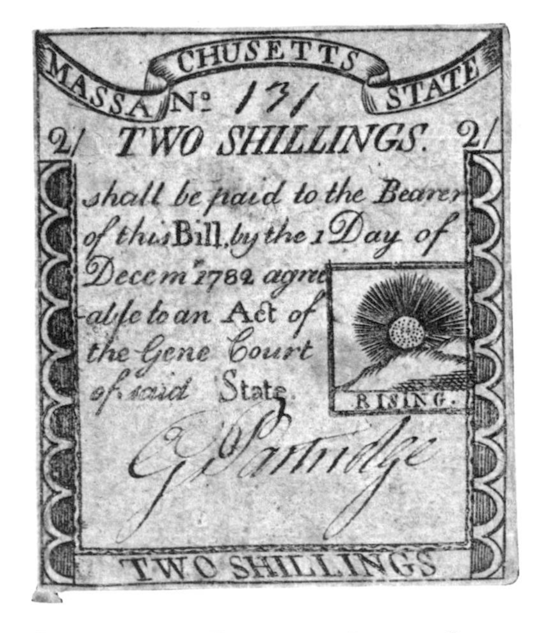

PLATE 77. BILL OF OCT. 18, 1776, AND REVERSE. BILL OF OCT. 16, 1778, AND REVERSE. RISING SUN BILL OF 1779, AND REVERSE.

issue of October 18. The bills of 6 shillings and over were to be signed by any two of the committee and the smaller bills by any one.

Paul Revere submitted his charge to the House on December 2, 1776, Nathaniel Hurd on December 7, and John Gill on December 30 (House *Journal*, pages 180, 190, 205), but in no case does the printed record state the nature or amount of the charges. The Committee on Accounts, to which the bills were submitted, could make the payments without reporting to the House.

In the year 1777 there were five varieties of notes issued. They all carried an elaborate engraved border on the two sides and at the bottom; a circular design at the upper left made by a coiled snake, enclosing a figure with a sword in hand and holding a scroll with the word "Independence," and the motto "Ense petit placidam sub libertate quietem;" the words "State of Massachusetts Bay" at the top, with penmanship scrolls, and the words "No" and "1777." The above were all engraved. The entire remainder of the wording of the note was in type. The size of the note was seven inches high, by over seven inches wide. The engraving was done by Nathaniel Hurd, copying exactly a border of a note which he had engraved in 1769. On a specimen of this earlier note, dated April 10, 1771, in the American Antiquarian Society can be seen in minute lettering on the left border, "Nath. Hurd Sculp. 1769."

The first issue of notes was enacted on May 2, 1777, and the *Journal* of the House includes several references to the fact that Hurd engraved it (*Acts and Resolves*, 1886 edition, Volume 5, pages 638, 720). This note was to be paid May 10, 1782. The next issue was enacted October 13, 1777, with one variety of notes to be paid March 1, 1781, and the other March 1, 1782. In these two forms of notes the words "Committee" and "Witness my Hand" were engraved instead of set in type. Another issue, also payable March 1, 1782, was enacted on October 22, 1777. A fifth variety of the notes of 1777 had the same Hurd border and engraving, but was made payable June 1, 1780, in lawful money, in Spanish milled dollars, or in coined silver and gold. The American Antiquarian Society has specimens of all of these notes. Although they are sometimes carelessly advertised as engraved by Revere, they positively were engraved by Hurd. Since they were not engraved by Revere, less attention is here paid to the details of their enactment.

No emissions of bills of credit were authorized or enacted in 1777. The General Court had reached the conclusion that money could be raised only through loans and taxes, and that the depreciation in paper money, complicated by frequent counterfeiting of the larger bills, constituted a serious danger to the State's economic system. Therefore on October 13, 1777, the General Assembly passed an Act for drawing in the bills of credit that had been issued and redeeming them by Treasurer's notes. An exception was made for small bills of less than one dollar, which could continue to be circulated, and also for bills upon which the State had promised interest. The notes were to be for sums not less than £10. The bond issue was for £250,000, a larger amount than any previous loan. Bills had to be handed into the Treasury before January 1, 1778.

Several towns in the State voiced opposition to the Act, believing that it worked a hardship on holders of small bills and that too short a time was provided for redemption. After listening to a number of petitions from the towns, stating grievances, the General Court passed an Act, December 13, 1777, extending the time for exchanging the bills until April 1, 1778. On December 15, 1777, the House of Representatives authorized the preparation and printing of a handbill explaining the reasons for the Act calling in the bills of credit. It was printed in a folio leaflet of four pages, and copies are to be found in the American Antiquarian Society and other libraries.

In 1778 the General Court decided to call in all the small bills, which had been excluded from the Act of October 13, 1777, redeeming the larger bills through an issue of notes. The new Act was passed October 13, 1778, the preamble stating that "the currency of the small bills of credit emitted in this state before October 18, 1776, suffers much from great numbers of them being much torn and otherwise defaced." The Act provided for an emission of £28,000, with denominations of 2, 3, 4, 6, 8, and 9 pence, and 1, 1/6, 2, 3, 4, and 4/6 shillings, with thirty thousand of each denomination to be dated October 16, 1778. They were to be "stamped on the copperplates prepared for the last emission," with the same form and device except for the change of date from October 18, 1776, to October 16, 1778. The Treasurer was authorized to exchange the new bills for all bills of less than six shillings which had been emitted before October 18, 1776, and penalties were provided for those who did not turn in the bills before March 1, 1779. Thomas Dawes, George Partridge, John Greenough, Richard Cranch, and Jonathan Brown were appointed a committee to number and sign the bills, any one name being sufficient. The final date for redeeming the bills was later lengthened to June 1, 1780 (*Acts and Resolves*, pages 906, 995).

Although the engraved face of the plate was not changed except for the alteration in the date, the reverse, being merely printed, was changed from "Boston: Printed by John Gill. October 1776" to "Boston, October 1778," also with alteration of printer's ornaments. The faces of the plates were much weaker, because of overuse, and in some bills the lines are very faint. Any engraver could have performed the simple task of changing the dates on twelve plates, and there is nothing on record to show who did it, but they were certainly Revere's plates which were altered. The American Antiquarian Society has all of the twelve bills in its collection, as does the Massachusetts Historical Society and F. C. C. Boyd. The Historical Society also has a restrike of the reverse of the plate, showing all twelve bills with the date of "October 1778." This restrike has the autograph inscription "Presented by Mr Thomas Fleet the printer 14 Septem 1799," indicating that it was Fleet who printed the reverse of the plate, in place of John Gill who was the printer of the previous issue. (See Plate no. 77.)

The House soon discovered that the impressions from the old plates were not satisfactory. On January 7, 1779, it was ordered "That the Committee appointed to sign the Bills of Credit, ordered to be emitted by an Act passed the last Session, be a Committee to bring in a Bill for repealing so much of the said Act as they shall judge necessary, and for procuring another Plate for the Impression of said Bills" (House *Journal*, page 89). This resulted in an Act, passed January 26, 1779, altering the tenor and denominations of the Act of October 13, 1778. The new Act stated that "the copperplates are found insufficient for stamping the number of bills required." Thirty thousand of each denomination was evidently too much for the plates to stand. Therefore the Act provided for a new plate with a new set of denominations as follows: 1, 1/6, 2, 2/6, 3, 3/6, 4, 4/6, 4/8, 5, 5/4, and 5/6 shillings. Of the £28,000 of the previous emission, £20,000 was to be paid in bills of the new emission (*Acts and Resolves*, 1886 edition, pages 921, 1010).

The same committee which had signed the bills of October 16, 1778, was authorized to sign the new bills.

This was known as the "Rising Sun" emission, because of the device of a crudely drawn sun set in a square on each bill, with the word "Rising" underneath. There was a border, in design, on either side. The bill was not dated on the engraved face, but stated that it was redeemable December 1, 1782. On the reverse was the amount, the familiar pine tree of previous issues, and at the bottom "Boston, 1779," all enclosed in a border of type ornaments, and all set in type. The Boston Public Library (Chamberlain Collection) has the original bill from Revere to the State of Massachusetts Bay for 1778, as follows:

	To Engraving a Copper plate for a State Note	£ 20-00-0
Nov. 16	To Engraving a Copper plate over again for 12 small bills	72-00-0
	To printing 8000 impressions at 6 pence	200-00-0
1779 May	To Engraving a Copper plate for 12 small Bills of the emission of 16 Oct. and the plate	108-00-0
20	To printing 9400 impressions at 8 pence	355-00-0
		£755-00-0
	Errors Excepted Paul Revere	
	Deduct for error	41-13-4
		£713- 6-8

Received the above in the full, by an Order on Mr. Benjamin Sumner one of the Collectors for the Town of Boston.

Boston Octo'r 7, 1779. Paul Revere

Thos. Dawes
Jon'n Brown
Richard Cranch

Among the Revere coppers in the State Archives Division is the original copper of the emission, 12¾ by 8 inches, showing all the twelve bills, but with blank reverse. Both the American Antiquarian Society and the Massachusetts Historical Society have restrikes from this copper. In the latter collection is also a restrike from the printed reverse plate, showing the twelve bills, with "Boston, 1779" underneath, and all in type. Inscribed in autograph on this restrike are the words

"Presented by Mr. Thomas Fleet the printer 14 Septem. 1799." This might indicate that Fleet, who printed the *Journal* of the House from May, 1777 to May, 1779, was the printer of the reverse of the bill instead of John Gill, who had printed the reverse of the issue of October 18, 1776. Of this 1779 emission the American Antiquarian Society collection and the Boyd collection have all of the twelve issues. (See Plate no. 77.)

There is no evidence that Revere engraved any notes or bills of credit from 1779 to the close of the Revolution. He was busily concerned with military affairs, especially in the summer of 1779 when he was one of the officers commanding the Penobscot expedition, after which he spent nearly three years clearing himself of charges connected with that unfortunate campaign. The notes from 1779 to 1783 were for lotteries, advance pay for officers, and various needs of government. Some were engraved, including notes signed by J. M. Furnass, and some were printed from type metal. The only issue of bills of credit was authorized May 5, 1780, was guaranteed by the United States Congress, and was printed by Hall and Sellers of Philadelphia. Revere's work in engraving for the State was confined to the earlier part of the Revolution, and in the later years he returned to gold- and silversmithing, and even ventured into trade as a merchant. The Boston Public Library (Chamberlain Collection) has an original bill from Revere to Massachusetts Commonwealth for 1781, as follows:

Sep'r	To Engraving a Brass Type for the Treasurer	1-4
18	To repairing it twice	1-4
		£2-8

Dec. 26, 1781. I hereby Certify the above service was performed for my Office.

H. Gardner Treas.

The statement has been frequently made that Revere engraved the Continental Congress issues of paper money of 1775. It apparently was first made by Benson J. Lossing in his *Pictorial Field-Book of the Revolution*, 1851, Volume 1, page 317, where he describes the issuing of bills of credit by the Continental Congress in 1775 and says: "The plates were engraved on copper by Paul Revere, of Boston." But Lossing evidently changed his mind. He wrote an article on "Continental Money" for *Harper's Monthly Magazine* for March, 1863, page 436. It was an anonymous article, but in the general index to the volume it was credited to B. J. Lossing. Here Mr. Lossing says that the United Colonies "employed Smithers, a gun-engraver (who had come to Philadelphia, from England, two years before), to prepare the plates. It is believed that Paul Revere engraved some of the later ones. They were rude specimens of art. The ornamental portions were engraved on type-metal, in the style of wood engraving introduced into this country by Doctor Anderson twenty years afterward; while the body of the lettering was in common movable type."

An anonymous *Review of the Article on Continental Money, in Harper's Magazine* for March, 1863, privately printed, 1863, and signed "Antiquarian" scathingly attacked the article in detail, and said: "We would also like his authority for *Smithers*. The general impression borne out by the Journal of Congress, is that Paul Revere was the engraver of the notes; *he* appears, and also in Force's Archives, but *Smithers* we cannot find anywhere. Where did he come from?"

The printed record in the *Journals of Congress*, authorizing the issues of May 10 and November 29, 1775, makes no mention of an engraver of the bills. The first issue, although dated May 10, 1775, was authorized, as to denomination and form, on June 23, 1775, and a committee of five, John Adams, John Rutledge, James Duane, Benjamin Franklin, and James Wilson, were ordered "to get proper plates engraved, to provide paper, and to agree with printers to print the above bills." The total emission was for two million dollars. On July 21, 1775, a committee of three was authorized "to superintend the press, and to have the oversight and care of printing the bills of Credit ordered to be struck by this Congress." On July 25 a further emission of one million dollars was ordered, to be struck in bills of thirty dollars each; and twenty-eight signers, not members of the Congress, were appointed to sign the bills. On October 3 the account of Frederick Bicking for fifty-six reams of paper for printing the bills was deemed reasonable. On October 10 a charge of David Rittenhouse for "36 cutts for the continental money amounting to 48 dollars" was allowed. The definition of the word "cutts" is uncertain. On November 29, 1775, a second emission of three million dollars was authorized, to be printed from the same plates used in the previous emission.

An exhaustive search in the Federal archives, both in the Library of Congress, in the National Archives, and in other record offices, fails to reveal any committee report or document referring to the engraver of either of the two emissions of bills of 1775.

The assumption that Revere engraved the Continental Congress bills persisted. Goss, in his *Life of Paul Revere*, 1891, Volume 2, page 424, states boldly "The plates were engraved by Revere," and in a footnote credits his authority to Lossing's *Cyclopedia of United States History*, 1881, Volume 1, page 320, where the author resolved all previous doubts by saying "The plates were engraved by Paul Revere, of Boston." W. L. Andrews, in his *Paul Revere and his Engraving*, 1901, page 19, follows Goss.

Yet all of the above authors apparently failed to notice the earliest and most important reference to the engraver of the Continental bills. William Dunlap, in his *History of the Arts of Design*, 1834, Volume 1, page 156, states positively: "Smither engraved the blocks for the continental money." Dunlap, born in 1766, knew personally most of the artists and engravers of the late eighteenth and early nineteenth centuries, and had unparalleled opportunity to obtain facts. His word counts for much.

James Smither was the one engraver in Philadelphia in 1775 to whom the Continental Congress would have turned. His advertisements in the *Pennsylvania Chronicle* of April 18, 1768, and January 16, 1769, show that he was skilled in all forms of engraving and even had conducted a school for drawing and design. The design and composition in the Continental Congress bills of 1775 are totally unlike Revere's work. The bills bear no characteristics of Revere. William Dunlap's statement made in 1834 that James Smither engraved these bills can well be allowed to stand.

Francis Hopkinson, although he had nothing to do with the engraving of the Continental bills, undoubtedly was concerned with designing them. In a letter to the United States Board of Admiralty, May 25, 1780, he stated that he had designed "7 devices of the Continental Currency," and "the Borders, Ornaments & Checks for the new Continental Currency now in the Press" (see George E.

Hastings's *Life of Francis Hopkinson*, 1926, page 240).

As will be observed, the above chapter makes no attempt to write a history of Massachusetts paper currency. The only concern is with the bills and notes which Revere did engrave or may have engraved. Most of his engraving for the Province and for the State is supported by documentary evidence. In a few cases committees handled the business of obtaining engravers and printers and their reports are not on file. A close student of Paul Revere's engraving can generally identify his work through the formation of his lettering and by the use of designs which were characteristic with him. It is to be hoped that documents will be discovered in the future which will add to our knowledge of his engravings.

Index

Index